MARKET AND THOUGHT

Brett Levinson

MARKET AND THOUGHT

Meditations on the Political and Biopolitical

Fordham University Press New York 2004

Library of Congress Cataloging-in-Publication Data

Levinson, Brett, 1959–
    Market and thought: meditations on the political and the biopolitical / Brett Levinson.—1st ed.
      p. cm.
    Includes bibliographical references and index.
    ISBN 0–8232–2384–1 (hardcover) — ISBN 0–8232–2385–X (pbk.)
  1. Capitalism. 2. Social change. 3. Political science—Philosophy. I. Title.
    HB501.L3975 2004
    320'.01—dc22

                               2004016808

Printed in the United States of America
08 07 06 05 04   5 4 3 2 1
First edition

Contents

Acknowledgments

This is my first book *not* about Latin America. It is nonetheless the one most shaped by Latin American and Latin Americanist scholars. I want to acknowledge first the influence of the Chilean philosopher Willy Thayer, whose book *La crisis no moderna de la universidad moderna* and whose generous dialogue have so formed my own thinking. Alberto Moreiras's work and person served as inspiration for this entire study. Special thanks go out to Harry Harootunian, who read the manuscript and offered valuable suggestions for no reason other than his good will. Gareth Williams, Horacio Legras, Marco Dorfsman, Lori Hopkins, John Kraniauskas, Nelly Richard, Kate Jenckes, and Mahnaz Yousefzadeh made important proposals as they read or listened to chapters over the past five years. My gratitude goes out as well to the faculty and graduate students of the Department of Comparative Literature at the State University of New York; their intelligence figures prominently in these pages. Finally, I want to thank Helen Tartar and Chris Mohney of Fordham University Press for their careful and wonderful editing.

Introduction

The State/Market Duopoly—Definitions Forthcoming

The following study does not pretend to present thinking—expert, inside, or otherwise—about the market. Rather, it asks whether the market *itself* names a certain kind of thinking.

Stated differently, this study does not analyze a socioeconomic topos, the market, in relation to an intellectual dominion, knowledge. In truth, the market is not simply either an economic or a social field. Nor is it reducible to a site of media explosions and corruption, multinational corporations, unbridled technological development, Western expansion, cultural homogeneity, crass individualism, cybernetics, or teenagers milling about the mall.

Instead, as I will try to illustrate, the market is itself a way of *comprehending*, of knowing the globe. Better said, it is a "sense of the world" that threatens to bring knowledge, even the need and desire for knowledge, to an end.[1] There has been much talk of the alliance between the global market and the "end of history" (whether the latter is perceived negatively or positively). But as I hope to show, a condition of the culmination of history is the termination of thought: the reduction of Being to a common sense that "goes without saying," and which cannot therefore be known, indeed discussed, further.

Phrased in still other terms, the market turns on knowledge since its direction and extension depend on the creation of a "neoliberal consensus" (a phrase I will define presently), established "naturally" or without negotiation—again, as an "it goes without saying"—that it (the market) is the destiny of man: inevitable and necessary. Once that is a given, oppositions and alternatives, which would demand knowledge of the market's bedrock (without it, the *essence* of the market remains unaddressed even by its critiques), can only appear useless, even absurd.

In casting the market as the site of a specific kind of thinking (or of nonthinking), I do not intend to downplay more obvious "market" concerns, such as the widening of the gap between rich and poor or the apparent impending elimination of fundamental public services (passed on to the private sector); indeed, the following pages offer extensive investigation into these matters. My purpose is rather to show how efforts to diminish the magnitude of knowledge in favor of a critique of "real social atrocities" in fact fuel them. The *separation* between knowledge and social inequity, within the market, helps yield that very inequity.

By "knowledge," I should also note at this juncture, I refer not solely to the way in which institutions such as the media, the university, or technology generate beliefs. My central concern is not the role of culture and education in the creation of a false consciousness that favors capitalism. Thus the present study does not undertake the kind of investigation found in Samir Amin's *Spectres of Capitalism: A Critique of Current Intellectual Fashions*, which provocatively analyzes the link between contemporary knowledge production and capitalism in this manner.[2] The foundations of market thinking are located less in culture or cultural influence than at the material limit of that influence: limit as the force that culture must appropriate if it is to generate the "intellectual fashions" upon which Amin deliberates, but which—as border—is not proper to those modes.

Indeed, this work resists as much as possible the entire "culture versus economics" debate that underlies much recent scholarship on globalization. What should be the central focus of intellectuals who at least agree that our current political condition does not result from "the nature of things"—who rebuff the theory that the totalization of the free market is the natural completion of history? Should scholars concentrate on the way in which culture—language, the media, the university, literature, religious institutions, popular or mass creations—generates a homogeneity that backs capitalism? Should they posit the economic or "material" base as the ground of political and social relations? Or should contemporary thought work through the dialectic of the two positions?

However, if cultural production and the economic/material base are in fact in conflict, or even if they are integrated, and if this discord or accord in some way founds analysis of our contemporary sociopolitical situation, then *something* separates or joins the two fields. This "something," irreducible to either domain, nonetheless touches upon both. It is their boundary (although we must determine the proper name or names for this boundary): the limit of cultural constructionism and economic materialism, their incapacity, even together, to account for the world. This frontier is what demands thinking and what thinking demands—assuming, of course, that the market can be thought at all.

Now, any sense of today's world requires that one carefully interrogate assumptions that the ground of the political has "lately" (since 1989?) passed from the state form to the global.

Even when the assertion is extremely nuanced, as when Michael
Hardt and Antonio Negri contend in *Empire* that in recent years
the universe has witnessed a swing from a disciplinary society (a
mode of state power) to a control society (the mode of globalization), the assertion must be questioned.[3] In fact, it is neither the
state nor the market but their interplay, a state/market *duopoly*—a
term I will also soon define—that sustains and explains both.

Transnational phenomena such as AIDS, nuclear proliferation,
terrorism, pollution, new information technology, mass immigration, international courts, and the fall of the Communist bloc are
certainly signs of a changing order, a shift in the foundation of
politics, and a demand for a rethinking of the political itself. A
fundamental change has taken place; contemporary efforts to
"return" to the state (especially when reduced to a given notion
of the "local") as a means to combat the global are consequently
suspect. All the same, the sovereign state (however defined), in
tandem with the market, retains significant force despite and even
because of these alterations.

Indeed, it is the aforementioned concept of consensus, rather
than that of the waning state, that offers the most apt means to
tackle our shifting political terrain. I am by no means the first to
say so. In *Disagreement: Philosophy and Politics,* Jacques Rancière
uses the notion powerfully, concluding that "consensual postdemocracy" (his name for the politics of our epoch) necessarily falls
"short of democracy, short of politics."[4] Rancière's more thorough
definition of *consensual postdemocracy,* which we will later flesh
out, runs as follows:

> The term will simply be used to denote the paradox that, in the
> name of democracy, emphasizes the consensual practice of effacing
> the forms of democratic action. Postdemocracy is the govern-
> ment practice and conceptual legitimization of a democracy *after*
> the demos, a democracy that has eliminated the appearance,
> miscount, and dispute of the people and is thereby reducible to

the interplay of state mechanisms and combinations of social energies and interests.[5]

As for the term "neoliberal consensus," it is a decidedly Latin American one. I appropriate it from Chilean scholarship, in particular from Tomás Moulián's *Chile actual: Anatomía de un mito* (Chile Today: Anatomy of a Myth) and from Willy Thayer's *La crisis no moderna de la universidad moderna: Epílogo del conflicto de las facultades* (The Unmodern Crisis of the Modern University: Epilogue on the Conflict of Faculties).[6] In Latin American nations, the notion of a neoliberal consensus (*consenso neoliberal*) lies at the core of nearly all leftist readings of the transition (*la transición*) from the dictatorships of the 1970s and 1980s to the so-called democracies of today. A major belief is that this transition marks, not the advent of a better state, but the completion of a neoliberal process (which commenced prior to the dictatorships), one in which liberty from terror (dictatorship) and "deeper" entrance into the market (a.k.a. democracy), freedom itself and free trade, become synonymous.

The effort to tie political, individual, and collective liberty to unfettered commerce has obviously developed, over a long period of time, into the spoken or unspoken mission of many states, many internationalist endeavors. Indeed, in Latin America, despite leftist interventions, this association has grown so powerful that it seemingly transcends both analysis and critique, even knowledge. Thus arises the *consenso neoliberal*, a name for a general agreement—"it goes without saying"—that the market is the only possible path to freedom. Consenso is the centerpiece of all diligent thought in the region. And although the present study is not about Latin America, it too argues that *consenso liberal* and the market are the domains to which intellectual labor ought now attend.

One might then inquire: Which intellectual labor? For some scholars, if only a few, humanities undertakings seem the ones most capable of market intervention. For instance, the devout Marxist sociologist Moulián dedicates much of *Chile actual* to demonstrating how the discourses of the social sciences, within *la transición*, only reproduce the language and ideals of the consensus itself. For him, the social sciences must be radically revamped, through an infusion of the lessons offered by the humanities, if they are to respond to (rather than merely recite) the market culture in which they now emerge.

Moulián's reproach of the social sciences, one intellectual's response to neoliberalism's dominance, can be compared and contrasted to the more prevalent and authoritative gesture: a wide-ranging *sociologization* of thought. In *The Ignorant Schoolmaster*, through a (not so) oblique strike against Pierre Bourdieu, Rancière forcefully addresses the matter: sociologization precludes thinking, philosophy, pedagogy, indeed, the practice of politics. And even though I will not directly analyze Rancière's thesis on the "sociologization" of both philosophy and the political, I want to reference my source.[7]

"Sociologization" signifies, in general, the presentation of the social—humanity's world, signs, and production—as an *object* of study for a *subject* of inquiry. (Yet "sociologization" is not a comment on sociology as a discipline; the critique of sociologization is not a critique of sociology.) In the chapters that follow, however, "sociologization" specifically denotes the way in which the humanities increasingly sociologize the philosophical, linguistic, cultural, psychological, and literary concerns that lie at the heart of many of the strongest intellectual pursuits of the late twentieth and early twenty-first centuries: endeavors that posit the world as irreducible to its subject of inquiry. Unsure of their role, even of their necessity, and perhaps in a quest for relevance, the humanities have made a turn or return to "society" or "the social"; and through the back door of this maneuver, humanists labor to claim the site that today seems to possess the highest bearing: "the political" (even if many seek to challenge the value of politics in the name of another concept, such as "the aesthetic," politics remains the value to contest).

Sociologization, in brief, is the humanist's marketing of the political. It plays to and for the very consensual postdemocracy that, most frequently in the name of leftism, it strives to undermine.

And yet terms such as "market," "late capitalism," and "neoliberalism" have themselves been so deeply sociologized that their deployment cannot but fall within existing definitions and limitations. Consequently, the humanities, including their many interdisciplinary ventures, cannot easily discard, rename, and then rework "the market" and its related nomenclatures. Perhaps it is too late; certainly, the sociologization of thought will not be undone any time soon. Still, if one judges, as I do, that the market is a "sense of the world," fundamentally a matter of knowledge, one does well—at the very least—to redesignate the field one strives to *know*, to labor "in the name" of other names, even if the "old" designations remain unavoidable (and they do). In this study, "neoliberal consensus," wrenched from its Latin American context, and "consensual postdemocracy" are those "other names."

I will address this consensus from a particular, even peculiar perspective, one of many that might have been selected: consensual postdemocratic or market thought, if indeed it is thought, can be best elicited by turning toward the still unexplored intersection of two projects, two visions of the expansion of the West: (1) deconstruction and (2) Marxist/post-Marxist theory. I say "still unexplored" not because this bond has never been investigated. If anything, it has been scrutinized, indeed dissected, all too often. And yet nearly all such explorations have been taken up *on behalf* of one of the projects: deconstruction or Marxism/post-Marxism. Best intentions notwithstanding, the goal has been to subsume leftist politics into deconstruction or vice versa. The objective, in other words, has been more to justify the theory than to ponder the relation or junction just mentioned: to justify the *theory* more than to think the thinking of our time.

It is paramount that we pursue this last assertion in greater detail. Christopher Fynsk opens his 1996 work *Language and Relation . . . That There Is Language* as follows:

> The linguistic turn in modern thought tends to sweep right by the most basic, but admittedly elusive, fact—the simple fact *that there is language*. Thus the questioning that should proceed from this fact, the question, to start, of the "essence" of language, is left to the residual obscurities of a few guiding texts. The result is a general impoverishment of all the analyses that have been enabled by this linguistic turn and the notion of the linguistic construction of identity—analyses throughout the disciplines of the humanities and social sciences that have been of immeasurable importance for cultural and sociopolitical study.[8]

Fynsk's words recall those of Jacques Derrida in *Of Grammatology*,[9] a text written thirty years before, which note that never has the issue of language been so much discussed, yet so profoundly evaded by intellectual enterprises.

Derrida's comments are mainly directed toward the structuralist movement, Fynsk's toward the linguistic turn (in the humanities and social sciences). Both scholars suggest, however, that the last fifty years of thinking have been largely dedicated to "sweeping by" the question of language that plainly lies at the heart of this thinking. The suggestion could not be more crucial today. For if the completion of the market turns on a consensus that "goes without saying," then the amplification of the "saying," attention to the "fact that there is language," is fundamental to any disruption of that totality. Conversely, the "sweeping by" of the "saying," its avoidance, cannot but feed consensus and neoliberalism, the "it goes without saying" itself.

When faced with intense and difficult meditations on language— Heidegger's, Blanchot's, Derrida's, Benjamin's—one is always tempted to ask: Why should we care? What is the importance of language, irreducible to representation, communicability, or culture (and this irreducibility is the fundamental focus of the just-named thinkers), for our time in particular? I offered above the response that I will pursue, one that I will clarify during the course of this study: resistance to the market and to the ends that this market spells—to history, politics, human relations, ideology, activism— hinges largely on the maintenance of language. It turns on a certain "speaking up" that consensus (which holds that the market is the only way, and which offers this "fact" as so obvious that it need not be spoken) strives to rub out.

Let us briefly review the fundamentals of the linguistic turn that Fynsk interrogates. These involve, above all, the move from the sig- nified to the signifier. Saussure taught generations of scholars that this signifier (or any set of signifiers) represents a signified arbi- trarily. Meaning or representation is the product of two factors: (1) repetitions, conventions, and rituals that naturalize and normalize the arbitrariness of a given signifier/signified tie, making it seem essential; and (2) the relation among or difference between signi- fiers. "Black" means "dark color" only within a system in which it is not "white," "red," "hack," "bladder," or "African-American," due to context, syntax, grammar, dialects, spelling, culture, habitus, and so on.

The first component of meaning (factor 1) fixes, limits, or "essentializes" both the connotation and denotation of the sign. The second (factor 2) exposes this meaning as relative, not neces- sary, and thereby as ever changing. (Of course, it is by now well known that one could easily reverse these two "steps," demon- strating how factor 2 essentializes what factor 1 destabilizes; but the point, important as it may be, does not alter the ideas I am here trying to present.)

In fact, the word *black* is not, and is not even like, the color it designates. And yet one says "black," and an image of the color often emerges, as if the meaning were itself natural. If it is natural for a subject to hear "black" and to think automatically of a specific color, then the signifier has grown into a part of that subject's "true nature."[10] The signifier has yielded to its essence or "true being": its signified, and ultimately, its *subject*. However, given the arbitrariness of the sign, this "nature" or truth is easily exposed—unconcealed—as an unnatural, therefore deconstructible ruse. This, of course, is a minor point when dealing with the color black itself. But it is a major one when addressing, say, race.

In sum, the linguistic turn, adopting for cultural analyses linguistic constructions and representation (the signifier) rather than presuming an authentic prediscursive site (the signified), discloses three matters:

1. the arbitrariness, contingency, displaceability, and constructed character of all meanings, truths, and laws;

2. the fact that these conventional stances, acting as if essential, bar alternative truths, therefore alternative subjects, from emerging; and

3. the alternatives themselves which, when liberated from the established or essentialist certainties that have concealed them, when *emancipated* from the signified or dominant discourse and *added* to the field of legitimacy, create not just another fact but a plurality of potentially valid statements and positions: plurality as synonymous, now, with the given, equality, truth, and universal freedom.

For Marx, "the proletariat was 'the classless class' whose emancipation was the touchstone for the liberation of humanity as a whole...."[11] Various groups, Marx intimated, could potentially bring about the *political* freedom of society. Yet they could only do so by abjecting from this social sphere the working class, "the one particular class . . . which gives universal offence," having committed "the *notorious crime* of the whole of society."[12] The political emancipation of society is thus the emancipation of a particular group *called* "society," to wit, the bourgeoisie; and it is so at the expense of another collective. Therefore (while it is indeed a necessary step, according to Marx), "social" liberation is not that of the whole. Societal/political liberty, stated in distinct terms, is the oppression of those who do not pertain to society or the body-politic (the state) but to a more general "humanity": the proletariat, stripped down to no possession but this, its raw humanity. If the classless class, almost without qualities (for it is a mere quantity), overcomes its condition, it will therefore do so as the "*total redemption of humanity*," of the "mere" humanity that the proletariat represents. "This dissolution of society as a particular class [therefore the dissolution of class itself] is the *proletariat*."[13]

We will explore whether plurality or multiplicity, the *political* ideal that lies behind the linguistic turn, pertains to this last emancipatory thrust. Is the representation of formerly unrepresented subjects, and the subsequent multiplication of signs, discourses, and political forces, a path toward a general emancipation of humanity (though not, perhaps, humanity in the Marxist sense; Marx's idealization of the notion of humanity possesses its own set of problems)? Or are these proliferating representations the situating of more and more parts into individual slots (the establishment of more and more identities), into autonomous properties that never touch, contaminate, or alter one another, much less the totality: properties that represent so many capitulations to a preestablished accord that operates effectively *because* it permits a multiplicity of entries and competitors?

Should one argue—or not—that increasing diversity and input offer a "freedom permit" only as long as parties take their correct place, in proper order, within a (civil) society that leaves a good part of the whole *untouched*, indeed "imprisoned"? Should one then speak of a novel collective, other than the proletariat, that today stands for the "*notorious crime* of the whole of society"? Does the emergence of more "free selves" affect more than the self itself, more than the (collective or single) individual: the self as the ground exclusively of *society*? In brief, what really occurs when all of humanity takes its place in the world as so many particular identities, when "the equality of anyone and everyone becomes identical to the total distribution of the people into its parts and subparts"?[14] Is this occurrence, at the least, a stride *toward* radical democracy? Or is it the last step into and *within* "consensual post-democracy"?

Whatever our responses, we should note that the linguistic turn, this divisive and decisive shift from signified to signifier, from truth to cultural constructions, did not spur the precise debates that one might have expected. The conflicts that ensued, at least within intellectual circles, did not take place between dominant and marginal voices, central and peripheral perspectives, canonical and non-canonical analyses, Same and Other. (Nor did the linguistic turn widen the supposed gap between a "conservative" but practical general public and an "out-of-touch" liberal Academy; the Academy was and remains a rather conservative place even—though not simply because—it has opened its arms to multiculturalism, pluralism, and the like.) These latter disputes, to be sure, may *seem* to be the central focus of the many current projects (such as critical race theory, cultural historiography, cultural, queer, and postcolonial studies) that tie themselves, deliberately or otherwise, to the linguistic turn. But as I will illustrate, what actually materialized from this turn was the fierce quarrel between the signified and the signifier themselves—words and things, ideology and economics, culture and materiality, reading and activism, image and reality—and the subsequent reduction of the humanities to the terms of this quarrel. Under the influence of the linguistic turn (and various other discourses, including if not primarily deconstruction), the radical intellectual promise offered by structuralism grew into a struggle between thought that addressed its material *object* (conflated with the "fixed" signified) and thought that tackled its *subjective* beholder (associated with the floating, "relativist" signifier). The linguistic turn's overall yield was the sociologization of thought.

Indeed, the link of contingency, in the form of floating signifier, to freedom renders the linguistic turn, despite its antihegemonic aspirations, a highly conformist operation. But this incongruity, if recently affirmed in a newly massive and public way by contemporary institutions and technologies, was exposed much earlier. For example, in the mid-1930s, Heidegger posited change as the root of uniformity and conservation, indeed, of nihilism: "fleetingness as the basic law of 'constancy'. . . restlessness of the always inventive operation, which is driven by the anxiety of boredom."[15] Given Heidegger's well-known political ties at the time of this statement, there might be the tendency to link the philosopher's disapproving view of change to a reactionary stance.[16] Yet to do so would be to miss, not only the essence of Heidegger's work, but any conceivable thought of the nihilism that most touches us today: that of the market, of neoliberal consensus.

Because it, first, adopts the signifier and representation, thus mutability and diversity as its ground, and, second, distinguishes these from the signified, immobility, imposition, and unity—because it demands that intellectuals, like shoppers, choose from the signs before them, assume their proper place in the *order* of representation, thereby support unawares a market arrangement whatever discourse or idea they select—because of all this, the linguistic turn tends to "sweep right by" *saying* as the counter to the "it goes without saying" of consensual postdemocracy. Our concern for language, to repeat, lies here: in saying this topos which runs most efficiently without any saying, indeed, which makes all saying increasingly difficult or scarce even as it creates avenues for more and more voices—to wit, the topos called "the market."

Like the market itself, a "total" neoliberal consensus is not, then, a discourse: it cannot be broached, must less understood, by discourse analysis. It is what will surface—if it has not already—when there is no discourse. Within a "completed" consensus, the way of the world is the way of the world. It is what is and what will be *because* there is nothing to say about it, because all talking, writing, and analyzing is essentially immaterial. "At the end of the day, proof of the right of state power is identical to the evidence that it only ever does the only thing possible, only ever what is possible by strict necessity in the context of the growing intricacy of economies within the global market."[17] We speak of the foundations of the market solely if there remains a limit to this market. Yet one does not assert this point or "say so" because the market is limited, thereby unwhole. The market is finite only if one *can* "say so," if the "what is the matter," the "what is the problem" within consensus is "sayable."

The thinkers I address in this study tackle, critique, deconstruct, espouse, or fall for "the market" understood in this sense: as a topos that, because it is nearly our nature, almost goes without saying. To be sure, the discourses analyzed below are not just on the market. "The market" may not be a term they even use. Yet "the market," even if designated in an alternative way, is a more or less good name for one key topos to which these intellectuals all attend: any discourse or practice in which multiplication (of commodities, of consumers as "rightful citizens," and of identities and selections), transformation (planned obsolescence, the movement of intellectuals from one theory to another), and liberation (free market, open debate), naturalize, reproduce, and extend the Same, rendering it more and more "the only way possible." The work and working of the *limit* of this logic (again, the logic, not of the signifier, but of the quarrel between signifier and signified), when attempted by these scholars, is therefore an effort to mark the nontotality—*because* finite—of the "way of the world," hence the sheer possibility of something more or something else.

My goal lies here. I cannot name this "something else." The period is not right for that word. I will not be able to describe, much less forge, the "outside" or "after" of the contemporary scene. I only want to show that there *could* be this something else. I hope solely to expose this "could," this possibility: not one that might one day be actual but one that is actual *presently*. I want to prove that, for us, possibility itself remains, here and now—that it remains to be spoken and thought.

It remains—but not without enormous exertion. Consensual postdemocracy is a very potent site, a powerful duality or duopoly. I want to rename, for the sake of clarity, the two fields. On one side of the divide lies the state form, akin to the logic of the signified. It turns on the production and acceptance of contingency as necessity. It imposes arbitrary and fixed limits through which it includes and excludes people, actions, speech. Yet in repeatedly doing so, it both naturalizes and essentializes those grounds so as to construct a groundless rule of law that permits it to operate.

On the other side sits the market form, allied with the logic of the signifier. Its entities are only arbitrarily fixed, thereby float with little regulation or rule. Just as the meaning of the signifier is relative to other signifiers, value here is relative to other values, relative pure and simple—therefore remarkably alterable.

The values of the market form slide, like the pure signifier. The values of the state form are unyielding, like an absolute signified. However, we live today in a state/market dyad in which relativism and absolutism, contingency and necessity, deregulation and law, circulation (a key topos of the market form) and production (a fundament of the state form), unfixity and fixity, work together to form our social, political, cultural, and intellectual domains.

Indeed, the possibility that the market offers, and one reason it ensnares the citizen-consumer, is a subject position that is protected by the absolute law; and one that is unrestricted by law, that is determined only by its relation to or competition with other positions: by will to power. Our times, those of neoliberal consensus, simultaneously promise the freedom *of* law (of the One) and the freedom *from* law (of the Many). The subject who as private individual is liberated *from* law wants also to be a public figure, among multiple competitors, protected and guaranteed *by* law. The subject yearns for relativism so as to be able to alter "truths" and add "positions" if need be; and for absolutism so as to prevent relativism and lawlessness (like capitalists in "bad times," subjects typically recall, when need be, the laws and regulations they just as typically scorn). In other words, neither the state nor the market, law nor lawlessness, constructionism nor essentialism is liberating or imprisoning. Neither side, on its own, bears responsibility for our consensual postdemocracy. Only in tandem do these two nihilisms—of absolutism and relativism—operate.

If deconstruction and leftist thought are today "impoverished" they are so because, ultimately, they bank on this same binary between contingency and necessity, relativeness and absolutism. They play off each other in order to speak both for a "real" materialism that is free from cultural relativism; and for "theory," for a progressive thought that is liberated from the dogmatism and absolutism of empiricism.

Nonetheless, and as already argued, these dichotomies do not and cannot complete the global picture. The condition of possibility of the signifier/signified relation, of any binary, is the slash between them, irreducible to either. This separation, bond, border, or limit is that which the linguistic turn, because conflating *language* with signifiers and signifieds, has "swept by." The bond is, as we will see, an index of language itself, language as such. Certainly, like the words "language," "language itself" or ". . . that there is language," the "/" is a sign, a signifier with a meaning, a signified. As such, it betrays the fact that the finitude of representation, hence of the linguistic turn—like the finitude of the market—cannot fail to fall into the very turn that it cuts off. The finitude of merchandizing cannot avoid ending up as merchandise. But the "/" or language—even as sign or product— does not fall without making a statement, without a *saying*: without stamping the frontier of the "it goes without saying" itself.

As to deconstruction *and* leftism, something similar applies. Each effort to think the relation of the two discourses or practices must make a statement about this *and*, about the copula that belongs to neither. The thought of the *relation* between deconstruction and leftism cannot, by logic, be deconstructive or leftist.

Of course, just as the mark between signifier and signified is itself a signifier (hence a signified, too: the signifier *is* the signified), every discourse on the separation/bond between deconstruction and leftism will necessarily come out on one side or the other. The scholar—me, for example—does not take a neutral or balanced position between the pair because a tipping of the scale in one direction is the condition of that balance.

Let us then conjecture that Marxist/post-Marxist thinking *is* deconstruction. But neither deconstruction nor leftism can activate or *say* that which lies between the two, the site where the one contaminates the other: this *is*. Deconstruction and leftism have therefore failed: failed to address this site which *faces them*, and that *is* their front and fount. In bypassing each other, deconstruction and leftism bypass less language than themselves. Yet they could not *but* have failed in such a manner. The boundary between them, after all, is (as limit) the death of the two discourses. Deconstruction and leftism could only have succeeded, made the essential contributions to which Fynsk alludes, by virtue of their evasion of this, their demise. It is only by succeeding that they fall short: of their own being, of our being, and of our world.

The present analysis picks up at this point of triumph and breakdown. It is thereby composed of a series of readings of quite divergent intellectual figures and, by extension, of very distinct topics: the state, ideology, terrorism, human rights, psychoanalysis, the culture wars, the new media, revolution, ethics, sex. Yet despite the distinctions among the thinkers chosen, the book stands as a book. It introduces a single thought at the outset, and explores that thought to the end.

Chapters 1–3 present the main theses of the text—consensus, duopoly, biopolitics, language—by reading and rereading three figures: Gramsci, Foucault, and Rancière. Chapters 4–5, through analyses of essays by Derrida and Levinas that have rarely been addressed, discuss the shifting role of human rights—including their possible demise—as internationalism yields to globalization. The function of language in Marx, Marxism, and post-Marxism is the subject of chapters 6–8, which address works by Althusser, Laclau and Mouffe, and Negri. The final pages, chapters 9–11 and the conclusion, tackle the commodification of culture; focus especially on the possibilities that—despite all—the fetishization of the commodity offers; address works by Hall, Said, Negri, Hardt, and Agamben; and tackle the Althusser-Lacan-Butler nexus. This embrace of the commodity, if indeed a means toward an affirmation of the political even today, no doubt calls as much for a novel thinking as a new politics. Perhaps it *is* that call. I label it "neoliberal consensus thinking." My only problem is that I am not certain that we have a way even to speak of such a thing, that we have not arrived too late on the scene.

1.

Gramsci
Subalternity and Common Sense

Three components of Antonio Gramsci's work have spearheaded a recent resurgence in Gramscian studies: (1) his examination of how cultural representations and institutions of civil society[1] shape rather than reflect social realities; (2) his formulation of the "subaltern"; and (3) his notion of the "organic intellectual." This initial chapter will analyze certain trends in contemporary political thought through a reanalysis of these Gramscian topoi, focusing on Gramsci's observations on language rather than representation.

In "Language, Linguistics and Folklore" (a selection from *The Cultural Writings*), Gramsci condemns linguistics as a discipline, then advances a counterlinguistic, alternative theory of language:

> Artificial languages are like jargons. It is not true that they are absolutely non-languages because they are useful in some ways: they have a very limited socio-historical content. But the

same is true of dialects in relation to the national-literary language. Yet dialect too is a language-art. But between the dialect and the national literary language something changes: precisely the cultural, political-moral-emotional environment. The history of languages is the history of linguistic innovations, but these innovations are not individual (as in the case of art). They are those of a whole social community that has renewed its culture and "progressed" historically. Naturally, they too become individual as a complete, determinate historical-cultural element. . . . Innovations occur through the interference of different cultures. . . .

Every time the question of language surfaces, in one way or another, it means that a series of other problems are coming to the fore; the formation and enlargement of the governing class, the need to establish more intimate and secure relationships between the governing groups and the national-popular mass, in other words to reorganize the cultural hegemony.[2]

To begin, let me define one of the notions presented here: "language-art." And let me do so in a rather roundabout manner: by tying "language-art" to the term "queer" as posited and used in texts such as Judith Butler's *Bodies that Matter*.[3] Queer theory, according to Butler, recycles the derogatory "queer" of homophobia, deploying the "dominant discourse" (or, in Gramsci's lexicon, the "national-literary") so as to turn it against itself. This reversal occurs in two different ways. First, reintroducing the pejorative term "queer" into ordinary discourse accentuates the violence and bigotry of the mainstream ("normal" discourse, in fact, would prefer signifiers such as "gay," "lesbian," or "homosexual": less name calling, the thinking is, signals the new tolerance within society). "Queer," as used by queer theory, recalls the fact that American culture views distinction not as difference but as abnormality, deformity, illness, in brief, queerness.

Second, and no less important, when sent back to the center (its origin) from the periphery, "queer" highlights the inequity, hence nonnecessity of the discourse of normalcy. Being without a fixed signified or essential meaning, "queer" does not easily play into the hands of an "essentialist" definition, homogeneity, or compulsive normalcy. The signified for the "queer" of "queer theory" is ambiguous, floating. Does "queer" refer to gays and lesbians? To transvestites and bisexuals? To all who identify with oddness, whatever their sexual practices, indeed, with oddness outside of sexuality altogether? Itself formerly (and often still) part of an essentialist homophobia, "queer" reveals the potential nonessentialness or displaceability of any sexual or personal moniker, indeed of any word whatsoever, within the "norm."

As a "language-art" articulation, "queer" does not, then, supply the marginalized group—or what Gramsci might have called the "subaltern" sectors—with a more fitting appellation than the language of hegemony does. Nor does it offer peripheral peoples a proper name, that is, an identity. In fact, "queer" misnames these peoples. Like all language-art articulations, "queer" is actually inappropriate for the community it designates. Yet herein lies the political usefulness of a language-art. How so?

For Gramsci, the subalterns of Italy (the underclass, agrarian Southerners and Sardinians) are alienated, not because they are estranged, but because they are not estranged enough. They all too habitually—through a process of naturalization and ritual—locate their being in the homogeneity, the dominant center, in the names ("Southerner," "Sardinian," "backward," "agrarian") and order that downgrade and delegitimize them, aiding in their exclusion from political representation.

Language-art terms such as "queer," or, indeed, such as "subaltern" itself disclose the violence, injustice, and instability (displaceability) of this homogeneity or national "familiar sense," even as they expose the subalterns to, permitting them to sense, their alienation and exploitation. Not unlike expressions of bigotry within certain social sectors that no longer find these expressions acceptable, the "language-art word" acts as an "odd term," snatched from proper or conventionalized forms of representation, which can raise the subalterns' feeling of being misrepresented or wronged.

The operative word here is *feeling*. Intellectuals who argue for the "linguistic construction of reality" often find themselves trapped by this question of feeling, particularly of pain and suffering. The argument such scholars almost inevitably face runs as follows: "Yes, cultural or ideological beliefs may be to a large degree structured by language. But a hit over the head with a police stick is not linguistic! Hunger is not linguistic but material!"

Yet pain is by no means given or experiential, as these exclamations suggest. Even from empirical evidence we know that beaten children at times become so traumatized that they fail even to sense the physical agony that they endure. Anorexics who are "objectively" starved (in terms of caloric input) may feel stuffed and bloated; likewise, malnourished individuals may "overcome" their hunger after consuming an altogether inadequate portion of food. This is to say nothing of those who feel little in the face of the brutality of others: who do not "feel for the Other" when they "should." And such reactions are not "abnormal" responses to what is "objectively" agonic. Coping mechanisms that mitigate, diminish, or even erase apparent suffering are in fact quite "normal."

Thus nothing is "objectively" hurtful. Pain does not happen in the object but in the subject. Police sticks do not hurt; skulls hurt. In other words agony, like any feeling, requires consciousness; and consciousness demands language and knowledge. It also demands aesthetics, images, and signs. These "raise the feelings" that induce people to engage the world or change their situation. Language, in brief, neither "constructs" nor misses the pain of a subject. It is, by logical necessity, suffering's condition.

Suffering, then, is not a nomination for a pure material experience that takes place exterior to representation or the concept. If, using Lacan's topoi, the Symbolic is the conceptual world, and the

Real the resistance to Symbolization, then this Real is precisely *not* that which hurts. For Gramsci, the case is just the opposite: without the consciousness that results from concepts and images—from apprehension, names, sense, knowledge, art, media—there is no suffering in the first place. Feeling outside of a concept of feeling, ironically enough, is feeling in the abstract: no actual affect. The absolute repulsion of the "aestheticization" or "linguistification" of suffering and oppression is aestheticism itself.

Thus Gramsci writes, this time in *The Prison Notebooks*: "The popular element 'feels' but does not know or understand; the intellectual element 'knows' but does not always understand, and in particular does not always feel."[4] Gramsci here recurs to the Hegelian triad of feeling, understanding, and knowing. These are intimately linked, in Hegel, to another hierarchy: family (feeling), civil society (understanding), and state (knowledge). The quotation marks that Gramsci places around the word *knows*—the "knowing" of an "intellectual element" who does not always "feel"— indicate that one does not *really* know without feeling, just as one does not *really* feel (or, as Gramsci writes it, "feel") without knowing. Feeling, understanding, and knowing together make up the domain of sense, and are thus codependent. We will presently see how Gramsci's movement through feeling, understanding, and knowledge parallels the subaltern's shift from a peripheral group or family into a participant in the political state through civil society. For now, though, I am only emphasizing this bond of sense and sense, sensation and knowing, suffering or joy and representation.

Yet, for Gramsci, if the raising of ill feeling (the sense of being wronged) by means of language-art is a condition of political awareness, the first stage of a subaltern political intervention, this feeling is nonetheless insufficient. In fact, the "queer" or subaltern term that induces feeling as consciousness necessarily comes from and recycles the hegemonic or "straight" idiom that it disrupts. "Subaltern" itself, after all, is a military designation for a subordinate officer. Language-art repeats, ritualizes, thereby normalizes and markets the aberrations within the national-literary, the degrading idiom it seems to have exposed. The discomfort of the margins or underclass is a priori co-opted for the representations and concepts of the center elite. "Queer" is always already a program; ill feeling is already comfort; subversive displacement is already alienating consolation.

The staging of exclusion (by means of the "queer word" or language-art), in brief, is the condition of both discomfort and its removal. Without the naming, representation, or the aestheticization of the subaltern, political "progress" cannot begin. Aesthetics (naming) raises the emotions, the ill feeling, the desire for change, just discussed. But with this aestheticization, the "progress" is already truncated as the feeling is lifted up onto an image, onto an outside and epiphenomenal space, off the body, away from the affect. Again, ill feeling and its eradication coincide.

This point, of course, belongs to one of our oldest theoretical narratives. Aesthetic creations, particularly when representing the painful or tragic, do indeed help construct the emotions, the ill feeling that, for Gramsci, forges passion and inspires action. But also, aesthetics detaches the oppressed or sufferers from this same affect since the ache happens (in a drama, for example) *to* the aesthetic object, *to* an art form. The *staging* or representation of the affect relieves "real people," embodied by the public, the potentially politicized subjects, from the very discomfort they experience— only the actors endure the pain; the pain is never actual. The injury is "not really real," meaning that the public, the people who feel the hurt in a secondary or detached manner, who *empathize*, does not "actually" experience it. The "bad feeling" of the subjects is thus also their pleasure: the removal of and *from* ill feeling.

The famous "aestheticization of the political," then, may well merit the critiques it has invited. But let us not forget Gramsci's counterpoint to the argument, which we have just discussed.

Without the aesthetic (e.g., the tragic), without the production of ill feeling that can collapse into apathetic consolation, there is no political: "There never has been any 'aestheticization' of the politics in the modern age because politics is aesthetic in principle."[5] Aestheticism, Gramsci warns contemporary thought *avant la lettre,* may be bad for politics, but without aestheticism not even this bad politics exists. There is no politics.

In this context, dialects, which Gramsci situates among the language-arts, are of considerable interest. They point up another means by which a language-art represents a potential intervention, particularly in light of Gramsci's statement that "every time the question of language surfaces, in one way or another, it means that a series of other problems are coming to the fore." We cannot assume that a dialect, in and of itself, is made up of "odd terms." It does not necessarily form a language-art. After all, a dialect is not generally viewed as odd, or as outside the common sense, by the person who uses it. Southerners' consciousness of their dialect as dialect, in fact, comes to the fore only through contact with the "national-literary," through some kind of awareness of the distinctions and similarities of two modes of speech or writing. The dialect is never a dialect in and of itself but by means of its relations to a "norm."[6]

The wish of the national-literary idiom, of course, is that the difference between it and its variations (its dialects) materialize as right is to wrong, cultured is to uncultured, progress is to backwardness. The users of the dialect are incorrect, hence "lowly," and should seek to correct themselves: a corrective measure that, if taken, would itself perform the rightness of the national-literary.

But cast in a distinct, Gramscian manner, as a language-art that is both set off alongside and a relation to the national-literary, dialects do something else entirely. They potentially allow the subalterns to sense, first, that their speech is not outside but *somewhat like* the national-literary (wrong is *like* right); and second, that the "correct idiom" is "proper," not because of any intrinsic quality but because of this "likeness": owing to its link to and binary with the regional utterances or national (or transnational) dialects. The center's rightness is relative (to the dialect) and not absolute, limited and not the whole of right or correctness. Its speech borders on an alternative subaltern linguistic space that, because *like* the national-literary, is itself also at least somewhat, or relatively, right. Thus, when the Southern or subaltern dialect is misrepresented as inferior by the national-literary, and when the consciousness of that misrepresentation arises, the way is opened for a sense of the limit and relativity of the center's right, thus the potential for an alternative right, an alternative politics.

Gramsci is careful to distinguish the emergence of dialects or language-arts from the individualism of artistic production, from "originality" or "agency": a dialect is never the product of agency but of a shift in social and political demographics, of "other problems coming to the fore."[7] To see what he means, let us take as an example the Chicano dialect, distinct from English and Spanish but connected to both (and to other languages as well). This idiom results from specific border crossings (themselves a response to shifting social and economic situations), and the subsequent formation of immigrant communities. Such mass immigration, of course, does not stem strictly from agency or "the choice to move" (individual or collective) but from forces that push people about. The same can be said of the resultant dialects, which materialize when distinct languages collide due to this push. As Gramsci notes rhetorically: "Who can control the linguistic innovations introduced by returning emigrants, travelers, readers of foreign newspapers and newspapers, translators, etc?"[8]

The terms, neologisms, gestures, and rhythms of a Chicano dialect, even if invented by particular subjects, are thereby never simply the productions emitting from subjects or individuals (as is an artwork, in Gramsci's eyes). A dialect must circulate, and then catch on; and the catching on exceeds every individual or collective impetus. An (individual or group) agent can surely put a word or phrase in circulation. But this "putting in play" in no way assures entrance into collective speech patterns. Such entry comes about only if social conditions, or new social collectives, surface in such a way that the phrase is "catchy," hence is appropriated.

Yet, with Gramsci, a linguist by training, one must always be ready to reverse this hierarchy (the "which comes first") of language shifts and alterations in social demographics. It is true that, whenever the question of language surfaces, it is because new social relations and conditions (thus also new dialects, which bring up "the problems") are emerging. But it is equally certain that whenever the question of social conditions surfaces, it is because linguistic alterations are taking or have already taken place. The Chicano dialect results in part from the social and economic conditions that yield border crossings. Yet this dialect, as such, could not have come into being in the complete absence of the term "Chicano" (which, most likely a truncated version of "Mexicano," is a good example of a language-art word), for it is this signifier that aided the formation of a Chicano family/community, the merging of collectives (the "demographic shifts"), and the civil rights movements that were instrumental in the formation of a Chicano "nation." "Chicano speech" does not gather into a unity and system the linguistic patterns of the extremely diverse Mexican-American groups that preexist them. "Chicano" helps bring about that coming together. It collects the new community under a single rubric; and this union leads to new means and methods of communication— hence to novel manners of speaking.

Although it is clear that social demographics and economic conditions, rather than individual agents, yield language-arts, these very language-arts are the requisites for the creative forces that drive the social movement. To put it another way, just as brick is the material condition of a brick wall, language-art is the material condition of the social reality, the social movement.

Thus a dialect—like or as the Gramscian language-art—can serve as a tool within civil society or the public sphere, much as the phrase "African-American" functions as a device for various social efforts in the contemporary U.S. space. Set off from other terms ("African-American" is implicitly contrasted with "black," "Negro," "colored," "Anglo-American," and so on), and not entirely conventional, it awakens a certain self-consciousness. Bringing together peoples who, through the collective activity, grow aware of themselves—or create themselves—as a community with a shared history, idiom, and territory, the dialect turns into a mechanism by means of which peripheral worlds initiate actual rallies and realities. Public practices, new institutions, popular art forms, and regionalisms all might materialize through the new articulations.

Yet a fuller analysis of this notion of a "mechanism" or "tool" is needed here. We have already established that the subalterns cannot *not* reuse the center's words or ideas, even by revamping them. In essence, the subaltern can only "break into the master's house with the master's keys." The fact that the masters possess such tools (here, keys), however, is itself of great importance. If they need tools to maintain their "houses" or position, they cannot also be "naturally" whole. If they must resort to "extra, nonnatural helpers," or tools, they are not by nature self-sufficient, not true sovereigns. The tools, which are means by which the center beats the margins into abject submission, also expose the center as "inherently" incomplete, hence weak, which is why a subaltern "break-in" can occur in the first place.

Let me put this idea in other terms. As the central power, the masters bank on thought/instinct, mind/body binaries. The masters must stand for the idea (or they do not stand at all). They must exist outside or beyond the physical realm or of work, in a transcendent sphere. Masters who require tools in order to build or maintain the space of right, however, are exposed as tinkerers rather than as thinkers, as mechanics laboring on the state apparatus and on themselves. Their right is not an intrinsic property, as is a hand. Artificial and constructed, it swings on extensions of the hand (tools) that, as not proper to the body itself, not the body proper, could be lost or stripped (even rightfully).

Yet once more, this analysis can and must be reversed if we are to understand Gramsci. The masters' need for tools potentially discloses their contingency. Yet oddly enough, when the subalterns, in an effort to break into the exposed master houses, are caught with those same tools in hand (for example, the language of the center), the masters (now relieved of their tools) are resituated onto their transcendent perch. Damaging binaries are reinstated: reason/nature (the subalterns use tools, the body, not the mind), property/impropriety (subalterns construct themselves through property that is not their own but is "stolen"), real/artifice (the tool is artificial), original/copy, wholeness/lack. The subalterns at once overcome their resignation through language-art as instigators of feeling (and later as tools) and inscribe themselves back into the positions they had begun to overcome.

Nonetheless, during this process important events have taken place. Not only has the national-literary idiom shifted so as to accommodate the new dialect or language-art. But also new political movements and representations have been assimilated into the center. We have now worked our way to and through a second stage of the process of hegemony formation: the subaltern's move from feeling to understanding, and by extension, from "family" to or through civil society.

At this juncture, according to Gramsci, a "whole social" community (the Italian nation-state) "has renewed its culture" and "progressed historically." The "progress" occurs because the "national-literary" takes in or smooths over the outside sectors—

regions that, having "sensed" their unfamiliarity within the legitimate state "family," squirm somewhat uncomfortably, perhaps a bit enraged. The metropolis, because it does not want the margins or underclass to feel their ill feeling or alienation—this could eventually lead to disturbance or even rebellion—must thereby appropriate, make proper, the language-arts that, when apprehended in a certain way, bring about the "bad sense." The ill feeling, through the appropriation, is temporarily cured. Yet it is so only because the center or the national-literary moves and is moved. It has appropriated the subaltern by "adding a foreign element" to its previous infrastructure, hence at the risk of its stability. The homogeneity of the center turns into a dynamic hegemonic operation that, to be sure, smooths out the "bump" in the machine, restoring the unity. But something has happened in the meantime: the state's center has had to struggle, shift its foundation, "progress."

Progress, as Gramsci (who, in the above citation, places the word *progress* in scare quotes) understands it, is thereby less a matter of the "dominant discourse" including the subaltern than of homogeneity yielding to hegemony: "the formation and enlargement of the governing class, the need to establish more intimate and secure relationships between the governing groups and the national-popular mass, in other words to reorganize the cultural hegemony."[9] The Italian state, Gramsci laments, is not too hegemonic; if anything, it is not hegemonic enough. Rather than constantly shifting, and moving toward a unified "ethical state" (Gramsci's term) through the introjection of the Italian regions, regionalisms, and underclass, the monarchy grows stronger and stronger at its center, while never doing the work of a hegemonic state: of translating this center so that it works for the subaltern periphery, and of translating the periphery so that it works on and in the ceaselessly decentered center.

Now, it must be emphasized that a language-art is not the language of the popular class. It is neither rooted in "folk" nor in the speech of the subaltern. Gramsci, in fact, views the popular, including popular speech and art forms, as a prime example of common sense (this is why some still see Gramsci as an elitist). In other words, folklore and folk speech are no less party to the monarchical state than is the "national-literary." For Gramsci, indeed, it is the binary of popular sense and elite sense, center and periphery, and not either "side," that produces a stagnant homogeneity, the common sense. A language-art, on the contrary, results from the articulation of the *bond* between "folk" and "national-literary." It is the creation of an uncommon idiom, at the limit of these two established senses, that exposes subalterns to their own alienation, creates the ill feeling that, in turn, raises the possibility of a political intervention.

In this context, it is interesting to meditate upon Gramsci's thoughts on the "national-literary" in terms of contemporary debates about the "canon." One might easily conflate the two. The national-literary, indeed, is similar to the canon in that it operates as a particular form of representation that can stand both for the whole and for legitimate language, thereby delegitimizing popular, regional, and folkloric expressions. Yet actually, a canonical or classical text (whose greatest example is no doubt *Don Quixote*), if representing the state, does not generally exclude the popular. On the contrary, the modern canonical text is canonized precisely by the way in which it stylizes and aestheticizes—but nonetheless takes in—this marginal or popular sector. The popular often gains entry into a national tradition precisely in this fashion: as it is cast by metropolitan artistic modes, such as the great novel.

But herein lies the key to the dialectic that Gramsci demands. He would like the popular, regional, or subaltern peoples, having gained rights to the advantages of the center, to be educated enough to access the canon, not as "proper culture," but as the national-literary that stylizes or misrepresents the popular. Their sense of misrepresentation would initiate the processes described above.

The subalterns must be "canonized" (enjoy passage to the canon) so as to locate themselves as the wronged or misrepresented ones within that canon. It is in the canon that the relation of center and periphery, as other than one of right (center) and wrong (margin), is disclosed to the underclass. Thus the canon, often disparaged, is in actuality a condition of subaltern knowledge—not because it contains the truth of the nation, but because it counts upon the relations between the national-literary and folk that reveal this truth: the truth of and as those relations.

Now, within Gramsci's thought and lexicon the person most responsible for effecting this sort of education, insofar as Gramsci links such education to the question of the subaltern, is the "organic intellectual." Contrary to a "natural attitude" toward this term, the Gramscian organic intellectual is not the one who is born and raised in the margins of the nation: one who is organic to a subaltern place (much as an accountant qua organic intellectual might seek to gain knowledge that, while exterior to accounting itself, emerges from and is organic to the work site). In fact, the condition of the Gramscian organic intellectuals as subaltern intellectuals is that they leave behind their nature, their birth site, their "native knowledge," and travel to the center, to the home of the national-literary.

This holds not because such a truth is located in the center more than it is in the margin. As noted, truth instead surfaces through the dialectic of center and periphery. The subaltern organic intellectuals grasp their peripheral origins solely by working through the center/margin relation—the condition for which is the acquisition of the center's sense—since the margin *is* that relation, and so too is the center. Through the education supplied by the center, the subalterns learn to grasp the beings or speech patterns fixed by the national-literary as relations (to the margins, to dialects), as relative, not essential.

The prototype of the subaltern organic intellectual, in short, is Gramsci himself: as Southerner and dialectician. Like Gramsci, subaltern intellectuals forge knowledge of their own nature (i.e., the knowledge that both their world and that of the center are relations) by going away and returning. They do not come to understand their being by leaving, through metropolitan learning: that is elitism. Nor do they possess the truth prior to their journey, through "folk learning," which they then bring to the center as an alternative to the "dominant discourses": that is anthropological idealism. The departure and return themselves produce the consciousness of their relation, hence the truth (of the state as a whole) to which the organic intellectuals endlessly aspire. The subaltern intellectuals who depart without retracing their roots are neither organic nor intellectual, for only in the (re)tracing does the intellect grow. And the same can be said of the homegrown thinkers who never depart (but let me emphasize that one can depart in many ways: physical departure, as opposed to the departure of the imagination, is only one such possibility). They never gain access to the relation that their world is, to their actual "nature."

It is well known that Gramsci believes that the traditional intellectual makes a claim on a classless, hence *general* good, language, taste, and knowledge. This is why Gramsci rejects such a figure. The traditional intellectual passes off the transcendence of class and the nonrecognition of regions qua regions as the political and moral good, both cajoling the underclass into striving for this ideal and thwarting any political alternative.[10]

Although Gramsci's subaltern intellectuals, floating between classes and social categories, may appear quite like such an individual, they do not in fact overcome their particular class, but precisely demonstrate that their "particular" status or sector is an abstraction. The particular exists not "by itself," nor even necessarily through a relation to or dialectic with the universal. It exists through its bond or link to another class (and to many other relations as well: to gender, race, religion, political affiliation, sexual orientation, and so on). The organic intellectual, then, exposes less the class nature of knowledge than knowledge of the nature of class: of class as class relations.

But what is the political responsibility of the "subaltern intellectual"? Where do learning and politics precisely meet? These intellectuals' job is to articulate the relation between the center and periphery that they, as travelers, have gleaned. Yet since neither center nor periphery can supply the words for this link—neither can capture the to and fro between them—such a language must be forged. Language-art names, for Gramsci, this "hinge" idiom wherein which "innovations occur through the interference of different cultures."[11] Subaltern intellectuals intervene into *two* common senses, that of center and that of the periphery—they have no great tolerance for either of these idioms—in order to phrase their relationality through the odd term, and hence to spark the ill feeling, the entire hegemonic process we have been discussing in this chapter. Yet as soon as a language-art signifier, such as "queer," is assimilated into the national-literary, into *state knowledge*, it becomes part of the established, legitimate field of erudition or homogeneity. Politics then demands a new language-art articulation, a substitute, so as to again raise the ill feeling, again push the homogeneity into a hegemony. Politics does not correct or redress wrong. It ceaselessly demands that wrong be *addressed*, and it *is* that addressing.

Thus, within Gramscian "progress," feeling is not the lowest step on the ladder to knowledge. Family, likewise, is not the lowest step on the ladder to the state. Although, in one cycle, feeling (of the subaltern family) indeed climbs up toward and disappears into knowledge (the state), in the next "spin," knowledge must extend up to (ill) feeling, so as to restart political interventions. Gramsci's dream is that the Italian state (a monarchy at the time he was writing) come into being, not as the dichotomy of the empowered and the powerless—the monarchical (rotten) core and the various regions that remain unincorporated into the state—but as a process, brought about by civil society, in which all peoples gain access to the benefits of an ever-changing center, the result being an "ethical state."[12]

One has to imagine a procedure in which all individuals or groups come to know themselves in the reigning legitimized knowledge, a knowledge that shifts each time a new "member" gains access to it, or each time a "subaltern word" settles into that field. The "law from above," which governs the margins with little understanding or even acknowledgment of those people (and vice versa: the law is not understood by the people it governs), with violence, hence for no reason, is replaced by the law of reason, in which legislation is created, dismantled, and reconstituted on good grounds. Every novel intercession by civil society, every popular political practice, is the potential reason for a new rule, and for the rule of a new reason. During the movements from feeling to knowing, or from family to state, the hegemonic state/knowledge has engulfed all interventions. But if the state performs this act on enough occasions, then it itself grows more and more into the collection of those interventions. The "engulfer" resurfaces as the "engulfed."

Gramsci's subaltern intellectuals, to state the above points in a different form, are at once poets, thinkers, readers, and activists: poets because they invent the language that links center to margin; thinkers because they do not accept the paradigms of the reigning common sense—which count upon a center/margin binary, and which result from discourses from both sites—hence must *think*, given that there is no existing paradigm, no existing sense that will supply that thought for them; readers because their activity is initiated not by the realities in front of their eyes but by the center/margin ties they must piece together and interpret; and activists because the forging of language through thought induces the discomfort that potentially de-alienates those on the margins of the state, initiating political practices.

This articulation between senses ought to be understood as "language as such": that part of communication which, occurring between fields of representation, between central and marginal realms, does not fall within either domain. It is the portion of speech or writing that does not represent a group, is not a mimetic reflection of the worlds that result from common sense—from separate metropolitan and peripheral domains, hence from a state that banks on this separation—or from the naturalized references that emerge through convention, concepts, and rituals. If language-art were such a reflection then it would, like all "mere" reflections, stand as an epiphenomenon whose truth or "as such" would be the existing material universe. It would not be language but next to nothing. As the "between" of those worlds, on the other hand, "language as such" is itself material. It is language not as reflection but as itself: poetry, invention, language-art.

But one should not speak too hastily. I suggested above that language-art is *always already* aesthetics. The displeasure with the system, hence the desire for social change that language-art generates, coincides with the satisfaction (and the subsequent apathy) with that very system. This, of course, is just another way of saying that the condition of the "language as such" (language-art) that interrupts representation is representation itself (the national-literary): the proviso of the force that prevents the state from endlessly reproducing the Same is that very reproduction. If, indeed, "something happens," if a shift within the state takes place by means of language-art, if language as such generates an event, it is not yet clear in *what time period* that event takes place since the condition of the interruption of common sense is common sense itself. The intervention that compels the state to change is the very "thing" that this state, which must always progress in order to maintain itself, *immediately* appropriates. The force that intrudes is the sustenance that preserves.

Nonetheless, the amplification of language as such, the creation and use of language-art, remains a key task of the Gramscian subaltern intellectual. Through this production, the center/periphery binary, which reduces the language-art to an inferior or epiphenomenal reflection, does not lose the trace of the limit, the between, that prevents the binary (and all its brethren: reason/instinct, modern/backward, thinker/laborer, etc.) from completing itself, hence the central government (which, now limited, bordered by the slash, stands as a relation) from representing the state as a whole. Responsible for the institution of education within civil society, indeed, for civil society itself (if and when civil society is something other than the private sphere), the subaltern organic intellectual is also responsible for language.

For Gramsci, then, the politician who is not an intellectual is no politician but an ideologue. Indeed, the activist who only leads people into action will most likely lead them to perform and repeat, hence normalize through that action, the status quo. Pure collective activism is pure ideology; and fascism, for Gramsci, is its greatest manifestation.

Gramsci does not imagine that politics ultimately lies outside books, language, and the humanities, in the "public sphere": that texts, for those interested in political activism, are *pretexts* to take "outside," to go "beyond." Words are not training wheels for a ride on reality. Intellectuals have a particular task within language, and it is one that only they can undertake—precisely because that, for Gramsci, is what intellectuals are, wherever they may work, whatever their origin: the safe keepers and creators of the language-arts. Who else will undertake the task: the politicians, the police, parents, the priests, the rabbis, the ministers? Any in truth could, any could be an organic intellectual. But only the intellectuals *must* (else they cease to be intellectuals).

Gramscian subaltern education does not simply involve the "progress" of the subaltern classes or "folk" as they access the knowledge of the center. It is not reducible to a movement in which the commonsense or (lowly) "feeling" of the people yields to the knowledge of the metropolis (or vice versa, for that matter: metropolitan knowledge of the people). Rather, Gramscian education can only be a teaching about and practice of the border or between of all common senses, this limit being "language as such": the most common and the least common. Knowledge, like politics, attends to the "inter": to that which is common to all sense but at home in, the property of no common sense. After all, if knowledge were just a matter of common sense, we would not need an institution called "education," for the social good would go without saying, hence would require no teaching, and no civil society either.

The question then emerges: Is "subaltern" (as Gramsci permits us to grasp the term, not necessarily the way he *meant* us to grasp it) a possible figure, today, of "language-art," of language itself? Might it serve, now or one day, as the figure of the most common *to* all and the least common *of* all: language? Alberto Moreiras, in *The Exhaustion of Difference: The Politics of Latin American Cultural Studies*, has gone the furthest in examining such a query. At first blush, Moreiras's response seems to be no. "Subalternity," through the project of subaltern studies that has marketed itself so well, has already been reduced to an included but separate part of consensual thinking, identity thinking. If once uncommon, "subaltern" is now proper to common sense (or, and what amounts to the same, to the senseless).[13] Yet (and this, to me, is the key) because we can disagree with the use or meaning that subaltern studies gives to "subaltern" (Moreiras outlines that disagreement), we can read the term rightly and reasonably but differently from previous interpretations. This very fact, which shows that disagreement is still possible, that consensus is not complete, also indicates that politics, and therefore a practice whose initiating force is the figure of the subaltern, also remains possible.

I began this chapter by noting Gramsci's relatively recent resurgence. The three Gramscian concepts that have inspired the resurgence—the organic intellectual, the subaltern, and Gramsci's particular understanding of civil society—have done so in large part because they lend themselves to the work of "cultural studies" (in the humanities) and the "linguistic turn" (in the social sciences). This work, at its best, demonstrates (1) that, when culture emerges, in essence, from a civil society that is a reflection of the state, or from state-form institutions that are reflections of the West, it often produces oppressive hierarchies through its representations, creating actual material realities; (2) that these hierarchies can be "deconstructed," precisely because they are cultural constructs rather than truths; and (3) that novel understandings of the social, through the inventions of the organic intellectual, or through ones that emit from a subaltern space, are possible, indeed, already operative as forces that upset the neoliberal consensus.

Gramsci's early twentieth-century "common sense," which produces and reproduces the state-form, is the precursor to the early twentieth-first-century "neoliberal consensus." Can one therefore maintain that Gramsci's theory of the interruption of common sense through the subaltern word, his notion of an articulation "between" center and periphery, is already *on the way* to a thesis on the limit, therefore on the incompletion, of a consensual post-democracy that swings on a similar exchange—not between center and periphery but *between* locality and universality or *between* state and market? Can one at least introduce the thesis that Gramsci's thoughts on the state, Marxist but a bit *odd* for a Marxist thinker, are moving to and through a thought of the market (consensus), and are at the same time irreducible to this market? The work of Rancière, as I will illustrate in chapter 3, supplies a timely response.

2.

Biopolitics and Duopolies

Toward Foucault's "Society Must Be Defended"

Recalling our fundamental question—how does a state/market division reproduce a global and globalized neoliberal consensus?— let us begin this chapter with a brief reading of Carl Schmitt's *The Concept of the Political*.[1] I intend to address only one of the most salient points of this provocative work, however, leaving more extensive analyses to others.

Schmitt argues that politics is, by definition, "state" politics (although he defines *state* not only as "polis" but also as "status"). "State" politics in turn is confined to the acts of a sovereign. Schmitt's point here is less that the state is sovereign than the reverse: that which is sovereign is a "state," whereas the state as traditionally understood is not necessarily a sovereign or political domain. Schmitt thus suggests that international groups *might* exist as a "state," as a political site, if or when they form a sovereign coalition.

But what, then, is a sovereign? According to Schmitt, the sovereign is rendered so through the right to posit and physically kill an enemy. The privilege is exercised most obviously during war, when a nation or coalition slays either people of another state or internal adversaries—both now "the enemy"—"rightfully." The *right* to kill the enemy (not necessarily the killing itself) defines the sovereign, and is the condition of all politics. Thus, for Schmitt, confrontations among political parties are not generally political operations. They would not be unless people in one party gained the right to exterminate those in another (which, of course, sometimes occurs).

The friend/enemy division is thereby the fundament of Schmitt's "political." A completed globalization or global market, conversely, would mark for him the end to politics. For within this single global "economy," there would be no enemies, hence no politics. Perhaps wars and competition would remain, as when we speak of the "culture wars." These liberalist confrontations, however, would reveal precisely the waning of the political since, in them, one collective does not possess the right to decimate physically its adversary.

The world has clearly not yet arrived at this completed globalization. In fact, nowhere in *The Concept of the Political* does Schmitt argue that the end of the "state," thereby the end of the political, is eventual (in fact, he seems to regard this end as inconceivable). Schmitt views even the "global" as the name of a politics that casts or will cast new enemies—and new kinds of enemies—who can be killed rightfully. Globalization remains purposefully inconclusive. Indeed, proper to its being is political will: the will to never end politics, or the friend/enemy rift.[2]

Still, Schmitt does suggest that, if politics *were* to come to an end, it would do so through the completion of a process that subsumes both friends and enemies. What would that completion look like?

One might speculate that such an end would hinge on the emergence of an absolute homogeneity, one in which no outsiders exist. For Schmitt, however, the case is just the opposite. The end of politics turns not on the elimination but on an intensification of plurality, multiplicity, and liberal competition: on an increase rather than decrease of differences.[3]

The work of Jean Baudrillard, Schmitt's oddest heir in the critique of liberalism, but his heir nonetheless, permits us to survey such a thesis. Battles between Pepsi and Coke, Baudrillard argues in *Symbolic Exchange and Death*, serve both companies.[4] First of all, they create selection. Given these market wars, consumers do not believe that the stronger product, Coke, possesses a monopoly. They do not feel forced to buy or swallow Coke. They choose Coke freely, often convinced that it tastes better. (This conviction, which can become an actual taste difference in the consumer's mouth—for what it is worth, I myself prefer Coke over Pepsi, and my preference is real, not an illusion—says a great deal about the relation of the global market and aesthetics: I will return to this relation.) Indeed, without Pepsi, or a strong substitute, Coke would likely emerge as an "ugly monopoly," and thus as an enemy of the free market that opened the way for Coke's successes in the first place. That is, if Coke actually ousted its chief competitor, it would lose, not win.

The point is this: in the *duopoly* between Coke and Pepsi, everyone seems victorious. Coke, by winning in a fair competition, emerges as a powerful but relatively appealing, safe product/company. Pepsi also triumphs because, by being linked to Coke, it "defeats" all the "minor" soft drinks, reaping large profits. And the consumer wins because the competition both controls prices and allows for selection.

But the overall champion is the market. Through the competition, this liberal market not only manages to sustain itself. It becomes the object of desire for the citizens and noncitizens it would seem to exploit. This would include persons who, perhaps due to political objections, do not make a purchase, claiming a space outside the market. Those who do not buy, "buy in" most forcefully. It is, after all, choosing itself—to buy this or that, to buy or not to buy, the difference is nil—that inscribes subjects into the market. Merely by choosing, subjects exercise their self-determination, thereby emerge as themselves: liberated subjects.

Stated in other terms, the market attracts and, through the attraction, generates consensus, by granting to consumers their real object of desire: themselves as transcendental beings. The acceptance of the market as the "only way" is a product of the selections by means of which subjects, whatever else they may pick, pick *first* their individual, unalienable, and "free" place. The market, then, is necessary insofar as it grants to subjects precisely themselves as that necessity: essential and permanent rather than contingent and mortal, sovereign rather than bound to the other, emancipated rather than enchained by social relations.

Typically, Baudrillard's renowned concept of "simulation" has been viewed in terms of the commonplace theory that images have replaced reality; the false is the true. If this reading is in some fashion correct, it nonetheless bypasses fundamental steps. The point, for Baudrillard, concerns not simply images, representation, and commodities but their hyperpropagation. The latter yields the assortment of ideas and cultural forms from which subjects select: select themselves. Images or commodities *as such* are not real; they are, as Marx was fond of saying, in fact worthless. Real and invaluable are the transcendental subjects, who capture in these images (*because* they are plural) their essentialness. There is no illusion here; simulation is not false representation. The subjects who can choose *are* the true subjects, the real thing, truth itself. And their tastes, beliefs, and convictions—for example, that the market is necessary— forged by these choices (again, I *really* like Coke), are also true.

The result of the duopoly, of multiplicity and selection, is thereby a potentially infinite number of free, transcendental individuals.

And as transcendental or essential, all are *guaranteed* their position. To be sure, the subjects must circulate to maintain such a slot. They enter the fray since only as potential challengers do they partake of the plurality that liberates them. Yet it matters little whether they conquer their adversaries since the mere circulation, the sheer contribution to the assortment of selections, promises the transcendence, the permanence.

It is noteworthy that the precondition of any subject's position, within the duopoly structure, is a *place* from which to effect confrontation. This point holds even for the numerous identity discourses that have emerged alongside, albeit in opposition to, neoliberal consensus (be the agreement termed "the market," "globalization," or "Western hegemony"). I am referring, for example, to all statements concerning "voices for the voiceless." Despite associations of this voicelessness with "being without a space," the actual a priori of any such participation, voice, or "speaking up" is a separate forum from which to articulate one's complaint (many in the world, needless to say, lack such a forum), from which to compete: private property.

The free market, after all, does not assure all subjects that they will make gains. It only guarantees that they will perennially enjoy the right, the *space*, to do so. They are free always to compete, thereby to reap benefit. Stated in other terms, what the market pledges to subjects, the reason it entices them, is the eternal entitlement to an empty, already given (waiting for them) lot: an immaterial space, external to all others, that they will eventually inhabit. The restrictions if not oppression of capitalism are felt daily by so many—to be sure, by some much more than by others. But because capitalism extends the right to a property outside "crass and transient capitalist worth," to a "higher" land lacking proprietors that *you* (given this lack) can occupy, its restrictions are also assurances of liberty: of a free property. The unalienable (and empty) because transcendental slot—in essence, the eternal values beyond those of money: self-determination, identity, truth, the good, equality, freedom—serve as the ground of capitalism, even and especially capitalism at its most crass. "Lack" or "vacancy," this base (which, of course, is first and foremost the placeholder of the subject) is a lure even and especially for those capitalism subjugates. Indeed, if *you* have not benefited from capitalism, this is only due to the anticapitalist states or forces that prevent the market from completing itself, therefore from emancipating *you,* too. Thus the lack or oppression of a "few" within, even *by* the global market, manages to operate as the demand for more of the market, for the completion of our neoliberal consensus, so that *all,* including *you,* can be liberated.

Possessing the interminable right to *compete* (for Schmitt, in essence, competition is the opposite of the friend/enemy strife)[5] for this territory that is yours, to eternal life itself, sooner or later you will "score" within capitalism: the place for this reaping is held out to *you* everlastingly. The battle without engagement, relation, friendship, risk, end, exchange, or eros (there can be no erotic life without the death drive) on the part of the individual identity— herein lies the "end of the political" as cast by Schmitt and "the end of the social" (a world of individuals without relations) as recast by Baudrillard. The subjects of plurality and selection, the transcendental subjects, are liberated from death, danger, or risk, hence from the political, through a market they therefore find increasingly attractive.

It has been said that the global includes (so as to build a controlling pluralism), whereas the state excludes (so as to maintain homogeneity).[6] This thesis bypasses the simple fact that the logical condition of inclusion is exclusion. The global market *must* exclude if it is to be. What it excludes, though, is not the foreigner or outsider (the Other as object) but death (the other Other as *non*object), and more tangibly, the peoples who embody death: not the "lower human" but, as we will come to understand, the inhuman (death as the "thing" the human cannot determine, as the limit of humanism).

Among these are the utterly impoverished (so near *absolute* loss, so close to existing outside the range of choices that sustains the market), the homeless, terrorists, certain immigrants, and AIDS sufferers: any who recall or *perform* mortality.

If the market must both include everything and exclude something, should it not exclude the no thing, or death? And who stand for such a death if not the ones *imagined* to be unable to insert themselves, *properly*, into the field of exchange? Who index fatality if not certain unmarketable "bodies of this death":[7] the destitute who possess nothing to offer (for sale), not even a ravaged body for labor; those "Communist," monarchical, or poor nations that cannot insert themselves into "proper capitalist commerce" due to their geopolitical choices or circumstances; the AIDS victims who are "supposed to" withdraw from sexual exchanges; the state in possession of nuclear weapons that refuses to *trade them in* for full acceptance into the world market with a promise of deterrence, and so on?

Now, the thinker who most rigorously addresses this last issue—the possible (and impossible) death of death as the end of the political—is Baudrillard's intellectual foe, Michel Foucault. I am thinking particularly of Foucault's 1975–76 lectures on biopolitics, recently published in English as *"Society Must Be Defended."*[8] Here, as elsewhere, Foucault analyzes the genealogy of the West through an investigation into three types of society, separate and intertwined (like a spiral): sovereign, disciplinary, and regulatory (the last type is sometimes designated by Foucault as "governmentality").

Foucault defines *sovereignty* in a manner not entirely unlike Schmitt's: the sovereign is so through the right to kill the other. Foucault's main focus, however, is the historical moment when sovereignty breaks up into related or relative forces: when, for example, the monarchy of the French absolutist era summoned the strength of the bourgeoisie—acknowledging and producing a pluralism of might: that of itself *plus* that of the bourgeoisie—in order to defeat the insurgency of the nobility, which had begun to overstate and overstake its claims (pp. 88–111).

Thus, as always with Foucault, the performance of power generates (rather than represses) the alternative (the bourgeoisie) that upsets this very power. How? Because, Foucault explains, power is exercised by a "small group," not *against,* but *over against* others; it is a relation of forces that, itself, "has no force" (p. 168). The revolt of the sovereign or monarch against the nobility, by enlisting the bourgeoisie as its arm, turned this class into a veritable challenger. The means to the reestablishment of the sovereign actually brought about the demise of that sovereign position (now relative to the force that it raised, therefore no longer absolute).

How and why, then, does power remain fierce and frequently awful? Foucault emphasizes that power invariably overcomes the relation of forces that it is. Forceless, "ultimately, this power becomes the strongest force of all" (p. 168). The execution of might, that is, performs the absolutism ("the strongest force of all") that is structurally impossible (structurally, as we have noted, power is the relation of forces) but historically operative.

Let me clarify by restating these last issues in other terms. There is no abstract power. Without a claim or performance, without the physical, cultural, sexual, psychological, or economic overpowering of another, power is not. Yet this execution does not simply obliterate the other in the name of a world without others: of absolutism. To be sure, the demolished or mortal other, because "defeated," testifies through death to the immortality of its opposite (the sovereign): to the latter's totality and invulnerability. But this same execution is also power's publication, its representation (for Foucault, of course, the classical era I am here describing also ushers in that of representation). Therefore, power's operation on the other/victim/body must be recognized by *another other*, a public *witness*, in order to work, in order to make the sovereign *actually* appear. (This is true even if the sovereign I, which kills, functions as its own witness: the I that sees and the one that acts are not of the same order.)[9] Power, vanquishing alterity through its exercise, nonetheless turns alterity into a force. (Here, the witness possesses this force, one that arises from the sovereign's dependence on the onlooker's recognition.) In sum, power's presentation of the conquest of the other is the performance both of its sovereignty and of the frontier that precludes sovereignty: of the exposure to the threatening exteriority that this absolute must check if it is to stand.

The sovereign's fall, its self-construction as one among a plurality of forces, its production of emergent strengths, therefore of multiplicity, does not then yield emancipation. The fact that Foucaultian power *produces* rather than represses does not mean that it *liberates*. It, in fact, gives way to a new form of control (one, to be sure, that is not without its freedoms): disciplinary society.

It is by now well known how discipline functions. It individualizes, classifies, and categorizes bodies. In the realm of knowledge, it creates separate fields, each with its own rules of authority. In other words, it generates *experts:* those who "know" solely within the limits of their domain, and who construct and maintain those limits so as to protect the authority of the expertise that grants them their proper intellectual and social place.

Thus, as disciplines grow in number, those seeking knowledge—"students" (in the most general sense of the word)—need not engage the territories of proficiency that they deem "useless." They can instead turn to another specialist, every bit as legitimate as the rejected one. Expertise in any one discipline, indeed, is expertise as such, sufficient unto itself: useful in that it supplies the expert or expert-to-be a social slot. Conversely, comprehension of the *relationship* of expertises, the acquisition of knowledge that is irreducible to any single proficiency, surfaces as an inefficient, complex, and time-consuming means of entry (it requires familiarity not only with *two* fields but *also* with their relation, which pertains to neither field), and thus as a relatively valueless task.

A discourse fits or does not into legitimate and legitimizing groupings; "knowledge" is restricted by these confines. Truth is obedience to an order. Thus another consequence of discipline: truths, once absolute, emerge as flexible, exchangeable, and reversible. One expertise, based on norms, modes, and technologies— all of which easily shift—displaces another. A plurality of acts, facts, and specialists surface but are managed: not through the repression of the illegitimate but through the ever-expanding and ever-changing cataloging and separating out of the disciplines.

Likewise, bodily or sexual practices within disciplinary society are not legal or illegal; they are charted as "normal" or "abnormal." On the political front, the sovereign as such ceases to dictate. Instead, a dispersed and imaginary gaze monitors the social, inducing individuals to situate themselves within a correct order or site.

For discipline, then, the marginality that power as a nonrepressive operation produces—that which is *classified* as "delinquent" or "marginal," for example, the barbarian in the New World as discussed by Foucault (pp. 195–97)—works for the disciplinary good. The "outsider" falls to and thus affirms classification and science themselves.

Here the scientific revolution, essential to Foucault's understanding of discipline, enters in. It has little to do with "new discoveries." It is connected instead to methods of taxonomy that are deployed by and that define all disciplines. In advance, these posit unknowns or outsides as "classifiable." Science, in other words, does not—during or around the "classical era"—displace philosophy as the former "knowledge of all knowledge." It is not itself a kind of knowledge but a *technique* that, covering all, *replaces* knowledge.

Take the character of the masturbator, a figure Foucault addresses throughout "*Society Must be Defended*." Masturbation itself, of course, did not emerge during the "age" of discipline. What materialized was the categorization (rather than knowledge) of the practice. Cast as dangerous or innocuous, depraved or blameless, unwell or healthy, the *figure* of the masturbator, the *subject* of masturbation, came into being at this juncture.

If discipline does not repress but invites "abnormal" or marginal practices/forces such as masturbation, it does so by constructing each of these forces as an individual exercise, as a distinct body that can be labeled and weeded out from other bodies. By walling off one subject from the other, discipline generates a plurality of operations but inhibits relations among them, thereby politics, ethics, or, in Baudrillard's terminology, "the social." And that is one main way by which it effects control: discipline keeps all subjects in their individual places, unto themselves, even when the number of places and subjects grows.

Apparently. Yet none of the above alters the fact that discipline does indeed produce the alternatives to the power that it exercises. All forms of power, according Foucault, do so. And even though we have not yet been able (we will be soon) to glimpse precisely how those alternatives function—they seem to be incorporated in advance as categories; hence they appear to be without any function except that of the reproduction of the already extant—the fact of their emergence necessarily escorts in, *demands*, another means of power and management. Foucault calls it "regulation" or "biopolitics."

In Foucault's terminology, "regulatory society" governs, not bodies or individuals, but the "population" (pp. 239–64), which does not represent an individual or a collection of individuals (such as the literal family or the family as metaphor for the state) but the species. The "population" is, in fact, too complex, murky, and ill defined to yield to discipline: to the classification and categorization of bodies. Banking on tactics such as statistics, however, regulation can govern and thus normalize a field. Life expectancies, ethnic demographics, kinds of sexual practices, sizes of families, and so on—these charters and polls are the mechanisms of a "governmentality" that standardizes a population that neither government as such nor the private sector nor civil society nor international organizations can actually "count" or "account for."

A key aspect of regulatory society, however, lies in a slightly distinct matter. As a biopolitics, regulation's foundation is not the right to kill the enemy (the sovereign's right) but the right to life: to the biological "living on," not of the individual, but of the subject as *species*, of a humanity that must avoid falling prey to deadly outsiders or "contaminants." Biopolitics is a hygienic operation above all. In the interest of the supremacy of life, biopower strives to erase from the scene the one "thing" it cannot reach, to wit, death: "Death," writes Foucault, "is beyond the reach of power, and power has a grip on it only in general, overall, or statistical terms. Power has no mandate over death, but, it can control mortality [mortality rates, and so on]" (p. 248). Indeed, as we will come to understand, regulation's power rests, not in the murder of the enemy, but in the murder of the *dying* that some "other" embodies.

Statistics, then, do not necessarily or merely aid in the construction of the norms that, in theory, they only chronicle; they are not tools of discipline. According to Foucault, as the "base" or model of the nation shifts from the family to the population, statistics construct life or health as the matter that must be managed and maintained. Political beliefs, ethical models, and cultural norms—in effect, control—emerge as by-products of the statistical link between social demographics/practices and the population's mortality. Which sexual routines are healthy and which are not? What is the proper number of children per family? Are school programs fitting for the youth? When X percentage of the people are counted as obese, should we characterize obesity as an infirmity? What is the ethnic composition of a given group: the poor, the intelligent, the hale, athletes, gays?

Each gauge is taken in the interest of the wellness of the population. And each produces real social, governmental, intellectual, economic, and personal positions. Thus, for example, those who through statistics "prove" that the "poor" tend toward "drug addiction"—even though no accurate count of these two fields (the "poor," the "addicted") is conceivable since their parameters cannot but be arbitrary (addicted to what?)—might draw conclusions about the "natural lack of will" of certain persons/groups, therefore about the "naturalness" of a society in which the division between wealth and poverty is wide: a "nature" that culture/politics should or should not correct. In this as in all cases, the *bios* (the [ill] health of an underprivileged subdivision prone to substance dependence) of the population surfaces as the factor that determines who or what is natural, just, right, good, normal, and what is to be done about it all. A healthy society is taken for a just one.

Biopolitics consequently feeds racism, the true name, according to Foucault, for all modern state injustice: "Once the State functions in the biopower mode, racism alone can justify the murderous function of the State" (p. 256). Why racism and why racism *alone*? Why, indeed, does Foucault insist that, according to Marx, the *race struggle*—the battle between the species and its contaminants—precedes both the class struggle and racism itself (p. 79)?

AIDS victims may not "officially" be a race. Yet, for Foucault, the "gay life" so facilely associated with these sufferers is ostracized or marginalized precisely as a "race" that menaces the population by (according to the imaginary behind the idea of "the population") sexually and *biologically* blending "its" fatal illness into the population's "well-being" (and also into the "sanctity" of propagation and the "clean pleasure" of "good" sex). Within biopolitics, masturbators are also seen as a "race." They are the signal of a biological degeneracy—one passed down through the generations—that will eventual spread throughout the human pedigree, infecting it (p. 252). Immigrants, refugees, and foreigners, likewise, "flood" the nation with cheap labor; as a biological *race*, they "take food out of the mouth of," thereby killing, not the state, but (once more) the "species." An unhealthy society is taken for an unjust one.

I want to emphasize that fear of these peoples (AIDS victims, masturbators, immigrants) is not rooted in the possibility that "I," my body, family, even country will be damaged. The fright sprouts from the idea that "humanity itself" will be ruined, even if "I" am not affected. Thus, for example, given massive urban immigration, antipathy toward the city is often voiced by those who do not live in, indeed rarely visit, metropolitan areas. The concern here is not for one's own body (as in disciplinary society), untouched by the city, but biological "well-being" as such.

Alarm about terrorism operates in like manner. "We" are not threatened by terrorists. The "population" is. President Bush (if I may use a contemporary example: winter 2003) need not prove that Iraq will do damage to actual American people with horrible biological agents. To make a case for war, he must instead convince Americans that Iraq puts the *species* at risk. Bush (or his administration) consequently presents a litany of *statistics* concerning the tonnage of weapons of mass destruction for which Saddam Hussein has not accounted. The numbers are far too large, and the weapons far too abstract, for us to gauge how these "arms of mass destruction" might affect us (any of us) personally. Yet the numbers and weapons are "just right" for a demonstration as to how humanity is imperiled. Therefore it should come as no surprise that, at the precise moment that Bush publicly sells the massive threat, he instructs all residents or citizens to "go about business as normal." Individuals are not in danger here; they should not worry. They should, however, remain deeply concerned for the biological species, hence advocate war against Iraq.

For Foucault, the "race struggle" thus names regulation's defense against death, or rather, against all those who remind society of death. The excluded within *real, existing racism*—and here

Foucault echoes Baudrillard—is not the Other life or identity but the *Other of life* (death), the biological incarnation (to repeat, AIDS sufferers and terrorists are among the best examples) of the physical corruption of the entire species: death "has become the most private and shameful thing of all (and ultimately, it is not so much sex as death that is the object of a taboo)" (p. 247).

The death of all is the dirty secret of racism. For Foucault, the other that the market, or homogeneity in general, most fear is life that, like a damaged section of DNA, a corrupt computer byte, or an undiagnosed computer virus—bad information in any case—might "out" the death, not of an individual, a state, or even a race (such as the white race), but (once more) the species.[10] This other, lacking an identity or emblem, cannot be tracked. It therefore invades unmonitored and uncontrolled as the corruption that imperils humanity as a whole.

Indeed, bad DNA and computer viruses serve as excellent metaphors for this "minimal life" within the biopolitical field. The "new other" is the outside that is not outside but, instead, is the species' indecipherable, pulsating interior, one that must be eradicated in the name of the species' well-being. Public but unreadable, such life may well be imaginary. What is certain, though, is that its existence can be and has been displaced onto real peoples, breathing bodies. These represent unidentifiable, untrackable, or unremarkable life: life without place or tag that, because of this (non)quality, can assume its place anywhere, subsume the everywhere (akin to a disease), overtake not this or that people but the entire "population." Without a "without," without any "out" at all, control society consequently devours itself—humanity devours humanity—in order to rid itself of the interior menace that it cannot "make out," thereby manage. In Foucault's work, racism names this entire biopolitical process.

Having moved the discussion of race and racism from the field of the visible and representation over to the domain of biopolitics,

Foucault is then able to define racism as "revolutionary discourse in inverted form" (p. 81). Racism surfaces, he contends, precisely when the state "fails" to manage the life of the nation. After all, bound to legal edicts and financial interests, the state cannot but permit "bodies of death" (for example, "foreigners" as cheap labor) into the midst of the population. Racism thus revolts against the state, the law, or both in order to protect life, on *moral* instead of legal grounds. In other words, the "racist revolution" desires something loftier than the "perfect sovereign" or "perfect State" (Nazi Germany, which is Foucault's prime example, possessed precisely this desire: not for a perfect Germany but for a perfect species in the wake of the *overcoming* of Germany). It seeks the nation as a faultless, hale genus.

The "nation" of nation-state, a concept that emerges in or around the wake of the French Revolution, must therefore be viewed as both a disciplinary and regulatory operation. On the one hand, such a nation *represents* (in the many senses of the term) the state. It is the collection and relation of, as well as the separation between, disciplines, individuals, and institutions (for example, those of civil society and the private sector) by means of which the state effects its rule. On the other hand, the nation stands in opposition to the state. It—the terrorist *and* antiterrorist nation, for example—exempts itself from state edicts and limits, extends itself beyond the state, in order to defend against contamination (death, embodied by "other" races) in the name of a larger, "global" matter: "life." Either the nation produces/reproduces the state or it displaces (a displacement that can be Left- or Right-leaning) state law in the name of a "higher" rule.

Although not confined to the state, consensual postdemocracy is likewise composed of a dynamic between disciplinary methods and biopolitics. It confines each being or body (or each body confines itself) to its own place as the subject of discipline: as a part that is a counted or represented part. But this gesture is insufficient since the wall or boundary between any two subjects, which renders order possible, is also the contact of one with the other. As the "inter," such a divider is therefore the "source" of a potential "biological" contamination (where there is contact, there is possible contamination): of the death of each body, of the species. Biopolitics is thereby called upon as a means to wipe out these walls, this exposure of self to a "toxin" (the "races" that, if mixed in, act like toxins): to remove the same barriers that disciplinary society constructs in order to contain its bodies. Without lines/boundaries/borders, there is no discipline; there are no "cells." Without the removal of these betweens (as stamps of contagion and fatality), there is no regulation or biopolitics.

Consensual postdemocracy requires partitions *and* the erasure of partitions in order to stand. It demands nations or states that mark friends off from enemies; and it requires a body without borders that, because the condition of contamination (the boundary that friend and enemy share: a fence, yes, but also a site of crossover) is absent, stands for the absolute health and pure life of the globe.

Indeed, consensus revolves around this il-logic, resolving it. It casts the world as the duopoly of discipline and regulation, of the finite and the limitless, of the subject as at once bounded (a particular identity/property set off from other identities/properties) and boundless (universal, the site of the choice among identities/properties that transcends them all), of sharply defined regions and of a whole without segments—preserving, without reason, as what goes without saying, all players in the process.

Foucault's regulatory society, then, permits us to grasp globalism and the market (which thinkers such as Giorgio Agamben, following Foucault, have now begun to do)[11] in a manner distinct from "the end or decline of the state" topos. Indeed, it should come as no surprise that Foucault, already in 1975, casts biological warfare—a globalization matter if ever there was one—as a key topos within the biopolitical.[12] These biological agents are, of course, part and parcel of the scientific experimentation (biotechnology or biomedicine) whose purpose is both the multiplication (cloning?) and preservation (new cures) of the species. But as life added to life, such "medicines" cannot but yield the very phenomenon, in the form of new and dangerous germs or figures, that they strive to keep off scene: mass death. In fact, efforts to build remedies for bioterrorism require the fabrication of new viruses—which can escape laboratory control—so as then to craft the antidote. Thus, on the one hand, biotechnology generates the divisions or limits (between those who use the technology for "good" and those who use it for "evil") that sustain the new world order; and, on the other, it promises an unlimited, deathless species that overcomes all divisions and ends—and that also, though in a different way, sustains this new world order.

Biopolitics, at least in part, names an affair that strives to maintain the frontier between the correct and incorrect, the proper and improper, the civilized and uncivilized deployment of biotechnology. It strives to stand as a disciplinary site, one that marks off, on the international stage, friends from enemies. But the frontier of biopolitics, as frontier, also points up the division, borders, the internal contamination, the perilous breakdown of discipline as such. As it turns out, the educated biomedical expert can be as improper (dangerous) as proper, as civilized (dangerous *because* civilized) as uncivilized, as much an agent of unimaginable death as of eternal life. The terrorist enemy and the enemy of the terrorist materialize as competitors for the same space of the *bios*. Biomedicine and bioterrorism are not two fields but intersect to form a single field: the biopolitical. Differences between the two, to be sure, exist. Yet since both bring the biological death of the species onto the global stage, the seemingly real wars that such distinctions (between nations who deploy the *bios* for good or for evil) apparently encourage only simulate market skirmishes (which, of course, makes them no less real). The opposition, in this case, is not a "fake" enemy that, when eliminated, leaves the actual enemy (and thus actual politics for Schmitt) to be killed. This "enemy" is instead the competitor simulated. The determination to kill the adversary thus leaves reality untouched: reality as the *actual* competitions—which, by generating sides and choices as the freedom of every One, relieve all subjects or the entire species from death—between cooperatives (say, oil companies) *within* the species and *without* enemies. War is the simulation of the market; competition between capitalism's powers is mimed by the friend/enemy divide of state combat. State law (discipline) falls; market regulation assumes control of war itself.

But we should examine Foucault's biopolitics from still another angle. I indicated previously that consensual postdemocracy differs from other models of consensus (such as Habermas's) since its backing is not "democratic" negotiation (however rigorous or complex) concerning the good but a good that "goes without saying." How, then, is the exclusion of death, which for Foucault and Baudrillard defines contemporary politics or biopolitics, also about the exclusion of this *saying*, of *language*? One might rephrase this query in light of the above analysis: How is the resistance to language actually the resistance to a biological contaminant that could destroy the species? It will take some time before we can respond; for now, we pick up the aforementioned discussion of Rancière.

3.

The People, the Uncounted, and Discardable Life in Rancière

It is now the moment to expand upon Gramsci's thoughts on the subaltern by relating them to recent theses put forth in Rancière's *Disagreement*:

> Politics exists wherever the count of parts and parties of society is disturbed by the inscription of a part of those who have no part. It begins when the equality of anyone and everyone is inscribed in the liberty of the people. This liberty of the people is an empty property, an improper property through which those who are nothing purport that their group is identical to the whole of the community. Politics ceases . . . wherever the whole of community is reduced to the sum of its parts with nothing left over.[1]

These words can be understood as follows. Politics, for Rancière, concerns not the fair or unfair distribution of the parts of society or of the state. It addresses the allotment of the "in common" that members of a political community share as the condition, in the first place, of the community's division into sectors, properties, and parties. "It is an order that determines the partition of what is common"; or "the political begins precisely when one stops balancing profits and losses and worries instead about distributing *common* lots and evening out communal shares. . . . "[2] One such common lot (though not one among others) is equality (equality before the law, for example: yet equality, for Rancière, is defined in other, more fundamental ways, as we will soon see). All members of the state, in fact, share this parity a priori—but only those who are counted. For there exist factions that are not included in any such count: "the part of those who have no part." In a political community that grants equality to all, the sum of the parts that are equal, paradoxically, never adds up to the whole.

To grasp the paradox, let us consider the notion of "the people," one that Rancière analyzes in detail.[3] On the one hand, "the people" includes the whole community. No separate group *is* the people. If all are equally "the people," if the people is the all, it cannot also be a section.

On the other hand, "the people" refers precisely to an individual part or party. A statement such as "the people approve of the decision to go to war" testifies to this fact. It presents "the people" as one sector of the whole that opposes another, presumably a "nonpeople" (in this particular example, the nonpeople might be "the elite").

Now, according to Rancière, *this* "people," this subdivision named "the people," *represents* equality. It stands as and for "that which is equal," a point made most apparent when "the people" designates the "rabble," the "masses," the "horde": "The people are nothing more than the undifferentiated mass of those who have no positive qualification—no wealth or virtue—but who are nonetheless acknowledged to enjoy the same freedom as those who do . . . the demos attributes to itself as its proper lot the equality that belongs to all citizens."[4] The people as the "masses" (or as the *demos* of democracy) embody a sameness without a specific property. Nothing defines "this people" except the equality that *everyone* "possesses," meaning that it (the people) is not distinct. The words *the people,* it would seem, do not represent any identity or collective individual, indeed, anyone at all. A quantity (because a part) without a quality, the people represent equality.

This explains why, as Ernesto Laclau argues, "the people" can function as a tool for divergent ideological programs, ranging from the far Left to the far Right. Any specific ideology or affiliation that is identified with "the people"—with the all—will attract individuals/collectives by claiming to represent "all" equally. U.S. "liberalism" (Laclau would contend) best succeeds by casting itself as the "liberalism of the people," as the "liberal people." But conservatism works similarly; it prospers as the "conservatism of the people," as the "conservative-people." The parts/parties that attach the name "people," that are overdetermined by the "people"—the latter, calling forth the subject, operates not by itself but as bound to a series of equivalences/differences—are more likely to gain traction.[5] I should add that, although the inclination of a "politics of the people" can fall to the Left or Right, the difference is not random. For Laclau, when the people's actions (re)define class differences, when the all (the people) materializes as a specific part (the lower classes), "the people" inspires leftist interventions. Yet when "the people" designates a classless group, as it did in fascist movements, it tilts to the Right.

Whenever "the people," in a given context, does not merely *pass* as a name for a transcendent totality but instead is *inscribed* into the body politic as a part, politics emerges. Rancière writes: "Politics exists wherever the count of parts and parties of society is disturbed by the inscription of a *part of those who have no part.*"[6] When "the people," which plays the part of those who have no part—of the part that is the whole—situates itself into or appears within the totality *as if* one part among others, politics goes to work.

Indeed, this inscription of equality, of a "people" (a whole) that goes uncounted in the count of parts, discloses the wrong, the miscount within a sum or community that, as it turns out, is unequal to itself. All the parts, in a society where all are equally parts, are taken into account. Yet because those ("the people") who stand for "the equal" cannot be included among the portions, equality itself is left out of the equation. There is no (e)quality in equality. The task of politics is to address this problem. Political labor, in the face of the inscription of a miscount, reconfigures the communal arrangement so as to attend to the damage or damaged.

Rancière labels this inscription of equality or the people "subjectification," which is not to be confused with subjectivity, hence identity. In fact, "any subjectification is a *disidentification*."[7] He notes that

> the production through a series of actions of a body and a capacity for enunciation not previously identifiable within a given field of experience, whose identification is thus part of the reconfiguration of experience. . . . It is an operator that connects and disconnects different areas, regions, identities, functions, and capacities existing in the configuration of a given experience— that is, in the nexus of distributions of the police order and whatever equality is already inscribed there, however fragile and fleeting such inscriptions may be.[8]

These kinds of inscriptions—the nexus between sites and signs that also functions as the core force for the reorganization of a given experience—recall the operations of Gramsci's language-art. It is Rancière, in fact, who contends (as previously cited in chapter 1) that "modern political animal is first a literary animal."[9] The duty of the Gramsci language-art, as I have maintained, is to articulate or invent a name for the relation or common space between two or more discourses (properties, places, domains, classes). The language-art term designates (without being) the portion of each discourse that does not belong, as a property, to any: language as such. The "in common" that all signs, discourses, and fields of experience impart prior to any separation of bodies, language is the border or limit that simultaneously splits collections (of words, discourses, subjects, classes, cultures, lands, worlds, etc.) into pieces and recollects those pieces into wholes.

In other words, communication depends both on the severance of speaking parties and on their connection. This dividing/binding, which is not simply essential to language but language's very essence, is neither one idiom within the world's compilation of idioms nor one of the elements within a particular tongue. Nor does it sit outside these domains. It is what these various sites share without "owning." Heraclitus, Giorgio Agamben notes, labels the communicative nature of humanity "the Common": common to all, property of none—this is language's share of and in the social.[10] And just as Agamben deploys this idea of the Common/communication that comes between speakers (as split and link) to grasp contemporary politics, so also does Rancière.

The Common, then, this "language-art" partition that recalls language as such, always—necessarily—appears out of context. Perpetually removed "from the naturalness of a place," *anomalous*, it is not "identifiable within a given field of experience." Its "context," indeed, is the All, the contrary of any context, any *particular* time or place.

In and of itself, the actual articulation of this Common may not be peculiar. But because it "turns up" inside a territory (an existent context or field) where all other signifiers or parts seem more or less familiar, it "looks" out of joint (I will supply an example of this "look" presently). The effort to distinguish and make sense of the "previously" unidentifiable inscription "is thus part of the reconfiguration of experience": of politics.

A given sense, if I may continue to combine Gramsci's and Rancière's vocabulary, is at a specific moment marked by the representation of a part (say, "the people") that is at once too common (embodiment of equality, evenness) and uncommon (oddness). The "host" field then modifies itself—this is the task of politics—so as to render identifiable, include in its total, the extra. For politics to happen the unnatural or nonnative guest, the inscription or limit, need not adjust to a new home. The home needs to rearrange itself, reconfigure its naturalized habitat so as to address the inequity that the guest, as the marker of a miscount or inequality, embodies. Yet the guest—and this is key—is not the wronged being, but rather the *stamp*, the "outing" of the wrong that precedes the guest's advent, one this guest, too, must work to right.

Let us pursue these last matters by examining Rancière's analysis of an event at the 1832 trial of the revolutionary Auguste Blanqui.[11] Asked his profession, Blanqui responded, "Proletarian." He was first informed that this was not an occupation. But due to the cleverness of his reply, the judge found himself compelled to include "proletarian" among the professions.

Proletarian, in this example (and I do not want to extend the people/proletariat association beyond this one case), is an articulation that operates like Rancière's "people." As Marx argued, and as Rancière reminds us, the proletariat is an undifferentiated mass that stands for class itself, which everyone "has." The embodiment of class that, as such, cannot *simply* be counted among the division of classes (the parts) that make up the whole, proletariat is the indicator of class itself. Without a quality or *property* by means of which we could classify it as a separate category or political community, the proletariat drifts about undefined as the menace to—and as the potential disbanding of—all classes.

Blanqui, however, managed to make the proletariat *count* within a "field of experience," within a category, tally, or collective that was not, seemingly, its proper habitat: the list of *professions*. He inscribed "proletarian" into that account. "Correctly" amiss within the inventory of occupations, Blanqui's "proletarian" was nonetheless strangely counted in. It appeared, in other words, as the index of the *oddness* or inequality, the incorrectness, the wrong within a list as a whole in which all are supposed to be equally a part, a whole of a *citizenry* within which belonging to a *proper profession* was—and is—deeply tied to being a proper member. As a proletarian, Blanqui claimed to belong to "'the profession of thirty million Frenchmen who live off their labor and are deprived of political rights'" (p. 37).

But how precisely did Blanqui oblige the judge to make the proletariat and thus himself count? According to Rancière, he did so by taking "profession" to mean "profession of faith." He declared his "profession" to be an allegiance to a cause: that of the proletariat. In essence, he pronounced the word *profession* in an eccentric but legitimate and rational manner: rightly but oddly. For him, "proletarian" designated (in Rancière's words) an "interval between a condition and a profession" (pp. 137–38); it did not fall precisely within either of the two groupings. And the judge thereby deemed it both right and necessary to consign "proletarian" to one domain or the other—the interval, after all, was not one of his choices—in this case the catalog of professions.

By doing so, this official did not right wrong. He helped mark it. The actual wrong, within Blanqui's appeal, was obviously not the exclusion of "proletarian" from the list of possible jobs (or even from the list of classes). The proletariat's inclusion therein—indeed, the inclusion of any exclusion—therefore did little to address the dismal circumstances of "thirty million Frenchmen" (besides, even if the judge did make law that enhanced the lives of thirty million Frenchmen, he would not precisely improve the situation of Blanqui's wronged people: a proletariat that, by definition, belongs to no state or nation). The inscription of the unfitting member "proletarian" onto the chart of possible professions, rather than fixing an inequity, exposed the general inequality of the state's general equality, thereby calling for(th) politics.

In truth, not even the inclusion of all (rather than of a particular, such as the proletariat) would tackle wrong. "Full inclusion," for Rancière, is precisely not "democratic"; quite to the contrary, it is the signal of an apolitical "consensual postdemocracy" in which "the whole of community is reduced to the sum of its parts with nothing left over" (p. 123). Indeed, for there to be democracy or politics wrongs must be attended to, miscounts recounted, misidentifications accommodated. If there is no sign of such wrong, no part that is as well the whole, politics is not done; there is nothing for it to do. Rather than politics (justice), there is solely consensus (health).

In this consensus, then, wrong survives. But it draws no remark. It is unremarkable. Without the inscription, suggestion, or "digestion" of something "disagreeable" within the body politic, the consensus "goes without saying." It slides down well enough, with no ill feelings. The "field of experience" does not reconfigure its parts so as to include the uncommon Common that enters its midst. At best, it permits some "equality figure" to enter as the "other," as the difference of a universal diversity. This difference thereby materializes as a value (diversity), a part that is a healthy part of a healthy whole. It in no way induces the "current arrangements" to shift since those arrangements—though still the hosts of inequity—grow increasingly pluralist, and now seem more right than ever.

Because all-inclusive, the community looks healthy as it is: Why do we need politics to complicate matters? The desire for reconfiguration, in this context, would indeed appear somewhat perverse since matters are the only way that they could be: "State powe . . . only ever does the only thing possible, only ever what is possible by strict necessity in the context of the growing intricacy of economies within the global market" (pp. 112–13).

Within a pluralist consensus, in brief, one finds no "nothing that is not a part," no counter of the miscount, such as the people or the proletarian. One encounters only parties, each a part of the whole. Rancière's idea of consensual democracy is clearly indebted, therefore, to Hegel's notion of "bad infinity," which names an accumulation without limits, one that adds on indefinitely to itself, but whose additions never alter the whole.[12] This sum is, or builds, an unlimited pluralism that conserves homogeneity, the One. A poor absolutism, bad infinity is development and accumulation without cultural, social, or economic change, expansion that does not grow historically. (And what does not grow, according to Hegel, deteriorates.) The global market, as addressed by Rancière, exemplifies this bad infinity. Here the abysmal gap between rich and poor—the "haves" and the "have-nots"—grows and grows as more and more peoples are added into an increasingly efficient and pluralist economy: nothing is advanced in the advancement. Nonprogressive progression, the politics of progressive nonprogressiveness, bad infinity is a bad agreement or bad consensus—a neoliberal consensus.

We noted that politics commences, according to Rancière, not when the parts of society are distributed fairly but when the common lot of all is divided up, when the distribution of an original division takes place. Should one designate this topos, this communal share which is the condition of the advent of parts and parties— which "divvies up" and reassembles a territory that is not the original property of any "who"—"communication," "language as such," as I have previously?

In *Disagreement,* Rancière directly addresses the possibility through the central issue of the text, disagreement itself: "Disagreement occurs whenever contention over what speaking means constitutes the very rationality of the speech situation. The interlocutors both understand and do not understand the same thing by the same words."[13] A disagreement is always rational, with each interlocutor understanding a speech act differently. Both comprehensions must be reasonable if there is to be "disagreement" as Rancière uses the term.

Politics, for Rancière, is thereby set off from the mere "order of domination and the disorder of revolt" (p. 12). Domination and the subversion of domination (revolt), to be sure, often take place within political operations. But domination/revolt battles for power do not pertain to the essence of the political. (Rancière's point, in fact, is that the ground of politics, the "in common," is not itself a property of politics: the essence of the political is not itself political.) This is mainly because the condition of any "order of domination" is the order itself: a command. And the prerequisite of those who command effectively is the capacity for reason and speech of those who are commanded. The commanders, indeed, always already recognize the reason of those they control as they construct their order. To be directed, the "other" must be in possession of language rather than irrational babble, must enjoy, at the least, the capacity of being communicated to: of comprehension. Only because of this can the commanded process and perform instructions correctly, and thus be properly subjugated. The two parties, by the logic of their division into commanded and commanders, are equally linguistic. And that "in common," that part (language) which is not a proper part, a property of either side, is the requisite of disagreement, attendance to the disagreement, and thereby politics.

But we ought clarify: if the commanders and the commanded share speech, they do not share the *same* speech, the same understanding. B can hear A's command differently, oddly, not according to A's intentions, but sensibly all the same. The sharing or Common is then the rift, the discord that, failing to fall to the particular reason of either subject (but without which there would be no subject), renders politics—as the addressing of the dissonance between reasonable understandings and "understanders"—conceivable. Absent this allotment, conversely, there can be no such schism, and consequently "there is no politics. There is only the order of domination and the disorder of revolt" (p. 12).

Now, we noted that when Blanqui uses the word *profession,* he means "allegiance" rather than "occupation." He uses the signifier reasonably but in a manner that it is not easily "identifiable within a given field of experience" (not unlike a pun, whose "second" meaning is just as legitimate as its "first," yet frequently catches the listener off-guard, producing irritation, laughter, or other sentiments). This is made possible by the mise-en-scéne of all speech acts: "The interlocutors both understand and do not understand the same thing by the same words." The context (which includes the history of each party) in which interlocutor A speaks can never be precisely the same as the one in which interlocutor B listens (and vice versa). Therefore, B always can grasp a situation or speech act differently from A. B understands A and A understands that B possesses understanding. But B on occasion disagrees with A's understanding. A cannot understand how B understands as B does: that is why there is disagreement and not the simple domination of one party by the other.

Consensual postdemocracy, at a minimum, means the end of disagreement in this sense. Disagreement is indeed impossible if every presentation, word, act, or view "is the only thing possible, only ever what is possible by strict necessity" (pp. 112–13). To be sure, oppositions to this "only thing possible," the only right, the only way, will be voiced. Yet, according to Rancière, if by "strict necessity" power takes the single achievable path, to speak or hear in a way different from this lone possibility is literally inconceivable. An oppositional voice, if it exists, cannot express a disagreement. Either it emerges as an additional party and thus contributes, as a proper portion of an overall agreement, to a controlled pluralism (consensus), to the accumulations of a "bad infinity." Or else it gives sound to an absurdity, to an outside din that cannot reshape anything: in Rancière's terms, to "noise" instead of speech, where the opposition is heard as the passionate or pathetic grumble of those who, because devoid of logic, cannot even disagree correctly. Such people can feel injury but cannot properly name its location, cause, or reason; they cannot make an appeal that might be addressed and possibly remedied.

Rancière casts this unheeded opposition, not as without language, however, but as without words. In fact, the "noise" that this antagonist makes is an element that all particular idioms and articulations equally share (even those of the deaf). The part of any and every speech act that belongs properly to no language, "noise," in Rancière's paradigm, is one index of language itself as the uncounted within every act of representation. It is the finitude of reason that opens the way for a reasonable disagreement, and that inscribes the possibility (but does not represent) of another reason into reason itself. The latter points up not a pragmatics of the irrational but the *promise* of an alternative reason, hence the coming of a reason irreducible to that of consensus or—and what amounts to the same thing—the advent of a politics irreducible to battles of power among parties, to rebellion and domination, or to revolution and counterrevolution. These last, in fact, no longer belong, if they ever did, to politics but to consensual postdemocracy.

A crucial question, which has been simmering beneath our analysis, now arises in full force: Is the part that is no part a *subject*, such as the "people" or the "proletariat"? Or are the "people" and the "proletariat" merely names that, in a particular context, incarnate the part/thing that is no part, to wit, language itself? Terms such as Blanqui's "proletarian," indeed, seem to represent two disparate entities. On the one hand, proletarian stands for the *who* of the "part of those who have no part." *Somebody* (some group) does not count within the body politic. On the other hand, as a signifier oddly deployed, at variance with its context, proletarian embodies the disagreeable "thing" that lingers within the common sense without ever forming a portion of it: language as the "*inscription* of the *part* of those who have no part."

As part or thing, "proletarian" would indeed stand for the Common that is least common, for an original sharing or collective zone that is also necessarily a site of possible agreement/discord. As linguistic figure rather than as subject—and all figures are irreducible to common sense because this is what a figure is: a sign or set of signs that are irreducible to common sense—it indexes the existence of language as the limit of consensus, as the rift among and *common* to all parties, and as the demand of politics. This does not mean, of course, that figures (poetic or literary language) exemplify "language itself." In fact, there is no example of "language itself." Each such potential example is a sign, the representation of a particular signified (but the signified is never "language"), when language is the limit, border, or "inter" of all representation.

But again, these last points may run contrary to Rancière's intentions. Rancière's part that is no part, after all, seems clearly to be an actual political *actor*: "Democracy is the designation of subjects that do not coincide with the parties of the state and of society, floating subjects that deregulate all representations of places and portions" (p. 100). But, on closer inspection, we note that as soon as the association between interruption and political actor is drawn, Rancière withdraws it by positing the force of intervention as a disagreeable *interlocution* that does not sit well within any discussion, and which consequently represents no subject, no actor. Indeed, this is how and why the enunciation, and not only "actors," itself acts: "It is not a discussion between partners, but an interlocution that *undermines* the very situation of interlocution" (p. 100; emphasis added).

How, then, can "people" and "proletarian," on the one side, and "interlocution" and "interval" (proletarian as the *interval* between a condition and profession), on the other, name the same idea: the part of those who have no part? They can do so, it would *appear*, if "people" and "proletarian" are figures (the specific figure is metonymy: the part that is no part for being the whole) that make the miscount of the whole, the wrong of the state, appear. "People" and "proletarian," to be sure, are human groups. But they *appear* (Rancière never ceases to emphasize the importance of this *appearance*), prompting politics, when or because they "come out" as language, as improper to the field of representation or subjectivity from which they surface. Blanqui's "proletarian," for example, ultimately names for Rancière less a collective of political actors than an *articulation* between two concepts ("an interval between a condition and a profession"). Thus, when language—not the "people" but, as the following quotation suggests, the *name* "people"—vanishes, so also does politics: "Consensus . . . is the disappearance of the mechanisms of appearance, of the miscount and the dispute opened by the *name* 'people' and the vacuum of their freedom" (p. 102; emphasis added).

All the same, we seem to be going in circles, leaving the fundamental query unresolved: Is the part that is no part a "who" or "what"? Is "the people" an actual "people" or just an example of a certain kind of name? Even Rancière's reading of Blanqui's intervention is ambiguous on this point. Although my previous partial quotation of Rancière's analysis emphasizes the emergence of the "proletarian" as an interval or articulation, the quotation in full also stresses the proletariat as a living assemblage, a community: "'proletarian' subjectification affirmed a *community* of wrong as an interval between a condition and a profession" (pp. 137–38; emphasis added).

A condition of Rancière's "society," we have repeatedly observed, is a being that does not count, that is structurally necessary but practically expendable. Let us imagine that one "who" or more than one "who"—a given collective or individual—embodies this entity. Yet because this "who," as part/whole, does not count, it can potentially be made to disappear without any party or representative being harmed, without any "real" wrong. In such a scenario political subjects "are disappeared"; but nothing noteworthy takes place, nothing of society *that counts* is lost.

Rancière's wronged subjects, in other words, fail to count if and when they *stand for* (as a trope) the sole material thing—language—that cannot be counted, that does not count, in any count.

Language is the common, the *equal sign* of the equation that cannot itself be added in to the sum total. Stated differently, the part that is no part is neither a who nor a what but any "who" that embodies a "thing" that is not a "what" (all "whats" can be tallied), that is not an object of representation (imaginary or otherwise). Politics starts, in short, when a given "who" appears as language, as the disposable offense within a whole that is itself wrong—not, however, due to this "language thing" but due to the whole itself, to its own miscount.

A key to grasping the political import of the withdrawal of the condition of *disagreement*, of language, lies here. (Yet withdrawal, as Heidegger and Derrida tell us and as we will later explore, leaves the trace that may itself be this very language.) When language is permitted to retract, without leaving behind any loss, guilt, or debt, it renders dispensable whatever part of consensual postdemocracy—whatever *who*—incarnates (or is cast as) that language. Stated differently, the expulsion of the Common (without which there would be no consensus, no agreement/disagreement), does not matter to consensual postdemocracy. Accordingly, nobody will be held accountable for the eradication: eradication as the liquidation of those who, because language (the common-to-all of personifying that stands for no one) at a given moment, are of no consequence. Herein lies the advent, to use a term that Etienne Balibar appropriates in order to discuss the matter,[14] of "discardable life," of a "who" who can be "disappeared" without the showing of any loss to the whole (since the who is a whatnot, of no meaning). The loss of discardable life is no loss but a wash.

With this materialization of discardable life, the trace of the most common, of language, rather than a body among neoliberalism's contentious consensus, we are no longer talking about the "objectification of the other." We might associate this last gesture, in fact, more with internationalist (rather than globalized) endeavors, such as colonialism, than with neoliberal or consensual ones.

For, as Hegel illustrated, this objectification discloses the necessity of the Other as *force capable of production* (and, of course, recognition), one without which no Same or Self, and no capitalism, materializes. (For Marx and Hegel, in fact, the objectification of the Other, far from making it vanish or rendering it incidental, is precisely the condition—the other as *force*—of the emergence of a political or revolutionary figure.) The other as "object" is *nondiscardable, indispensable.*

Can we then contend, with Rancière, that globalization constructs an alternative "other": the "other" as the incarnation of a living thing that, because it is not even an object or a "what," is expendable though unavoidable? Not merely a signifier, this "discardable life" is insignificant, unproductive, valueless to each and every subject. Nonetheless, like the slash between signifier/signified that renders the signifier (hence the subject of representation) possible, or like the Common that makes communication or sharing conceivable but itself sends no message, it is never *not* present on the scene. The equality sign, it indeed sets the scene.

So again: The slash is the mere trace of the Common, of the part that is no part. It is the living stain that blocks globalization's termination. But, because meaningless, it (the *bios*) can be eradicated without doing damage to anything consequential, and without leaving any trace of the violence (the final erasure of the trace would obviously be untraceable), any mark upon the guilty parties. Discardable life is not the *representation* of the globe's illness, the sacrificial scapegoat. Rather, precisely because it is unmarked and deritualized—for it is ritual that would render such "life" worthy and of worth, sacred—discardable life can be easily discarded. One scandal of the market is the deritualization, the unremarkability and "desacrilegization" of its victims.

Internationalism, to present a model that Rancière does not advance but does perhaps license, posits and subsequently strives to incorporate the outside: the outside by means of which it constitutes itself as a body. It operates according to a subject/object paradigm, which affirms the West or the state itself (not a particular state, but the state itself) as subject. Globalization, subtly distinct, enjoys no exterior or object, no "Third World." As a bad infinity, it is whole from the outset, although its wholeness includes a superfluous *part*: the whole itself, for which globalization never accounts. This part/whole is what internationalism wants either to "out" in order to manage it through the just-described subject/object binary, or to eradicate, so that internationalism is in accord with itself, so that it can stomach itself without feeling too full.

Consensual postdemocracy, then, occurs when the superfluous portion survives as the life that the "full" globe could do just as well without (for without it, it remains full), life that is dead to the global subject and serves no purpose—not because the Western imaginary erroneously sees things this way but because, for the globe, the limit/life or life/death is truly "unproductive" and "unserviceable." To reiterate, this last point does not make the elimination of such lives right but all the more terrible for drawing no necessary comment.

On the other hand, we should keep clearly in mind that even though, without bodies that incarnate discardable life, language's uncountability is of minor import, the reverse is also true: if "language itself" is the part that a community shares but that is no part's property—if it is the slice that is not a slice—then its departure, as *thing*, is no less central than the annihilation of the "who" (such as Blanqui's proletarian) who typifies it. For such a disappearance is a chief cause of the consensus: not that there is no matter to say, no "who" for politics to address, but no language in which to say what matters, to articulate a disagreement or miscount, thereby to initiate politics as Rancière defines it. If "No comment" is the last plausible reply to the demise of the *bios* that stamps language, politics becomes itself implausible. A language in peril signals the peril of every body politic, every body that desires a politics, and of politics itself: the "disappearance of the mechanisms of appearance, of the miscount and the dispute opened by the name 'people' . . . is, in a word, the disappearance of politics."[15]

In sum, the existence of politics as Rancière characterizes it is menaced by the disappearance of neither a subject nor a thing, but of a complex crisscross of the two: the living-thing.

Stated in very different terms, Rancière's work opposes two political models of globalization. One is that of the inclusion of more and more parts and peoples. Here, the Other is posited as the wronged party. Politics demands a righting or correction through greater inclusion. According to Rancière, such incorporation of a part that is just a part, rather than also the whole, only aids *management*. Indeed, globalization is most frequently precisely this: the management of the adjuncts. The additional Other increases choice, hence lends its hand to the formation of free subjects. Consensus thrives; an increasing number of individuals enter the fold. But they do so as subjects separated from a whole that remains wrong, that goes untouched by this entire process. New subjects are inserted into society, but the social space remains unaltered.

The theory that the Other cannot be engaged except through this practice of appropriation and control leads to the second discourse that Rancière rejects, one which contends that the wronged Other should be deemed an "outside," should be cast as the unspeakable or unnameable so as to preclude appropriation. This absolute Other, Rancière explains, can emerge solely as the whole that has no part, that does not and cannot participate. The logic of the last point—the Other as the unspeakable is the whole that has no part—will be further discussed in chapters to come. For now, I should emphasize that this exterior Other, because exterior, can effect no politics, though it may generate an ethics (precisely of the unspeakable) in the place of politics—an ethics that is problematic, according to Rancière, for this very reason: because it is a substitute for politics, a compensatory gesture for a consensual postdemocracy that has given up on politics.

Either the other is added on to the social, in which case this other is controlled by a market that foils politics in advance, or the other is negated, left out. Yet in either case, the other does not figure. No miscount, no wrong, is marked, and no politics is instituted. Rancière's politics turns neither on wronged-to-be-righted parts nor on the Absolute that lies outside all parts and participation, but on the part who/that has no part for being the whole (e.g., the language that Blanqui's "proletarian" indexes).

How to summarize all of this? Uncomfortable with the politics of the French Heideggerianism or "structuralism/deconstruction" of the 1960s, 1970s, and 1980s and aware that classical Marxism was no longer a viable option, Rancière works to distinguish his project from these (as he sees them) orthodoxies, although he does not completely overlook his direct and indirect debt to Heidegger. He remains keen to the idea that the menace to politics presented by capitalism, a capitalism that Heidegger grasped in terms of the question concerning technology, is deeply tied to the danger of language's disappearance. As Heidegger observed: "The widely and spreading devastation of language not only undermines moral and aesthetic responsibility; it arises from a threat to the essence of humanity."[16] Rancière thus analyzes consensual postdemocracy, or postpolitics, precisely in terms of this devastation, which threatens to leave behind a world of competitors who, through their competition, generate an absolute agreement, one that "goes without saying," has no reason to change, but is inequitable all the same. Whereas a thinker such as Alan Badiou, like Rancière in so many ways, sees language, and by extension Heideggerianism and post-Heideggerianism, as the unwitting agent of the capitalist domination which political philosophy must overcome (in Badiou's words) *"to the peril of language,"*[17] Rancière seeks a break from French Heideggerianism that nonetheless affirms, rather than resents and competes with, the strength of that thought. And Rancière declares the care of and attendance to language as essential to any intervention into neoliberal consensus. Indeed, this ceaseless affirmation, even when averring a certain sorrow about the future, is Rancière's signature—and may also explain his relatively small market share within intellectual commerce (although I am not sure he would agree).

4.

Dictatorship, Human Rights, and Psychoanalysis in Derrida's Argentina

One Discourse or Three?

It is odd, but not surprising, that for all the debates concerning deconstruction's viability within Latin America, Derrida's "Geopsychoanalysis . . . and the Rest of the World," delivered at a French–Latin American meeting held in Paris, has received scant attention.[1] Perhaps this is because the 1980 essay appears as little more than a harsh critique of the International Psychoanalytic Association's refusal to condemn the practices of torture deployed by the Argentine junta in the late 1970s, even though it was asked to do so by its Australian contingent.

The IPA contended that, given the plethora of human rights violations taking place around the world, denouncing only those of Argentina would be imprudent. The organization therefore opted for a general criticism of human rights violations occurring across the globe or, in its words, in "certain geographical areas." It declined to name Argentina. Addressed to "various concerned international organizations, such as the World Federation for Mental Health, the World Health Organization, the International Psychiatric Association, Amnesty International, and so on, and to various national governments," the IPA's statement reads as follows

> The International Psychoanalytic Association wishes to express its opposition to the use of psychiatric or psychotherapeutic methods to deprive individuals of their legitimate freedom; to an individual's receiving psychiatric or psychotherapeutic treatment based on political considerations; to the interference with professional confidentiality for political purposes. The IPA also condemns the violation of human rights of citizens in general, of scientists and our colleagues in particular.[2]

A general condemnation of human rights is probably better than nothing, Derrida notes. Moreover, a certain neutrality or nonspecificity is proper to any effective human rights declaration. Human rights groups, after all, speak not for particular political practices or for particular states but for universal values. In fact they operate with relative freedom—and, through that freedom, they at times accomplish vital feats—on the international stage precisely because they advocate values rather than political beliefs, the universal rather than the particular good (this advocacy of value over politics may *itself* be a main source of value for human rights). Would a statement specifically about Argentina (when Argentina was only one among many human rights abusers) not then go against the spirit of human rights? Is a general declaration, covering all cases, not more in line with that spirit? In fact, the Australian branch of the IPA, which raised the Argentine issue, was (and is) made up of many Argentine exiles and immigrants. Demand for IPA censure of Argentina's regime rather than, say, Chile's (whose human rights record in 1977 was as atrocious as that of its eastern neighbor) might well have grown from a certain self-interest on the part of these members, therefore on the part of the IPA itself.

The IPA's decision was not, in the abstract, wrong. Indeed, on strictly political grounds, the IPA might well have been justified in making *no* statement about human rights. After all, condemnation of human rights cruelty necessarily advocates the values of human rights, whose principles, however well intentioned, do not always serve the interests of "good politics."

Derrida stresses the latter point, which we have made previously, in "Geopsychoanalysis," yet he does so more strenuously in his famous essay on apartheid, "Racism's Last Word."[3] Condemnation of the human rights records of the apartheid government may have been crucial. Yet human rights brutality and activism were only one of a series of transnational affairs taking place in the South Africa of the period. Another was the free market: the private investments, not directly tied to the state, that nonetheless aided the social conditions sustaining both this state and its racist policies. The case is not simply that the denunciation of South Africa's human rights conduct, aimed at the government, did not address the market movements that wittingly or unwittingly backed the abusive activity. The censure, however unintentionally, lent a hand to the exploitation. By setting human rights abuse as the ground of wrong, human rights accusations in fact *licensed* other pursuits in South Africa that stood—over against human rights inequity—as relatively right, relatively "guilt free." Thus a right (human rights censure) ends up silently backing a wrong (certain investment practices behind the oppression). And as this example illustrates, those interested in the general political good *might*, at times, do well to refuse to denounce the abuse of human rights, decline to espouse the ideals or values behind such a denunciation.

None of these justifications validates the IPA's decision, however. This is because, when it comes to psychoanalysis, Argentina does not belong to some "general situation." The interests of psychoanalysis in this state are particular—and not only due, as we will see, to the sheer size of the psychoanalytic institution within that nation. And it is the reluctance on the part of the IPA to tackle this particularity that spurs Derrida's critique. Indeed, he sees in the IPA's determination to consider the Argentine military atrocities as human rights abuse in general a sign of the apoliticism of psychoanalysis. He does not deny the capacity of psychoanalysis to offer political models or theories. Rather, he decries its inability to present a "discourse *qua* ethico-political action or behaviour":

> The first obvious fact is that despite all commotion of issues as "psychoanalysis and politics," despite all the deluge of discussions on this kind of topic that we have witnessed over the last ten or twelve years at least, it must be acknowledged . . . that at present there exists no approach to political problems, no code of political discourse, that has incorporated the axiomatics of a possible psychoanalysis. . . . If no ethical discourse has incorporated the axiomatics of psychoanalysis, no political discourse has done so either.[4]

But what does this mean? What is "discourse *qua* ethico-political action"? Is it not discourse as *action* rather than as a field that only *informs* or *constructs* action?

We need not recur to Derrida to answer, at least within the human rights context. We know that when we speak today of "human rights abuse," we are referring, not to any violation of one human being by another, but to the physical brutality inflicted by a state upon people within its own dominion. This is why human rights organizations tend to be *international* bodies, even if they are based in a specific state. If a particular state perpetrates or is party to an instance of human rights abuse, that state cannot be counted upon to judge the offense. Its judiciary system, after all, is party to the wrong. Theoretically, only an "unbiased" (international) arena can adjudicate a state's attack of "its own."

In Jean-François Lyotard's view, because the state is in some way their abuser, victims of human rights abuse are denied a meaningful appeal: they lack an addressee, a real judicial body, for their

complaint, thereby cannot *speak* of the wrong that they have suf-
fered. In essence, these victims undergo a double abuse. On the one
hand, they are oppressed; on the other, they are barred from the
state judicial process. And it is this double affront, in Lyotard's
scheme, that defines an offense as a human rights abuse, rather
than as a crime against the state or a civil rights infringement.
There are many sorts of human rights abuses; but the cutting off of
speech is at the heart of all of them. (This is why censorship is the
most complicated of all human rights abuses: it is not one abuse
among others but this abuse's general condition.)

The potential value of an international human rights association
is that it offers a forum for precisely such an appeal. It thereby
makes way for the return of the abject: not of the one who is hurt
but of the one who is hurt and cannot register a grievance.[5] An
intercession into the discourse on international right operates as
political action, as intervention, by potentially granting to the
injured a language and forum in which to make an entreaty, to
speak of the damage: to overcome one material element of the
injustice—the structural impossibility of making a plea—seek
relief, remember, mourn, and move on.

Derrida, however, puts forth his own notion of this "discourse
qua ethico-political action." He notes that at its Thirtieth Congress,
the IPA divided the globe into three areas: the Americas north of the
Mexican-U.S. border, the Americas south of that border, and the
"rest of the world."[6] Derrida deems the map objectionable.

Already in 1980, prior to the fall of the Communist bloc,
Derrida viewed the First-Second-Third World "atlas" as outdated,
an "old world" (p. 160). In search of a substitute, Derrida appears
to demand that each international institution, because part and
parcel of a global network, construct its own map: a charter created according to the institution's particular *concerns* (a world
upon the earth). A given feminist organization, for example, might
divide the world into sites where abortion is legal, where its legality

is feverishly debated, and where no such discussion has even begun. A distinct human rights assemblage might devise a very different, but no less correct map: where human rights abuses are prevalent and where they are not; where they are debated and where they are not; and so on. Thus two institutions end up drawing two maps of the world, sometimes intersecting, sometimes in conflict—but two worlds all the same.

We can now understand why Derrida would only *seem* to insist that each international institution construct its own globe. Given that many institutions register their own worlds, and that there therefore exist numerous globalizations with distinct maps, no single "globe" can fail to encounter another globe "within" or upon its own orb. At any specific location, a world either coincides with another, creating a palimpsest of worlds at that point; or else this world faces its limit, its incapacity to account completely—another legitimate account exists—for the very site or sites, hence for the very world, it has mapped. One map cannot measure completely even its own territory, much less globalization itself. Therefore, not only are there many globalizations; each globalization is many.

One might imagine a specific international institution that advocates *both* abortion rights and human rights. It constructs one atlas based on the legality and illegality of abortion, and a second based on the protection and violation of human rights. At the center of the first atlas, it situates Latin American countries—or one country, Chile, say—where abortion is illegal (so, too, is divorce), and where activism in the name of abortion rights (assuming one espouses these rights) is most needed. In sharp contrast, Chile occupies a "relatively good place" on the institution's second—human rights—atlas. However atrocious other aspects of the politics of the nation may be, the human rights record of post-1995 Chile merits no special censure. Yet this good runs into its limit on the abortion rights atlas, a limit that splinters Chile itself, and any single locus within Chile, into a nation with a right and a wrong "side." The divide sets Chile off from itself; it cleaves not only this space but any world, any map, that contains it.

To map itself, if I may restate this last matter in different terms, psychoanalysis would not situate its undertaking on a pregiven globe, such as the one constructed by the United Nations or international human rights institutions. It would draw a map that would not only serve as an atlas of its concern, care, and responsibility—but also lead to encounter and engagement with other maps.

Yet the IPA has done no such "accounting," leading Derrida to contend that the psychoanalytic "global charter," its "geo," ought to be redrawn. At a minimum, it ought to include four, rather than three spaces since the "rest of the world" is at least double: "on the one hand, it covers Europe and all those places where analysis has taken firm root (broadly speaking, the cradle of psychoanalysis in the so-called democracies of the Old World); on the other hand, it also includes that immensity of territory, where for reasons of a particular kind but of great diversity, *Homo psychoanalyticus* is unknown or outlawed" (p. 160).

Derrida, in fact, considers in great detail:

> Those areas of human settlements where psychoanalysis that has made no inroads whatsoever—sometimes not even with the help of all the paraphernalia of colonization: almost all China, a good portion of Africa, the entire non-Judeo-Christian world—as also myriad enclaves in Europe and America. The size of these psychoanalytically virgin territories, in terms both of their physical extension and of their (present and future) demographics, means that they constitute a vast problem for the future of psychoanalysis. For that future is far from being structured like a space opening up ahead—a space yet to come, as it were, for psychoanalysis. (p. 160)

The sites on the psychoanalytic map that have not yet been "psychoanalyzed" constitute, for this charter, a "vast problem." Do they represent the future of psychoanalysis, the area for its development? The winds certainly do not seem to be blowing in that direction.

And yet, as a living organism, psychoanalysis either advances or dies. There is no "staying the same." The project's survival, its very being, turns on its future. What, then, is the future of psychoanalysis if it is not expansion? Is it death, a future without future?

To answer, Derrida offers a reading of the IPA's own covenant, in particular a discussion of its dissolution. If the IPA should dissolve, the charter states, its monies would be bestowed on the institution that most closely shares its fundamental beliefs (if none exists, the funds would go to charity). And yet, in the IPA documents, one discerns no outline of the foundations of psychoanalysis that would distinguish psychoanalysis from psychology, psychiatry, or psychotherapy. Indeed, there is but one word in the IPA's self-description that defines it as a psychoanalytic organization: "Freud."

According to Derrida, psychoanalysis, as its principal organization characterizes it, is the sole intellectual project whose base is a signifier rather than a concept or series of concepts (the IPA does not even cite "the unconscious" as a foundation). Its ground is signified by a proper noun, the name of the father of psychoanalysis. Thus it would seem that the IPA, upon its own death, can transfer its assets only to an association that shares this paternal figure, to one that belonged originally to the same family of associations as the IPA itself.

We will reconsider this last point later. For now, let us return to Derrida's "geo": "Another area—and another hemisphere—embraces all those places where psychoanalysis as an institution is firmly implanted . . ., and of which, though human rights are not universally respected (far from it . . .), at least it may be said that certain forms of violence, have not as yet, not in the period since World War Two, been unleashed with the ferocity, whether state-supported or not, that is familiar at various levels in so many Latin American countries . . ." (p. 161).

Proper to the IPA atlas, which contains Argentina as a major territory, is a seemingly foreign world: that of human rights. On one part of this map, a strong psychoanalytic institution coincides with nations whose human rights records, while perhaps not exemplary, do not cross a certain "threshold" (Derrida's word). Although all countries commit human rights abuses, if we did not set up some kind of threshold to divide the greater abusers from the lesser ones, a politics of human rights could not operate. If everybody offends human rights, it is not right to censure anybody.

On another portion of this IPA atlas, then, this threshold is passed, yielding the "Latin America of psychoanalysis" upon which the IPA, in Derrida's view, ought to have based its decision concerning human rights violations in Argentina: "What I shall from now on call the Latin America of psychoanalysis is the only area in the world where there is a coexistence, whether actively adversarial or not, between a strong psychoanalytic institution on the one hand and a society on the other (civil society or State) that engages in torture on a scale and of a kind far surpassing the crude traditional forms familiar everywhere" (p. 161). The case is not that the IPA, as an international organization with a Latin American outpost, should attend to the "human rights abuse" territory where (in Argentina) it finds itself, much as one nation should be concerned for another. Rather,

the kinds of torture to which I refer sometimes appropriate what I suppose we may well call psychosymbolic techniques, thereby involving the citizen-psychoanalyst, as such, as an active participant on either one side or the other, or perhaps even on both sides at once, of these abuses. In any case, the medium of psychoanalysis is in consequence traversed by the violence in question, and this, whether directly or indirectly, inevitably leaves its mark on all its intra-institutional relationships, all its clinical practice, and all its dealing with civil society or with the State. This is an area, then, where no relationship of the psychoanalytic sphere to itself can be conceived that does not bear traces of internal and external violence of this kind. In short, the psychoanalytic medium no longer enjoys any simple exteriority. We are obliged to acknowledge that this pattern—a dense psychoanalytic colonization and strong psychoanalytic culture coupled with the highest possible intensity of modern military and police violence—is at once *without equivalent* and *exemplary* in character. (p. 161)

The psychoanalytic world "no longer enjoys any simple exteriority" (to human rights abuse) both because psychoanalytic techniques—indeed psychoanalysts—have been deployed by the Argentine dictatorship and because psychoanalysts have been victims of the torture. Psychoanalysis, as globe and as global, is crossed in its entirety by this particular or local violence.

The "Latin America of psychoanalysis" map, in sum, graphs the psychoanalytic charter written across the human rights abusers charter, forming an atlas whose center is Argentina: the country where human rights abuse and psychoanalysis most clearly dwell together (at least they did in the late 1970s). Human rights and psychoanalysis intersect in Argentina, meaning that one map indexes the internal limit of the other. The crossing of the two plots indicates the incapacity of either to account not for Argentina but for itself since that self contains this other, foreign, nonfamiliar field and discourse within it. The weave of human rights abuse and psychoanalysis under the Argentine junta was, at the very least, a call for the IPA to do this accounting, to state its principles, to determine its role, to declare what it *is*—beyond the mere naming of the father. And that "accounting" would be a highly political act, as we will soon see.

Now, according to Derrida, the IPA—and, with it, psychoanalysis—is constituted by, and has profited from, its global circulation. This international body did not first exist "locally" in Europe, and then move out into territories such as Argentina. "Moving out" to Argentina, to other worlds, is how psychoanalysis, as an international body, grew into itself. Every expansion was always already both an addition to and fortification of the international foundation.

This fact unveils the origin of Derrida's inquiry. How did he come across the matter of the IPA's problem with Argentine human rights persecution in the first place? In the same IPA record where the Argentine rights debate is chronicled ("Geopsychoanalysis" is a reading of that chronicle), the IPA expressed concern over its voting procedures: Were they sufficiently democratic? Because "geographical and economic circumstances" do not permit them to attend the main meetings, the IPA noted, psychoanalysts in portions of the world are sometimes excluded from certain elections. As to voting, the IPA concluded, *"geographical and economic circumstances made it difficult for the Latin American societies"* (p. 146; emphasis added by Derrida). Should the IPA therefore rely more on votes cast in absentia through the post?

Derrida calls attention to this subject for two reasons. First, "postal questions" illustrate that, as an international body, the IPA faces "circulation problems." If it is to be a proper, democratic association, it must grant rights to its margins: to the outposts that, as we have noted, supplement the base of psychoanalysis, increase its strength. Yet these outposts, because located in areas that cannot always reach the center and that the center cannot always reach, are too often left out of certain procedures. Circulation or travel issues yield an unjust, even if unintentional, exclusion.

The health of the IPA as an institution, its democratic structure, is thus endangered by the mere presence of its own periphery. Yet without including this periphery, the IPA might not be democratic. Indeed, it might not even exist. How does one include the Other when full and fair inclusion, given the logistics of globalization and internationalism, seems impossible?

But Derrida points to the IPA's voting procedures for a second, more crucial reason. Derrida does not doubt that "geographical and economic circumstances" make it "difficult for the Latin

American societies" to partake fully in the IPA's decisions. Yet these very circumstances are experienced by members of many non–Latin American nations within the IPA charter. Why single out Latin America?

Derrida, as he peruses the paragraphs in which the voting is discussed, notices on the opposite page the Argentine human rights affair. He suggests that the *over*attention to Latin America on one matter (voting concerns) might indicate an effort on the part of the IPA to compensate for an *under*attention to Latin America on another. In other words, the IPA's odd position (why not point to all the nations who find it difficult and costly to travel?) taken on the voting topic must be a symptom of a different problem: the problem of Argentina.

This associative reading of the IPA document (in which Derrida purposefully mimes a number of Lacanian maneuvers tied to psychoanalytic "symptomatic reading," such as linking symptom and metonymy, that I will not trace here) is meant to raise the specter of the symptom itself. Latin America and Argentina in particular represent a symptom for psychoanalysis. The area stands as an outside-the-center, "foreign" object that is nevertheless essential to the body itself. It is, to use the old deconstructionist cliché, the outside that is inside. This does not mean that Latin America—and by extension, as will become apparent, human rights—is the illness with which the IPA must nonetheless deal. As symptom, it is only the sign or mark of that "disease."

The fact that the IPA corpus finds itself implicated in Argentine human rights abuse, as we have noted, is clearly not the result of an accident. Psychoanalysis, after all, cannot logically claim Argentina when it (psychoanalysis) expands, advances, fortifies itself and gains authority as a result of "travels" into this zone; and then disavow the Argentine territory when the deployment or exploitation of psychoanalytic practices/practitioners "gets out of hand" there. Psychoanalysis is responsible for the ways in which its "investment" in Argentina is put to use by the state apparatus since it made that use, through the investment, possible in the first place.

To confirm this thesis, Derrida introduces the idea of "wildness" (p. 157). Circulation into outside areas and future times, always already the condition of the present and of presence, nonetheless cannot be dictated by a present position. Psychoanalysis, because open a priori to appropriation, because accruing value through that reception, cannot prevent its rearticulation, displacement, destabilization, even perversion. The IPA must attach "geo-outposts" such as Argentina and receive a return from them if it is to maintain itself. Yet such outposts, "ailing or triumphant marginalities," are as likely to ruin as benefit the institution and discourse.

Circulation, then, is wild because, essential but beyond control of the institution/subject, it leads that institution into a foreign land, a "world of improvisation governed solely by its own currents, by isolation, by the determining inscriptions of biography, history, politics" (p. 156). It pushes psychoanalysis into an unplanned encounter with others who might (mis)use it for their own circumstances—by deploying it for human rights abuse, for example.

This is why Derrida notes, in reference to the spreading institution of psychoanalysis, that "the dissolution of the law which the IPA takes as its authority is already under way" (p. 157). The death of the project is the condition of its birth, hence life. Death through contamination by a foreign territory/discourse—in Argentina, the contaminants are a military regime and human rights abuses—always already lies in wait because "wild" circulation stamps the finitude of the rule of this home base, the boundary or border that exposes self to other.[7]

The psychoanalytic "infirmity" for which Latin America and deconstruction are symptoms is thus mortality itself. The death drive of the institution is proper to its foundation. The IPA is forced to address Latin America because its mortality and limitations, in the late 1970s, materialized in this particular (Latin America) warning sign. But why is this important?

The Argentine situation, Derrida argues, is for psychoanalysis "at once *without equivalent* and *exemplary* in character." It is exemplary, a model for psychoanalysis, because it exposes the situation of each psychoanalytic endeavor, to wit: every psychoanalytic discourse and intervention is contaminated by its "wild" outside, plagued by a border (porous, like all borders), by the finitude that exposes the body to contaminants—an outside project or discourse for which it must account. Psychoanalysis, to be, must reach beyond itself to reach itself, to know its own foundation: it must follow the example that the encounter of human rights abuse and psychoanalysis in Argentina sets. Yet, being without equivalent, being singular—solely in Argentina do psychoanalysis and human rights abuses so correspond—Argentina's military atrocities fall to no psychoanalytic model, indeed can be captured by no single paradigm at all. What can one say and do about this?

In 1975–76, the United Nations requested "that various agencies establish new international norms" (p. 154) about torture (other international organizations made similar appeals at or around this time). It noted that human rights definitions of such abuse were inadequate. As modes and methods of state torture radically advance, the human rights understanding of the phenomenon remains virtually the same. It is as if the means to address torture had "fallen behind the thing itself" (Derrida's description). Derrida contends that if any single international group should have jumped at the UN appeal, it should have been the IPA. For pain is the psychoanalysts' concern: "You ought to have essential things to say—and do—on the matter of torture," Derrida lectures them. Yet the IPA, an international organization whose very business is affliction, did nothing to aid the United Nations, human rights groups, and other international bodies in reshaping the meanings and maps of abuse.

Such a redefinition of torture would not be solely theoretical or discursive. State torture, when named as such by international human rights commissions with power, can actually alter international policy and encourage humanitarian aid. It happens—not often enough perhaps, yet it happens. If the global comprehension of torture expands, more or at least different people might be recognized under the moniker of "the tortured," thereby might gain relief.

Derrida, as I indicated earlier, defines "discourse *qua* ethico-political action" in terms of incorporation: "The incorporation I have in mind," he explains, "would not be a kind of calm appropriation: it could not come about without a measure of distortion and transformation on both sides" (p. 151). Psychoanalysis, for Derrida, could not act politically by "falling back upon the appeal to human rights" for the simple reason that the torture taking place in Argentina outstrips violation as understood by human rights itself. This is true, in large part, because state terror banks on psychic, not only bodily, torment. This sort of abuse lies exterior to the domain of human rights, but it is a matter about which psychoanalysis ought to have a thing or two to say—and do.

I said that the IPA might indeed have done well *not* to have made a human rights declaration in reference to Argentina, not to have spoken in the name of human rights and thus legitimized a project that, authorized through international circulation, as much lends itself to the authority of the neoliberal state as any other. Yet the opposite action, a solitary, purely psychoanalytic intervention on part of the IPA in Argentina, over against human rights organizations and ideals, would have yielded equally problematic results.

For one thing, psychoanalysis as an institution does not enjoy on the global stage the political clout that human rights organizations can claim. Whereas a human rights pronouncement by, say, Amnesty International or the International Red Cross can exert pressure on a given sovereign state, a declaration grounded in psychoanalytic principles, however sharp, possesses no such power. A political appeal based strictly on the concepts and specialized vocabulary of psychoanalysis would most likely be ineffective; indeed, it might even appear absurd. Thus the IPA, if it is to intervene politically as a psychoanalytic institution in Argentina, would best attach itself to or supplement other discourses, for example, human rights discourses.

The potential political benefits of such an intervention are not difficult to imagine. Psychoanalysts, human rights institutions, and various other international bodies meet in order to reconfigure torture by relating different understandings and paradigms, creating new terms, hence, new ventures. Out of this meeting emerges a refined notion of torture (one that addresses both psychic and bodily harm) that permits more victims—not only those who fall under the human rights understanding of victimization, but other sorts—to make pleas to international organizations, appeals that might in some fashion improve their situation. Ideally, new projects of transnational right and justice, with new principles of right and wrong, of torture and relief, materialize from the combination of international assemblages. These supply as yet unborn forums through which the injured can cast complaints—and here we should recall Lyotard's insistence that, for victims of state terror, the lack of a proper site in which to make a plea for justice is at the very core of that terror, a main cause of the suffering. Derrida reiterates the point in his own way: "Under given conditions, once a protocol is established, naming can become a historical and political act" (p. 162).

However, the convening of international bodies in order to rework international understandings of torture comes, for psychoanalysis, at extreme risk. Indeed, in taking account of that which is already internal to its world—human rights abuse—in redefining pain and torture, psychoanalysis could well expose its own foundational principles to their ruin, as these guidelines merge with and are replaced by others. The reconfiguration of torture could disclose the inadequacy, hence end, of human rights as the standard of global right and wrong. Likewise, the encounter of psychoanalysis and human rights abuses could bring about the fall of psychoanalysis, which might find its foundational principles inadequate to psychic hurt within the dangerous geopolitical world where it dwells.

Psychoanalysis could become its own contemporary, catch up to its own situation—its situation in Argentina for example—only by opening to the boundary that, in its global existence, binds it to human rights questions. Yet in making that political address, in becoming equal to its own circumstance, psychoanalysis could just as well render itself, its very grounds—even the name Freud—obsolete.

Note that I am not discussing the demise of an *institution* of psychoanalysis, the IPA, but of the project itself. In fact the two are inseparable. The more the foundational concepts of psychoanalysis remain in place, the more they are used in distinct contexts (such as literary studies or Latin American studies), the more authority and legitimacy they gain, and the more they lend themselves to authority, to the name of the father: to institutions such as the IPA, yes, but also to authorities such as the Argentine military state. The more psychoanalysis develops, spreads, legitimizes its main signifiers, the more it facilitates its own appropriation for despotism, for authoritarianism. Refusing to take part in the kinds of assemblages described above, psychoanalysis cannot claim that it has been misappropriated by a state such as Argentina, for it gives license to that appropriation when it declines to confront its own symptoms or nonrelations. It fails to reconfigure its family names in order to maintain all in the family. In other words, the more psychoanalysis advances conceptually within its own little family, the firmer and more refined its base of signifiers, and the greater its currency, the further behind it falls, the more it hands itself over to the backwardness of dictatorships, and the more it crumbles, as the world events in which it finds itself render its foundations progressively weaker. Developmentalism is not the cause but a tool of despotism, even the despotism of well-meaning undertakings such as psychoanalysis—or, for that matter, deconstruction.

Psychoanalysis, Derrida claims, is this combination of "backwardness and progress," civilization and barbarism. The more it improves its framework and technology and polishes up its vocabulary, the more it slips behind politically while "out in the wild"—indeed, perhaps more importantly, the more it slips behind itself.

For Derrida, discourse is political action when it opens its own foundational signifiers to encounter, to exposure, and therefore to death (for, through the encounter, names can fall) and reconstitution through the other's demand. The whole point is that, as signifiers circulate enough, they become their own referents, like proper nouns. Yet discourse must first *define* itself, determine what those foundational signifiers *are*. The downfall and reconfiguration do not just happen, however. We are not discussing change for the sake of change, of currency, as in the market. To reiterate: as the signifiers of one discourse—such as psychoanalysis—meet those of another, such as human rights, neither of the discourses can articulate the boundary, the border, that binds them. The bond is the limit of both tasks. Needed is a linguistic figure for this shared space, one that lacks a discourse and project, but is the condition of any such discourse or project. One does not create the figure as a diversion. Geopolitics petitions it; it is that petition. And such figures, the result of encounter, can outstrip the signifiers from which they emerge. They eliminate one set of grounds, possibly setting new grounds. They substitute for and displace, maybe mourn and move past, their own "fathers" and names.

What is the future of psychoanalysis? Either it passes itself on to itself (this is its tendency), advancing its current state and power, in which case it falls behind the world, falls from circulation—yet because out of step, "exhausted," it also lends a hand to despotic appropriations, to authority. Or else it opens itself to others, renovating itself, possibly preventing such appropriations because the newer psychoanalytic figures and articulations, as well as the institutions that they found, are less legitimized, authoritative. The future is death in either case: psychoanalysis embodies either the dead father that backs authority, or the finitude that opens psychoanalysis to the world.

For Derrida, then, attending to the circulation of one's signifiers by using them or using them up emerges as the political responsibility of the global intellectual. Politics is not a matter of reaching the public. Intellectuals do not become more political by speaking in forums such as newspapers or television. They are always already public; publication is their condition. Politics, in this context, is instead a matter of taking responsibility for the publicness, for the publication, that the intellectuals put in circulation, that represents them. For only by indexing the exhaustion of authorial signifiers through novel figures does one deauthorize these words, preclude them from playing so easily to state and international authoritarianism. You cannot stop circulation; but you can debase the authority of the words that you put in play, wear them to death, by working their limits.

The utility of language, indeed, the reduction of the entire world to a mere instrument or resource—to a technology—that can be manipulated by a human subject, is of course one of the key exercises of what Nietzsche and Heidegger call "nihilism." Nonetheless, and as these thinkers knew, language serves as an instrument whether one wants it to or not; that is its condition. As instrument, it is used, therefore used up. To use, to work *on* the meaning, use, and usage of the foundational statements of an institution—on the use of the institution itself—is to work *over* these fundaments, to ex-pose them as always already open to death and to the future or outside that is always already overtaking them: to the end of the institution as the thought of that institution. Technology, instrumentalization, naming itself—these preclude thought by situating that which must be thought into an order. Yet this same use or usage of language must also be affirmed, for it discloses the wearing away, the fringes, the death that open to thought in the first place, that make it possible, indeed, that demand it.

In short, only if the IPA had addressed and deciphered the limit of its constitution and constituency, *de-fined* itself and its mission, understood its exposure to Latin American military persecution as a symptom of itself, directed its energies toward its *usage* and "misusage," toward the *deconstituency* of its power, could it have met its political obligation. The root of the IPA's refusal to engage Argentina, then, would seem to be the disavowal by psychoanalysis of its own death. Latin America, represented by Argentina of the late 1970s, was a particular or "local" symptom of the fundamental and general "cause" that drives the psychoanalytic project: ruin, the death drive. Yet to call this symptom by its name—to map it, post it up for use—is a condition of possibility for the singular ethical and political responsibility of psychoanalysis.

When faced with the Argentine human rights situation, psychoanalysis declined to do any such naming. Derrida marks the nature and stakes of psychoanalysis's refusal to make use of itself:

> Under given conditions, once a protocol is established, naming can become a historical and political act. . . . This is a responsibility that the IPA has ducked at a particularly grave moment in history—the history of psychoanalysis included. Henceforward, should psychoanalysis wish to take measure of what is happening in Latin America, to measure itself against what the state of affairs down there reveals, to respond to what threatens, limits, defines, disfigures, or exposes it, then it will be necessary, at least, to do some *naming*. This is the first requirement for an appeal: a call to call that which has a name by its name. (p. 162)

He then finishes the task that the IPA could barely commence: "To call Latin America by its name, by what the name seems to mean for psychoanalysis today. At least as a start. All I could hope to contribute to that appeal today was the naming of Latin America" (p. 162).

5.

Levinas and Civil/Human Liberties after September 11
What's God Got to Do with It?

One might argue that, if prior to 1989 the world was split in three—First, Second, and Third Worlds—after 1989 the ideology that these partitions nourished is preserved, perhaps in altered forms, through the division between "human rights abusers" and "non–human rights abusers."

That situation may well have changed on September 11. Since then, transnational politics seems guided by the split between "terrorist" and "nonterrorist" zones. Human rights groups are well aware of the adjustment, as indicated by the statement of Irene Kahn of Amnesty International in the *New York Times*: "One cannot pick and choose countries where [human rights] abuses will be allowed to go ignored simply because they're being committed by allies in the fight against terrorism. . . . If this happens, the whole notion of human rights as global standard is damaged." And indeed, the damage could be most dangerous. Amnesty International notes, for example, that China is using terrorism as a pretext to justify human rights violations, as "an excuse to crack down on its Muslim and Uighar minority."[1]

At stake here, we should mention, is not whether terrorism has become, after September 11, a greater "menace" than previously. It is debatable—how could one possibly measure?—whether "more" terrorism or more threats of terrorism now exist (and for whom?). The current concerns of human rights groups, in any case, have little to do with such questions. They grow from a different though related issue: terrorism post-9/11 circulates as the *name* of evil as such. Consequently, distinct forms of abuse—human rights infractions being chief among them—receive increasingly less public attention and play a smaller role in international jurisprudence.

Of course, human rights practices have long been questioned (long before September 11, that is) by both intellectuals and the general public. (The Derrida essay analyzed in chapter 4 speaks to this fact.) I am not here referring to inquiries that take as their starting point the position either that "human rights are Western rights" or that "human rights are relative." For reasons I will not enumerate, such discourses cannot expose the foundational problems inherent to human rights ideals, problems more readily identified by a formula such as Rancière's: politics commences when the part that is the all and therefore no part is inscribed into the body politic.

For what occurs if this "part" is humanity? Indeed, Rancière designates the populace of consensual postdemocracy precisely as "humanity."[2] Unlike the "people" (of the state), this "humanity" (of the globe) possesses no part that is no part, no "nothing that is all." Abuse of "this humanity" takes place, although, as Rancière emphasizes, human rights and humanitarian institutions engage it, often effectively. Still, "the humans," because they form a whole that plays no part, cannot be addressed by any global *politics*. Human rights organizations, in fact, respond only to those beings who are *identifiable*—to parts or parties of a nation, ethnicity, citizenship, gender, sex, class, profession, or religion—never to "humans" or "just humans," who are not counted among these categories.

What is the issue? Human rights, Rancière contends, lends an arm to the administration of what we might call the "police globe" (as opposed to the "police state"). It *manages* the "just humans," first, by positing them as the excluded (as not a part, not even a part that has no part) and, second (if and when this second step is in fact taken), by including them as one identity (a race, sex, religion, etc.) among others, one party or power among the collection of parties or powers. Each victim, today, is dealt with as an identity, a property whose addition, *because* allowed to be added (by the market itself, of course), speaks to and extends the right of consensual postdemocracy. Within the field called "humanity," nothing that is not party to consensus can materialize since the condition of any such materialization is its management. In other words, at any given moment the "humans" of human rights are posited either as the absolute victim, the absolutely excluded, hence represent a transcendental ground—a theoretical foundation of globalization and the market to which no human rights undertaking can attend—or as an identity that, now rescued and appended, adds to the selection that supports this same market.

Marx's thesis, we recall, is that the proletariat—having been relieved of every other quality—embodies our sheer humanity from which all humans (including the proletariat) have been alienated. The proletariat's potential emancipation is therefore the emancipation of all humans. The freedom of the "just human" of human rights, conversely, is the potential liberation merely of this transcendent, albeit collective individual *from* or *for* the whole that crushes it, and not *of* that whole. Universal wrong goes untouched by the liberation offered to the "humans." At best, the human "part," when added to the parties of consensual postdemocracy, renders the whole *healthier*. Yet the whole remains no more *just* through the inclusion—one of the features of a bad infinity such as the market, and its neoliberal consensus, is that it can add to itself without being altered—since no marker or count of the whole's injustice, no part that is no part, emerges.

But one might then ask: If there is no global politics of the "just human," what is one to do about human rights abuses? Should one perhaps forget about "theorists" such as Rancière and, in the wake of the just-mentioned shift brought about by September 11, salvage human rights activism as among the "best things we can do for others," be these acts "political" or not?[3] Is globalization in fact a demand that we turn to ethics and abandon politics? Is it the end of any politics beyond identity politics?

In the present chapter we will address these questions through a study of Emmanuel Levinas. To start, let us review the "general human rights situation." Victims of abuse, those who cannot turn to state law given the fact that the state is itself their abuser, petition an international human rights body. They may request asylum, medical aid, justice, supplies, recognition. But whatever the nature of their appeal, it involves a minimum of three fields: those of the alleged victims, a human rights organization, and an intermediary. The intermediary may be a human representative of the injured, such as a politician, a prominent local figure, a lawyer, or simply a written or oral "document," a text, even a "cry for help"—sent by the victims—upon which human rights activists must base their decision to intercede (in some fashion) or not.

In all cases, however, the activism involves reading and analysis. Having to interpret the medium in order to make a pronouncement, the activist reads the pain of the other by means of a representation or substitute—that is, in the place of—the agony itself.

Levinas's ethics has proven enormously attractive to contemporary theorists, such as Alain Badiou, interested in overcoming both the naïveté of liberal humanism and the "apoliticality" of deconstruction.[4] Some of these theorists, however, have had difficulty reconciling Levinas's antihumanism with his religious, and indeed Jewish, foundations. Often, in fact, it seems as if God and Judaism are not *really* part of the Levinas enterprise but means by which Levinas deliberates on a general ethics and on philosophy itself.

To think the relation of ethics, God, and Judaism, let us address Levinas's essay "Useless Suffering." Here Levinas points to the uselessness, meaninglessness, and unjustified nature of the suffering of victims—victims, for example, of human rights abuse: "intrinsically, it is useless, 'for nothing.'"[5] The "meaninglessness" is not simply a result of the gratuitous nature of the violence that leads to the pain. For Levinas, it also derives from the mortality—a worthless mortality, for reasons that will emerge—of this other.

Stated in different terms, the other's pain is for Levinas the sign that this other, under siege, is vulnerable, could die, is prey to death. Indeed, when tormented victims petition a human rights group, or anybody else, they are pleading to be rescued from more torment, thereby from the death to which this "more" could lead. And it is precisely this death which is useless, valueless.

But pain as a sign of vulnerability, and vulnerability as mortality, are not for Levinas "given" to the victim by a knowable abuser: by the terrorist state, by other states, by global powers or capital, by another citizen, or even by some animal or machine. The other receives death prior to any mandate or act, indeed, is given death by God at inception. It is the gift but also the law, the commandment, the call that strikes the subject at the subject's origin, and which the subject cannot get around. In other words, according to Levinas, death is an unconditional edict, one that cannot be granted by collective or individual subjects, for it materializes prior to subjectivity. Assigned to the subject "earlier" than the subject's being, hence before the subject "has earned it," the law and demand of death marks out the subject's debt (even as gift: the endowment exacts duty), thus the subject's obligation—and responsibility.

The link Levinas draws between the other (*autrui* in his lexicon) and the absolute Other (*l'Autre*) now materializes. The absolute Other names God: the experience of God's law, of death. The other is the other human (other than the self or, in Levinas's words, other than the ego). Yet the separation of these "two others" is never possible since the other is always already marked by the absolute Other. Without the law, without finitude and death (*l'Autre*), there is no other (*autrui*). At the same time, this Other exists neither "above" the world nor above the other, but as proper to the ego's experience. Without an encounter (the ego's) with the other, there is no Other. And without the Other's *call*, there is no encounter. Other and other, irreducible, are nonetheless inseparable.

Death is not for Levinas any law, however. It is absolute law, outside the contingency of any human or state law. Levinas, moreover, posits this law (as gift) in terms of the Jewish tradition. As absolute law, it is one the "chosen person" cannot subvert, take back, undo, abdicate. The Jew as Jew cannot say: I choose not to accept this obligation (or debt), for Jews are Jews (in theory, anyway) precisely because they freely take this directive (because they take Torah), which comes directly at them from God the Absolute, right across their bodies, without mediation (the mediation of Christ).

"Taking Torah" means: exposing oneself to the other "via" the limit of human understanding, "via" the Word (yet "via" suggests a medium: God's Word, to repeat, comes without mediation) that— as God's utterance—exposes one to one's finitude, to the border, where one encounters an outside, another. The Other calls the ego to its ethical responsibility. The assumption of the law, in other words, pushes ego up against other through the bind and boundary (God, Torah, the Other, death) that the two parties share but over which neither is master.

Levinasian ethics, therefore, does not require that one "actually" read or address Torah. "Taking Torah" simply signifies that one has (been) opened to the absolute Word, God's law. Ethics, Jewish or otherwise, commences with the reading of the finitude of the human, written across the body of the suffering other.

Let us imagine a teacher who guides a student toward a certain "human" comprehension (as mortal, the teacher can possess no other kind of knowledge) of the Word, which indexes the finitude of this comprehension. Experiencing God as this limit, the student then seeks to know the Word further. The result, of course, is not "greater" knowledge of the Word or God (one is never closer or further from infinity), but a distinct comprehension of the world, an opening to this world at the world's limit. The ethics that results thereby derives not from the application of an established moral code but from a novel understanding (for the ego) of the good that the Other, across the other, ceaselessly demands.

Without guidance or understanding, without a human measure of God's word, without, in the above case, the teacher, there is no experience of the limit of human mastery, hence of God. *One* cannot engage the Word or God; the Word only comes between two. It is that coming-between.

So again, absent the Absolute Other, there is no ethical demand to attend to the other. Conversely, without the ego's encounter with an other, without community, the Other's call (the Word) as the condition of ethics never emerges.

Human rights are not Jewish rights. Far from it. But every human rights activist, to whatever degree, faces the Absolute Law as cast by Levinas. The activist attends to the other's suffering because petitioned by the death of this other (again, revealed in the call of the Other), which is the "root" of the agony. The suffering, therefore, is given by a decree that sits beyond the activist: independent of every state or international legal system, outside all agency, exterior to any human understanding. Human rights activism, because it includes the interpretation of the representation of pain and thus of mortality (the limit of this representation), always in some way is addressed by such a mandate.

The diabolic, according to Levinas, is marked by violations of this absolute edict. I wrongly transgress the law by turning the other's vulnerability or death into a human object of knowledge, capable of being grasped or justified from within human, that is, subjective paradigms, systems, and structures: "an order . . . which it [humanity] continues to think diabolic."[6] In such cases, I convert the other's pain into the reflection of my subjectivity, and thus affirm my totality, my absoluteness, the "fact" that the other's agony, which I "know" (how to fix since I "know" the true cause), is merely a mirror of my powers, knowledge, and reason. The subject converts the miracle of God's law as opening to the other, the treacherous marvel of revelation, into the reason of the human. The conversion is not itself evil; evil is the elimination of the obligation of self to other since, without that obligation, there is no good.

The other's distress is deemed as reasonable, as for good reason: "the justification of the neighbor's pain is certainly the source of all immorality."[7] I use the other's anguish as a way to justify my world and my acts, or for the benefit of myself. There is nothing exterior to me. Or rather, the exteriority—here, the other's suffering—is void, epiphenomenal. Indeed, within this humanist paradigm, which Levinas abhors, I can only apprehend and aid the other in pain, who is suffering to death, by essentially finishing the other off. I annul the force of the other's appeal, reducing the plea to an echo of myself, consequently—like all mere reflections—to nothing real. I am "unethical" for I get rid of the ethical situation itself.

In avowing knowledge of the other's suffering, I appropriate the absolute or God's law, which marks the limit of humanism. I claim as proper to my domain, as an object for my use and human use, the other's "useless" death, which I am therefore free to give or appropriate. I am "diabolic" for I play out the archetypal scene of humanism. Here the human subject assumes the position of the Absolute, of God who dwells over the All and who thus possesses the total right to bequeath or strip (or not strip), to save or damn, the life of the other.

For Levinas, the trace of God's law inscribed across the other is the "portion" of this other that, because singular, lies beyond comparison and calculation: "The fact that the identity of the species can include the absolutely dissimilar, a multiplicity of nonadditive, unique beings—that the unity of Adam marks the individuals of incomparable uniqueness in which the common species disappears and in which the individuals cease being interchangeable like coins . . . surely this is the trace of God in man. . . ."[8] The other's plight is incomparable, absolute in the Levinasian sense, thereby cannot be tackled through the given paradigms or conventions of right/justice: cannot be "figured" by any human figure.

I should emphasize, as Levinas well knows, that no ethical response is actually possible without this same humanist appropriation, without calculation. If I confront the suffering of the other as suffering, if I perceive it as suffering, I have already interpreted it, given it meaning. This suffering always takes place as a relation to other sufferings, hence within a semiotics of suffering. The other's suffering is never suffering as such but a *kind* of suffering: unjust incarceration, depression, a heart attack, the loss of a loved one, torture, exile. That is, every singular suffering is, for the "reader" of the agony, a sign within conventional definitions of suffering, with a certain intensity, level, value, or meaning. In other words, without humanism, without the appropriation or calculation of the other's suffering, there can be no ethical engagement at all, no limit to humanism: no experience of the Other's call and thereby no sense of the other's hurt, no *reason* to respond. Thus humanism is for Levinas what metaphysics is for Heidegger or what capitalism is for Marx: the condition of its own overcoming.

But if the human rights activist, when read from within Levinas's ethical paradigm, cannot respond properly to the agony of the other, which, rooted in God's law, is inhuman or at least exceeds human agency; and if such a response cannot avoid unjustly appropriating or "using" this pain, how does an ethical act actually take place? What kind of response or ethics is this, anyway?

I can begin to reply by emphasizing that Levinas's demand is not that the subject let the other be, not try to know the other, not impose, not appropriate. Levinas's is not an ethics of "letting alone." It involves what Levinas labels a "face-to-face" confrontation. To be good, you must make contact—the Other as Law/limit situates the ego as a being-in-contact—with the other. Not only can you impose, even appropriate. You must.

In the case of the human rights activist, the "imposition" as bound to action and the "imposition" as bound to knowledge are tied. As just intimated, the claim to know the other's agony may ground unethical actions; but no good is possible without it. The activist must strive to understand, make sense of the trace of the other's mortality: of the other's petition. An appropriate determination to intervene hinges on that proper judgment. Is this appeal genuine, is the person really suffering? If so, is the suffering due to human rights abuse or to other reasons, ones into which a human rights group has no right to intervene? If the other is the victim of human rights violations, are these sufficiently cruel to merit a condemnation? Are the "context" and "timing" correct for such a move, or might the human rights pronouncement interfere negatively in other global political negotiations?

And yet, as we have noted, the signs upon which the decisions must be based contain within their infrastructure a law (the law of mortality) that is irreducible to human reason, one that resists the sense-making process, and thus puts the agency of the activist, of human rights, on the line. Levinasian ethics consequently turns on bringing the subject position or discourse (of human rights: the judger and the judgment of the judger) to its own end or finitude: to the border or boundary, where activist and sufferer, self and other meet—to the ethical situation "in which the suffering of the suffering, the suffering for the useless suffering of the other person, the just suffering in me for the unjustifiable suffering of the Other, opens upon suffering the ethical perspective of the inter-human."9

The encounter is revelation. The reading of the appeal of the other, because the appeal is tinged with death of this other, is the revelation of God's call or Word, and thus of God himself, to the subject. God is revealed, of course, in all the revealed religions—but not in the same way. In Judaism (though not only in Judaism), God is so in the letter of the law (the appeal as bearer of the trace of mortality) that bonds subject and other. One cannot "know" God, just as one cannot "know" the other's pain or vulnerability, for God does not come from reason or for a reason. He is exposed in a law, in his call or Word whose reason remains unknown—it is a gift, a miracle—but which, as unknown, is the limit that renders ethics, the Good, the encounter with the other conceivable.

So, again, *what* good is this revelation? What precisely does it have to do with any "real" ethics?

In the present context, it is helpful to review once more the task of a "human rights activist" or the "human rights subject." This subject, obviously, is one whose parameters are set by the discourse of human rights. In facing the other's agony, the subject confronts both the limit of the human and the limit of this discourse: human rights cannot account for the All of global right and wrong. In addressing the suffering of the other, the human rights activist potentially opens to the death not only of the activist's personal subjectivity, but also of the project of human rights itself.

Here we might recall Levinas's famous point of contention with Heidegger. Levinas argues that, according to Heidegger, I can never endure the death of the other. I cannot experience death through another's, but only through my own. For his part, Levinas asserts that it is precisely through the other's death—the other's pain as the sign of death/God—that I am "out" before my own death.[10] I experience my finitude in the other's mortality, in the fragile other's call for aid. And we have seen why. The call signals the inhuman law that exposes my subjectivity to its terminal point: to the frontier that opens me to the other, an other with force, capable of an appeal, of hounding me.

Death, for the subject, is not (for either Levinas or Heidegger) a biological "fact of life" that the signs of the other's suffering "bring out." Biological death is not a "fact" at all but an abstraction, one that no subject can conceive (except through a metaphor derived from the world of the living), much less experience. Death takes on a real presence through signs and communication. I struggle to respond (one instance of communication or sense) to the other's distress; this distress reaches me through both the signs of the other's pain (another field of sense) and the call of the Other (communication at the limit of sense). These set off my own anxiety, exceed my understanding, and thereby expose me to my finitude: my death. This is why, for Levinas, the other persecutes me. The exchange of signals with the other, or communication, does not reflect but produces death as material entity, as a fact of my existence, as "the just suffering in me for the unjustifiable suffering of the Other."

Levinas labels the senses just outlined "the Said." He names the limit, or the encounter/communication between these senses, "the Saying." Every speech act includes a Said and a Saying, "human sense" (the Said) and the limit of both the human and sense (the Saying), signification and (the phrasing of) death.

Such ideas best explain both Levinas's "face-to-face" and his insistence on carnal or bodily metaphors to describe the contact. The other's petition is the exposure of helper and victim to their boundary, to an encounter that is without mediation since the limit that the two share situates them skin-to-skin—skin as the outer edge of the body—in complete intimacy. I am hostage to the touch, to the petition of the other, for I cannot be without that touch, without the call that, defining and delimiting me, puts me in contact: in a contact I cannot avoid and still "be."

We noted that the Absolute, or God's law as it stamps the other, marks the uniqueness or irreplaceability of this other. In so doing, however, it also exposes the "ego" or subject to the stamp (of finitude) that renders the subject, too, irreducible to another being.

This is why, as Levinas emphasizes on numerous occasions, nobody can take the subject's place in the ethical situation. The ethical responsibility is absolutely mine, and no one else can assume it, since the situation discloses the singularity (my death) of my being—revealed at the instant of contact—as my own only: "No one can substitute himself for me, who substitutes myself for all."[11] I give myself to all, but nobody but me can do that giving.

The question for human rights, when viewed from the Levinas perspective, now grows clearer. A human rights organization faces the appeal of the suffering other. Either it appropriates the appeal for its own sense of the good, claims knowledge of the other's suffering, thereby "uses" the other as a means to expand the legitimacy of itself, and of human rights in general. (We should note that if this deployment, as suggested above, is for Levinas "diabolic," it is also the condition of possibility of any "good deed" on the part of human rights. The good is diabolic at the core, which makes it no less good.) Or else human rights subjects, through the encounter with the other's appeal, run into the limit of their right and understanding, the death of their own project. Yet this is not the whole picture.

The human rights activist receives an appeal from alleged victims, which represents the suffering that is being endured. The activist must then announce or not announce, to one or various publics, human rights violations on the basis of the activist's interpretation of that petition. Such a pronouncement is the condition of any number of actions, ones that, most likely, the human rights group will not itself perform: the granting of asylum to the victims, economic sanctions, international humanitarian intercessions, more research into the area in question, even military intervention, to name a few.

The pronouncement of human rights violations requires reading, discussion, meditation. These are not the "thinking" that precedes the action but are themselves acts. After the intellectual or discursive human rights determination, a "physical" humanitarian, international, or military intervention may follow. Yet without the determination and pronouncement, such intercessions are not "legitimized," hence may not take place. The human rights decision, hardly abstract or "mere words," functions as one type of act that makes way for other types.

Indeed, during the interim in which the rights group weighs or "reads" the appeal of victims, the alleged abuses continue to take place. As human rights activists interrogate their object, hence hesitate before taking a position, they possibly permit offenses to go unchecked, for however short a period, and to however small a degree. (A quicker denunciation, on the other hand, could lead to misjudgment, causing extra harm.) The "thinking process," indecision, or "question asking" of the human rights group is, for the individuals who endure, say, electric shock during the interval, a determination to permit the torture to take place ("for now" perhaps; yet since the future is not at all assured to these victims, the "for now" is no consolation). It is not the vacillation that precedes the response but the response, the determination itself. In the ethical circumstance, one cannot hesitate before acting since the hesitation is an act.

This double bind is, for human rights as Levinas would address them, the condition of an ethics. It exposes the limit of human rights and the human rights subject—due to the very global circumstance in which it dwells, human rights can claim no unbounded right; this is true whether we deem human rights "universal" or "relative"—the border where self and other find themselves engaged, face to face, bound. The human rights activist cannot freely "choose" just right (the self-determination that would make the activist a subject proper) since the potential for creating injury is a condition of that right.

The case, however, is not simply that a human rights group or subject, because it must cast judgment on human suffering that, indexed by the inhuman (death), always exceeds its domain and right. Nor is the situation merely that the "right" pronouncement of abuse can end up doing more harm than good. Indeed, if human rights determinations are limited, potentially bordering on wrong, they also border on *other rights*. Outside any single right lie both wrong and these other rights.

Such other rights include, for example, civil rights. Abuse of these rights, roughly speaking, involves the unjust treatment of individuals or a group, often a minority or women, performed not by state government as such but by institutions such as the local police or private enterprise. Unlike human rights injustices, civil rights infringements need not involve detention or bodily abuse, although of course they can. However, the distinction between a civil and a human rights offense lies, not in the degree or type of offense, but in the nature of the appeal to justice. If the injured can petition the state for relief, then the injury (insofar, and only insofar, as we are distinguishing between civil and human rights) belongs to the realm of civil rights. If, however, no such petition is possible or potentially meaningful, if victims—to register their complaint—must reach out beyond the state since the state is itself the offender, then the injury belongs to the realm of human rights.

As I have emphasized, human rights organizations have gained legitimacy in large part through their internationalism. Being, in theory, unbound to any individual state law, hence, also in theory, unbiased or "nonideological"—speaking in the name, not of politics as ideology, but of values—they are deemed capable of casting judgment upon abusive state conduct in general. Civil rights do not enjoy this international status, no doubt in part because the term "civil rights" evokes the heavily politicized, "biased" environment of the 1960s. Does it not seem, however, that international bodies capable of addressing international *civil rights* injustices are now more necessary than ever?

This point became apparent just after September 11. The aggressive "profiling" of "people of apparent Middle Eastern descent" within U.S. borders, given the concerns about ethnic prejudice that the profiling evoked, seemed to call out, not only to U.S. civil rights organizations, but also to similar groups from other nations. After all, many of the subjects under investigation were and are citizens of or refugees from foreign states. Yet, because the profiling also led to secretive and possibly unjust detentions (the jury, quite literally, remains out), the profiling process was never far removed from human rights matters. Secretive and unjust detentions by a government are, in fact, one of the staple understandings of a human rights violation.

My intention here is not to condemn or condone the detentions but to pose a different question: What body possesses the right to cast the necessary legal or moral judgment on these acts? Will *all* the detainees who feel wronged be able to make a consequential appeal to the U.S. judicial system? Is this system too tied to post-9/11 antiterrorist governmental policy, too in league with the policy makers who sponsor the detentions, to judge (even to acquit) the potential offending agents or agencies? Or is perhaps the executive branch, in these times of "war," too powerful, thus rendering the judicial branch's determinations irrelevant? Should international human rights organizations take matters into their hands? Or are they part of the problem?

Interestingly, the controversy over these detentions has not actually surfaced as a civil rights (or human rights) affair in the United States, where government spokespeople, networks of civil society, and private citizens have quickly displaced the term "civil rights" with "civil liberties." The latter is a perfectly appropriate phrase. Yet the substitution was not innocent or simply "appropriate," but meant to avoid the political dissension that the phrase "civil rights" recalls, thus to cast the "terrorist" issues at hand in terms of the "protection of universal values."

Two major discourses on rights were thus destabilized on September 11. Civil rights lost footing as a political instrument, yielding to civil liberties. And human rights, a monitor of international right, gave ground to the "right to security against terrorism," regardless of human rights. Both rights still retain a place—no doubt a powerful place—in state and in international deliberations. Yet the September 11 attacks, and the reaction to them, shook their foundations: The event is a call for a novel, global Law.

Hence, in trying to gain popular, congressional, and international backing to wage a preemptive war in Iraq during the winter of 2002–3, the president of the United States could not use Saddam Hussein's human rights record as a primary justification for the action. He needed to present Hussein as a terrorist threat in possession of weapons of mass destruction. Later, when the weapons were not found, and when Hussein's terrible human rights record was highlighted as a reason for the war, the Bush administration still grounded these offenses in terrorism (human rights crimes "by themselves" were seen as insufficiently grave): Hussein gassed his own people, he used biological weapons against the Kurds, and so on. Without casting terrorism as the *true* name for or foundation of evil, President Bush could not initiate combat in the *apparent* name of human rights.

Human rights and civil rights groups both attend to the appeal of the suffering other, thus face, according to Levinas's model, the ethical situation: the call of the Other within the other's call, one that marks the limit/death of these two endeavors or subject positions. The case of the post-9/11 detainees in the United States, where the two rights collide, indicates that this limit is also a border, a mutual space. The sharing, in turn, points up the relationality of the two ventures: their nontotality, contingency, vulnerability, co-contamination (because they touch, the one contaminates the other), their "ill health" (an entity infected by an outside body cannot be perfectly well), or simply their being-in-common. The rule of mortality, or God's law as it underwrites the complaint of the detainees, is not some abstract or theoretical edict but the material collision of two missions, discourses, egos, subjects, projects, goods. It indexes the mortality not only of the "wronged" (if, in fact, wronged) individuals but also of the methods or discourses by means of which a "right" judgment might be cast upon them. September 11, in short, confirmed that both human rights and civil rights are inadequate to their own circumstances, worn out and fatigued, and thus in need of renovation.

Such renovations hinge on the articulation—articulation as act— of the bond between civil and human rights. If human rights groups are losing their status as the most legitimized monitors of global right and wrong, and if civil rights no longer represents adequate means to address certain acts of violence, what action more than the formation of a novel project of global right, founded on the "Saying" of the limit/border between human and civil rights (rather than the "Said" of both projects) would at once better aid victims and preclude terror/terrorism from becoming the very ground— unthinkable like all grounds—the very *essence* of global politics, indeed, of Being itself?

A possible answer concerns the two laws that Levinas describes: Absolute Law, the law of mortality, which no subject can avoid; and human law, which is displaceable, reworkable, and replaceable. September 11 in fact exposes the limit of *two* kinds of human law— state law (such as those of civil rights) and international law (such as those of human rights), for which neither kind can account: Absolute Law, or death. I do not want to suggest that the events of September 11 *exemplified* human vulnerability, or the law of mortality, more tellingly than have other atrocities. However, as doubts about the power of both the sovereign state and international jurisprudence grow increasingly prevalent, September 11 represented a demand for the articulation of the encounter among subjects/ethical projects, an articulation that in the future might result in a much-needed new means to attend to global and state wrong, means whose effectiveness would depend on the degree of legitimacy they have attained. A possible good emerges, then, when the civil rights and human rights activists meet over the demands to which the deaths of September 11 give rise, over the Absolute Law that separates and binds them, and that obliges them to come to terms with their encounter, for which neither can account. This obligation is neither political nor moral since politics and morality (Levinas would say) assume preexistent positions and cannot but materialize as struggles for power among subjects. It is ethical instead because the subject (the human rights subject, for example), exposed by the Absolute Law to the other, opens to this other through a practice that represents the irreducible encounter between the two (subjects), who are this very encounter: ethical subjects.

Is such an encounter an event? Clearly, the mere "bumping into each other" of two rights organizations—even if brought about by a singular atrocity—in no way guarantees the *event* of their encounter. Nor does it assure the exposure to and rephrasing of the limit. Indeed, it is just as likely that one site will subsume the other site. The exposure to alterity then becomes the pretext for the appropriation of the outside: for an expansion of the Same (this, for Levinas, is the tendency of both humanism and metaphysics). The division between any two institutions or subjects, in other words, easily yields the binary structure that allows one to transcend the limit, to take over the exterior, and to stand as essence itself through its development or developmentalism.

No singularity, no "unprecedented" occurrence by itself produces an event. The "limit" of our existing institutions and subjectivities, in fact, is only endured through concepts that appropriate in advance this limit for the already established. And that appropriation precludes the happening, as such, from taking place: when the other emerges as the pretext for the expansion of the Same and of Presence, the event as interrupter is itself interrupted, blocked.

One does not experience an event without the (pre)concepts that prepare for one's apprehension of it. The event does not take place, to be experienced later or not. It *is* that experience. Also, there is no experience, not even a "feeling" of the episode (one perhaps "lost" as it enters the field of representation), without the conceptual frameworks that subsume the experience in advance. This a priori conceptualization of the event, which is a product of tradition, culture and ritual, means first that the event never happens once or at once. When did September 11 take place? On September 11 only? Was not the legitimization of a fragile Bush administration, and the drastic international and national determinations that were initiated due to this legitimization, part of September 11, proper to the event? Are not the Iraq war, the abuse of Iraqi prisoners, the increasingly aggressive reactions of the Israeli government in its own "war on terror," the soon-to-be released film by Michael Moore, the rise and fall of Howard Dean, the intensification of the schism between the United States and France, and so on *also* part of September 11?

An event is not "singular" because it occurs once and for all. Conceptualization and thus repetition are conditions of apprehension: the event both happens at a given point and keeps on happening. It explodes once, but reverberates in waves over time and space. It does not end on the date of its occurrence but, insofar at it ends at all, when it is *dated*. And September 11, because it *names* rather than dates the event, was dated before its due date, or dated before dated. It was thus a poignant moment that has not yet taken place as *event*.

These issues are central to Levinas's ethics, whose demand emerges not from the agonic situation of the other, to which the ethical subject must attend, but from the transference of the other's pain to the subject, exposing the subject, too, to finitude and distress. What distress? As just noted, the event is always already consumed and erased by the (pre)concepts that, at the same time, allow for the event's experience. Thus the event strikes the other, not as the unfathomable, but, quite to the contrary, as one episode among others, as the iteration of former happenings that itself will be iterated by and in other historical chapters. The suffering of victims lies here: not in the impossibility of conceptualizing and thus communicating or understanding the extreme episode, but in the habitualization of the episode as the condition of its advent. It is cast too readily—that is a main source of an unwellness (one thinks of the many *good*, therefore disturbing books published about September 11 almost on that very day). The event cannot be shared except as an eventless story in a series. Victims, defined or redefined by their unshareable experience, are also set off from others by it. They communicate the extreme marker of their lives solely as an ordinary one. The sufferers are therefore alone; without a means of communication for what really matters, for what is truly material, they are without community. This *without* is their distress; it is the experience of their lives. Stated differently, the experience of distress is the victims' sense of the unsolvable nature of their mood. The solitude that marks out the pain seems incommunicable (it can be shared, but only through its reduction to the everyday, to the inessential). The loneliness and grief—which could be mitigated only through a sharing—seems in its essence unending.

The event, then, is neither a feeling nor a narrative. Feelings and narratives pertain to the realm of the manifest and the sensible, whereas the event cannot reveal itself within this realm. It is *affect* or *mood* in the psychoanalytic sense: a drive that may be translated into manifest emotions or signs, but withdraws or fades from each such translation. The event happens as drive, but appears to consciousness only in its manifest symptoms: feeling or representation. The responsibility of the ethical subject is to read and react to this event as mood, mood not as substance of or upon the other, but as the drive the sufferer harbors as trace.

The task seems impossible. Because they cannot conceptualize the other's pain, and thereby cannot act properly (in response to the trace of this inconceivability), ethical subjects, confronted with the other's mood, must face simultaneously their own. The other's mood materializes as "readerly" trace; the trace is the revelation of God; same and other meet over this, the co-affect of the Absolute Law. Human finitude as sharing moods, and sharing as this same finitude are the bonds between the two, the event of the two, a site of encounter that calls to be phrased, yet that every phrase misses. The collaborative effort to read and articulate the bond nonetheless results in an ethics: it offers relief, the potential invention of novel communication or new phrases that, as response to encounter, could well interrupt banality, point toward an expression of the damaging event, and construct a memory. Upon this memorial, the dating that—given the engagement of Same and Other that God bequeaths, and that renders material this very memorial—might one day bring the ill-mood to a close. The granting of that "one day," of the future to the victim by the ethical act, is the granting of faith and hope, of reprieve and release through the trace as the tender relief upon the body of the other. For Levinas, this act is the most profound performance of ethics possible.

In any case, nothing that happens, including "major catastrophes," is by itself the *source* of the happening. What "just happens," such as 9/11, is not the ground of an event. The happening takes place when the self encounters its limit, meets the other *over* the particular incident—and not simply by accident. Nor, however, can the meeting be willed by humans, by subjects. For that willing, that subjectivity, precisely wipes out the limit, extends the self infinitely. (Subjectivity *is* indeed that extension.) I am not saying that ethics and politics do not require will. Rather, I am suggesting that will responds to a call delivered by neither historical accidents nor the will itself. Will may come before power, but neither will nor destitution (will's opposite) nor power is to be found "at the beginning."

For Levinas, the call of God names this commencement: the commencement that never ends. We cannot act ethically without responding to God. God stands as the demand that comes from elsewhere, not from ourselves and not by accident. Only those open to this insistence can act, can *will*. God is not ethical. He is the call or mark that is the proviso for the encounter with the other. There is only one event for Levinas, yet it is one that never comes and never stops coming: the mood of revelation.

Even though September 11 exposed the U.S. citizenry to terror, to death at the hands of a menacing Other whom the *universal* market had promised to incorporate and thus eliminate such an episode is not revelatory or *eventful* unless it calls a human force to open itself to another human force: human rights to civil rights, for example. And we cannot at all be sure, after September 11, that the U.S. citizenry or indeed the globe itself has been opened in this manner. In other words, we cannot hold that September 11 was an event. We cannot be certain that it was not, rather, a trauma without distress or mood that was disavowed in favor of strengthening and justifying the pre-9/11 status quo, the Western ego.

Rancière dismisses ethics as a mere means to address the unsayable or unthinkable. It is a compensatory gesture in the absence of a certain "in the name of," a certain "political cause." There is, to be sure, an *un*said in Levinas's labor. Yet this unsaid does not feed an ethics that only fills in for an absent politics. The *un*said is not the unspeakable but the demand of a Saying that compels the ego to tackle the being that concerns it: the other in pain. Indeed opposed to "politics," Levinas's ethics nonetheless is not a response to the unsayable but to the saying of God, to God as call for encounter. God's gift to us is therefore exactly this: our potential to respond, to act. Take it or leave it, this is Levinas's position: no Good, no event, no encounter, no human or civil rights without God as the inhuman but living call. Those who say otherwise are, for Levinas, not without religion but, precisely, too religious, too moralistic, too political, and all too human besides.

6.

If It Goes without Saying
Notes toward the Investigation of the Ideological State Apparatus

Although few would deny that recent global developments demand a rethinking of the contemporary nation-state and, possibly, of the entire history of the state form, such a revaluation is easier said than done. Indeed, current efforts to recast the state through theories of transnationality or globalization tend to recuperate the traditional nation-state (often as part of a notion of internationalism) as their ground, hence to reassert the state form as the indispensable horizon of all political inquiry—either to subvert or embrace it. It is as if the state form holds the same sway over politics that metaphysics holds over philosophy: the instant a project escapes the state's clutches is the moment it most firmly falls into the state's grasp.

What is most needed, then, is not a rethinking of the state, but a thinking of a rethinking that, from Hegel through Foucault, has been materializing since the modern state's conception. In that regard, "Ideology and Ideological State Apparatuses: Notes towards an Investigation," the Louis Althusser text that has most influenced the post-1980 North American and British intellectual scene, deserves our careful attention.[1]

Relating the state of modern thought to thought on the modern state, Althusser's essay asks: How does production ceaselessly maintain, in distinct times and over many spaces, a similar worker/capitalist, subjugated/subject division, one that permits the capitalist/subject to exploit the worker/subjugated, thus preserving class difference? Which is to say, how is this key social component of the conditions of production, class difference, endlessly reproduced?

By way of explanation, the main sections of the essay present three complementary discourses: labor relations and labor exploitation (the Marxist section), cultural institutions (the Gramscian section), and psychological or psychoanalytic factors (the Lacanian section). Each is advanced to "pick up" where the others slip. Cultural analysis, or Gramsci, strives to explain what classical Marxism cannot. Psychoanalysis, or Lacan, promises to finish off what Gramscian deliberations only begin. Yet ultimately all the discourses fail to explicate the persistence of class difference.

Thus, in a postscript to the essay, Althusser struggles to recover a certain if slightly aberrant "classical" Marxist position. Where the body of his essay demonstrates how cultural institutions overdetermine the economic base (and vice versa), and how psychological factors overdetermine both culture and economics, "in the last instance," Althusser returns to the labor base as the ground of class difference. In doing so, however, he runs into the limit of the Marxism that created the need for the Gramscian and Lacanian sections in the first place.

In order to survive and thrive, Althusser notes in the first section of his essay, the capitalist must renovate machines, supply and resupply materials, and "restock" the workers by giving them "necessary" wages for "necessary" food, clothing, housing, and even for a minimum of luxuries (wine for the French, beer for the British). In other words, the capitalist must make sure that the workers' needs are met, that they can come to the workplace each day, in decent health and spirits, and that workplace conditions allow for maximum production, hence maximum profit and alienation.

Althusser exposes a contradiction inherent to this reproduction process. The conditions of production, using, say, functional machines, that must be reproduced by a capitalist are dependent on the production of these same machines by another capitalist, that is, on the relations among producers. Many facets of the production of a clothes maker, for instance, involve links—such as the clothes maker's link to the builder of sewing machinery maker—beyond the former's control. This sewing machine maker might, for example, alter the clothes maker's mode of production by forcing the clothes maker to retrain workers—a costly expense—and possibly to hire new trainees.

The process cannot be stopped, accelerated, or avoided. Circulation, as Marx himself emphasized, is both a condition of and a barrier within each individual site of production.[2] Even though the clothes maker can command, exploit, and alienate workers to the greatest degree, such exploitation, by itself, cannot reproduce the conditions of production; these are dependent on the circulation between producers and products, which no single producer can dictate. Althusser suggests, then, that no theory of the economic base, no examination of the way production brings about the alienation of the labor force can itself explain the persistence of class distinctions, that is, the reproduction of the conditions of production. In making these points, Althusser has shifted his inquiry away from the conditions, and toward the *relations* of production.

Thus, as Althusser enters the second section of the essay, his initial question has been altered: If production (labor exploitation, alienation of the worker) is not the force that reproduces the *relations* of production, how do these relations reproduce themselves? They do so, Althusser answers, by means of the "ideological state apparatuses" (ISAs), which overdetermine the economic base, and which represent Althusser's rearticulation and revamping of Gramsci's conceptualization of "civil society."

Like Gramsci, Althusser strives to emphasize the material reality of ideological ideals, beliefs, art, culture, and, ultimately, of concepts and knowledge. For Althusser as for Gramsci, ideology, thought, and aesthetics are not abstractions but manifest themselves physically, materially, institutionally. For both thinkers, the state is represented not only by the government but also by a series of institutions or operations that are "relatively independent," and therefore "relatively free," to make their own laws and decisions. Althusser lists a number of ISAs that play this role, noting that his list is not exhaustive: the Church (and other religious institutions), the schools, the family, the law, the trade unions, the media, and culture (the arts, literature). He holds that whereas, in former times, the Church was the most powerful ISA, in modern times, that position is occupied by the schools.

Let us look at the school ISA. The schools, Althusser holds, do not offer students knowledge but train them in such a way that they will assume their "proper" place in society. The Peruvian government, for example, does not instruct or persuade the author of a third-grade primer, designed to teach reading rather than ideas, to cast the maid in the story of a well-to-do Lima family as an indigenous woman. And no law forces the schools to select this particular primer. And yet not only is this text chosen; the issue of the maid is not even mentioned during class. Certain Peruvian social relations thus emerge as so natural and normal as to merit no comment. Whether a good reading manual or not, the primer "shows and tells" the students who use it the "correct" place for each "type" within Peruvian society, hence the "correct" place for each student. And the more unknowingly and "innocently" the book does this, the more natural and normal such places appear.

It is important to emphasize that this hypothetical portrayal of the well-to-do metropolitan Peruvian household with an indigenous servant is not false but, in fact, quite true to reality. Nor does the primer directly promote racial prejudices. In the tale the maid is a completely positive figure. She may even be the wise confidante of the children. The ISAs do not, as in the narrative of "ideology as false consciousness" that Althusser debunks, strive to pass off the false for the true, bias for objective fact. The actual conditions of Peruvian production (the divisions between the European Creole and the indigenous, family and maid, wealthy and poor, men and women) are already working in ideology's favor. All that is necessary is the innocent, "soft," but *persuasive* naturalization and standardization of that unjust reality, that "truth." The school ISA simply puts actual social practices and relations down in writing. It formalizes and institutionalizes them.

ISAs aid in the reproduction of social arrangements, not only through this process of standardization, but also through a series of binaries, the first of which is the ideological state/repressive state binary. The repressive state imposes its statutes and convictions through violence and strong law enforcement, sometimes through torture and war. Its power is extremely visible. It often administers its rule unjustly, and just as often openly advocates unjust legislation. Censorship and propaganda are two key tactics it uses to reduce freedom of expression and thought to a minimum.

The ideological state, on the other hand, "induces" the law through "relatively pacific" or "civil" means. Censorship is lifted, words flow freely, debate is promoted, unjust governmental policy or acts are condemned. Yet the most important way the ideological state manages to rule and pacify the public is by capitalizing on its difference from the repressive state. Its hope is that citizens who "know" this repression, who have experienced it, seen it on television, or read about it in newspapers, magazines, or books, will automatically, through the repressive/ideological comparison, come to associate the ideological state, which does not physically repress them, with improvement and—it goes without saying—with freedom and the good.

This explains why, within the media ISA of the United States before September 11 (see chapter 5), human rights abuses in foreign countries were constantly emphasized. Given that all kinds of violence were (and are) taking place in the world, why did the U.S. media focus on these *human rights* abuses—why did they not focus, say, on global *civil rights* violations? Because American "freedoms," as well as projects such as the New World Order, hinged (and hinge) on the distinction between the ideological and repressive state.[3] U.S. ideological control needed to cast human rights abuses as physical state violence in order to (1) "sell" its usually nonphysically violent domestic policies as progress and democracy—not another form of control; (2) mark the absolute separation between the United States and the "foreign" sites of these abuses, as if the U.S. economy (market exploitation) had nothing to do with the abuses; and (3) distinguish foreign nations that have signed up for the New World Order as a full market economy from those that have not (as progressive global democracy is to barbaric state despotism).

All of this tells us why, as Slavoj Zizek has noted, a statement or idea can be "true," accurate, but still ideological.[4] "Ideology as false consciousness" falls again on the face of its assumptions. Those who declare that "there is much censorship in Cuba" are correct; the censorship has frequently been rampant, random, and terrifying. Yet, because this declaration implicitly sets up the violence/control, United States/Cuba, democracy/Communism, censorship/freedom distinctions, it hammers home the U.S. ideology, indeed, the ideological state itself. The declaration about Cuban censorship, though not false "by itself," is nevertheless most often "ideological" since it does not emerge "by itself" but in a relation to other beliefs. It surfaces through the repressive/ideological binaries that ground the ideological state, aid in the creation of a national U.S. consensus ("better free press than censorship"), and, in turn, curb disturbances and maintain the conditions of production.

If it goes without saying that the humane, ideological, "soft" injunction is better than the repressive law, it follows that this benign system is better than political activism as well. This activity is often riotous. It easily commands, or brings about, a fierce, repressive response: the return of the abusive state, of a wrong whose agent may well be the right, but whose "instigator" (from the view of the ideological state) is leftist activism, now party to the harm.

Such points need not be emphasized, or forced home through the hard rhetoric of propaganda, which tactic belongs to the repressive state. The ideological state is ideological rather than repressive precisely because "the facts" go without saying, because it is obvious that a blow to the head from a police stick is worse than innocently absurd pedagogy, or the "unfortunate" withdrawal of funds from public schools, which at times yield that pedagogy. Ideology persuades "nicely"; repression coerces "meanly."

Here we might recall Foucault's argument that power must be executed or represented (by public acts or statements), embodied by a particular figure/practice, in order to materialize. Yet, as soon as power is visibly represented, it loses its transcendental, necessary status (as do all "mere" representations), emerging as relative, exposed to other forces, vulnerable.

The government of the ideological state, however, seems to get around such contradictions. It appears to exercise its power by farming out—to the ISAs—the practices of force that would expose it, bring it down. The less it acts, speaks, or shows, the more the government's positions are strengthened. Taken to its utmost extreme, the government of the ideological state would sell itself without publicity (the ISAs would do the state's "PR" for it). Government's off-scene existence and nonrhetoric would themselves serve as testimony to the state's nonintrusive, hence just nature. Since its consensus production is grounded in the "relatively private" ISAs, the ideological state manages to convey the idea that the people, not the politicians, autonomously determine the social: an autonomy whose conditions the state justly supplies.

It is a matter of common sense: nonintrusive law—law that never directly "touches" the bodies or rights of the people, and is fair because it does not—is the condition of the emancipation of the citizen (individual or collective). This "common sense," yielding consensus and tranquility, allows the state government to spend more time (hence money) on private matters (such as "deregulation") and less on curbing internal violence (a curbing that might well lead to "going overboard": human rights abuses), public works, and foreign policy (outside of war): less on government and more on the market.

Here one might ask: In the ideological or "hegemonic" state, do ISAs such as the media, the schools, or the family even *persuade*? Is persuasion not too close to propaganda, hence to coercion and barbarism? In the ideological state, as I suggested above, reason is to violence, and information to censorship/propaganda, as right is to wrong, progress to backwardness. The display of the binaries and of the values implied therein seduces the people toward the ideals of the ideological state—yet neither the government nor the ISAs really need to cajole since their key conviction is just a matter of common sense.

Indeed, ideology is to violence, not as influence is to coercion, but as the "it goes without saying" is to the persuasion/coercion binary. If the government of the ideological state must in some way push its own perspective at the expense of others, such force easily leads to dissension. The excluded persons do not identify themselves in "their" representations or representatives, and thus fight to situate their own vision therein. This struggle, in turn, can compel the "progressive" state to resort to violence—the dissension, after all, must be tamed—hence to slip into the barbarism from which it must distance itself if it is to reach its desired goal: the production of a natural consensus or "state of nature" that, being beyond dispute and thereby automatic, requires no public monitoring or regulation.

Thus the hegemonic or ideological state, as Althusser understands it, actually sustains itself by setting up three operations, and by playing one against the other two: (1) discipline through violence (police state, whether de jure or de facto); (2) control through persuasion (liberal democracy); and (3) consensus through common sense or "it goes without saying" (today's neoliberalism).

Public/private is hence the second binary Althusser's ideological state banks on. The idea is to posit the operations of the ISAs as "private and personal" matters into which the government, as the overseer only of the public sphere, should not intervene. The state divests itself from public services, delegating its various tasks to the appropriate "nongovernmental or private sector." The state welfare program (for example) is reduced. Corporations are then encouraged (with financial incentives) by the government to hire and train more of the workforce. As public domain after public domain is reborn as a private site, thus no longer a state responsibility, the state's mandates and laws fade further and further into the background. And this shift occurs (so the story goes) not due to the state's irresponsibility (an irresponsible withdrawal would be one that is too rapid, too violent) but because the nongovernmental or "independent" sector has taken matters into its own hands. The government need not talk about giving people liberties. The people themselves take those liberties, assume control of public existence, and hence perform the emancipation.

The "private" or "nongovernmental" forces that back the state and "reproduce the relations and conditions of production" now fall outside the state's jurisdiction. Thus, for instance, a Christian base (the Church) for the state is rejected as potentially intolerant or biased. Yet Christian ideals—in the form of "the moral majority" or "family values"—remain at the center of the political infrastructure through actual social practices. Their central positions grow firmer and firmer because they are set up as "out-of-bounds." To touch them would be wrong, despotic, abusive. Hence the state is free of the religious base in the abstract, de jure, but dominated by religion in fact, de facto.

Binaries such as public/private are problematic, not because they are false, but because they refuse the very differences they seem to advance, as is the case for all binaries. In the public/private binary, for example, the public is presented as a phase in the gradual maturation of the state. The public is to the private as the child is to the adult or as the "underdeveloped" is to the modern nation: not an actual operation or being, but an epiphenomenal reflection or object that will only realize itself, become what it truly is, when it disappears into the private. The public/private difference, in other words, is no difference. The public is the (not yet) private.

The third binary deployed by the ISAs is know-how/knowledge. The ISAs supply individuals, not with knowledge, but with the know-how necessary to run and get into the social machine: into the "proper" part of the machine. The instruction first builds up the belief that social conditions are given, beyond critique. One requires no knowledge of the operation of the apparatus (just as one can readily use computer software and programs without the least understanding of the way the hardware operates). One only needs the know-how, the manual, the information necessary for access.

Every use is, in fact, the performance and ritualization of the machine's rightness and justice, thus of the fact that it should not be changed: a change that would require, in any event, precise knowledge of the mechanism. If the social machine as given permits my entry, allows me to prosper, mature, become myself, then it is itself liberating and good. It supplies the know-how by means of the ISAs; and these grant me passage, freedom, and use. In the ideological state, it is the case not only that we do not need knowledge (of the machine) because the machine is already perfect but also that the machine is already perfect because we do not need knowledge, because every claim of the "no-need-for-knowledge" standardizes or "perfects" both the claim and the apparatus.

Our social conditions, so the belief runs, are flawless, as in nature, or better said, as in a state of nature.[5] They already form a site that, if exploited correctly through the know-how that the conditions themselves offer free of charge, allows for all creations, subjectivities, understanding, and liberties. Here are the implements, ready to hand. There is nothing else you need to know. Indeed, knowledge of the operation would only be a waste of time, an excess, a disturbance.

Although know-how first subsumes knowledge into production and information access, the know-how/ knowledge binary is necessary for this subsumption. Thus, if know-how were to take over or eliminate knowledge, it would lose the know-how/knowledge binary off of which it feeds: if know-how made knowledge vanish, know-how would also vanish.

Know-how, therefore, must set itself up, not as "mere" know-how, but as practical, thus essential knowledge: not as the other, but as the truth of all knowledge, as knowledge itself. Know-how accomplishes this portion of its task by establishing a productive/unproductive binary. It contrasts productive deliberation to theoretical reflection, which now stands for impractical, superfluous, spurious intellectualism. The spokespeople for know-how (the same ones who insist: "Everything I need to know I learned in kindergarten") present their argument: "After all, the essence of the social machine transcends the human. Those who would like to waste their time trying to understand this transcendental sphere are most welcome to do so. But these theoretical speculations—like theories that prove God's existence—are useless, dedicated as they are to a realm that lies outside human production. To be useful, we should understand the social only insofar as we can put that knowledge to work for better production, which is to say, better use of the machine. True knowledge, productive knowledge, is know-how: expertise."

Althusser contends the opposite. His insistence that the key ISA is education (his model is Gramsci) indicates to what degree Althusser ties knowledge and theory to activism. He holds that theoretical analysis (or "science" torn away from its rationalist impulse by Lacan) is part and parcel of practice. The knowledge that the capitalist machine—unlike an irrational animal—can be analyzed, that its operations do not transcend the human, hence are not absolute, essential, unmanageable, or given, is the condition of any political project. Either a practice grows from the knowledge that the capitalist machine is not necessary, and hence can be radically altered or displaced, or else practice can be nothing but a ceaseless production or reproduction—alienation—that performs capitalism's inevitability. Action is bound to theory because, without knowledge of the nonessentialness of the social apparatus, which theory best discovers, political undertakings cannot even begin.

Althusser's is not far from a classical Marxist narrative. Praxis and production accede to the level of politics only when teamed with consciousness (to which, however, Althusser adds the unconscious), when the "practical" (labor, the worker) and theoretical (intellectual) sectors (e)merge as a single force. But the ideological state has no patience for such theses on the "importance of knowledge." It assimilates knowledge into production and know-how in order to recast "the thing formerly known as thought" into "mere theory": into elitist abstraction that, preposterously convoluted, itself testifies to the value of know-how as "real" knowledge. It posits the making sense of operations such as capital and metaphysics (which can indeed be complicated and difficult) as gentrified, sometimes amusing, sometimes annoying, mumbo-jumbo. The know-how/knowledge binary repeats the practice/theory, materiality/thought divisions, divisions that, for Althusser, eliminate politics in advance.

But know-how does not end its operations here. The above arguments must be reversed to be maintained. Know-how, needing a know-how/knowledge binary to survive, passes for knowledge, disappears into knowledge, takes over knowledge. But if know-how turns into knowledge, how can it maintain the sphere of know-how, without whose mediation it cannot stand as knowledge? The answer is a tidy one: know-how, being no longer know-how but new genuine knowledge, invents *another* sphere of know-how from which it distinguishes itself.

Thus, for a certain contemporary imaginary, the computer programmer, the corporate consultant, the chief executive officer, the banker, the doctor, the lawyer, the broker, and the engineer are knowledgeable and productive. They understand the world; and they make that wisdom work for themselves and for society. The car mechanic, the nurse, and the homemaker, on the other hand, possess only know-how. God forbid the nurse—however nice, helpful, careful, understanding, educated, bright, and patient that nurse may be—should diagnose my illness, given the money I pay for my HMO. That task—it goes without saying—can only be performed by the doctor, who comes in for four minutes, looks at my tongue, shoves a light in my eyes, tells me my splitting headache is nothing, and then scurries off. Figures such as the nurse are (in this imaginary) productive, but not knowledgeable. If they were, they would be doctors. They are not involved in true production, or in the truth of production.

We now understand further how the relations of production—between, say, the clothes maker and the sewing machine maker—reproduce the conditions of production: class difference or the social. Class division is built and rebuilt by the oppositions that sustain the ISAs and that the ISAs sustain, ISAs that seem disconnected from any workplace. The workers repeatedly choose to accept the "order of things" not only because they are alienated by their labor, or by the production process proper. They opt for the consensus or common sense also because they have been trained to do so almost from birth by the ISAs.

One site of labor production need not control another. The clothes maker need not dictate the sewing machine maker's operations. The ISAs, which cross national and cultural boundaries, as well as scenes of production, assure the persistence of the dominant order (the boss is ahead of the workers), hence of the overall ideology, in all places of production.

But here an important query arises: If the ISAs reproduce, above all, the conditions of production, how do they reproduce one another? To grasp the nature and importance of this question, let us imagine a young, intelligent, enthusiastic thirteen-year-old boy growing up in Mexico City. His history teacher, a bright, charismatic, funny, admirable, inspiring man, posits the Church as a repressive force, and, taking what amounts to a commonplace intellectual position, then associates liberation, democracy, and progress with efforts to overcome Church dogmatism (a dogmatism that, working through the hypocritical ruling Party, the PRI, has taken control of many public and political sectors). The boy attends history class four days a week; he loves it. On Sunday, he goes to church, where the priest—whom the boy quietly dislikes—lectures the congregation on the evils of progress and modern society. How do the two ISAs relate?

For the ISAs collectively to function as a mechanism of social reproduction, the school ISA would have to "hammer home" the same lesson as the Church ISA. This does not mean that the teacher must repeat the priest verbatim, or vice versa. In the example above, it is obviously possible that the liberalism of the teacher and the conservatism of the priest differ, but also complement each other through a common link. The two authorities offer separate views. But both command obedience, and thus posit compliance to authority as a cultural value, beyond ideologies or differences of "perspective."

Yet nothing is to prevent the young man from drawing an entirely different conclusion. If one authority can say the exact opposite of another, then authority as a whole should be questioned. No authority figure can be assumed correct. Authority is not necessarily right. Two "heads" do not add up to a bigger head, to absolute command, but to a division within authority: to a rift that reveals that one authority is always relative to another, thereby vulnerable. Power is relational, contingent, not total or absolute. It thus can be overcome. Two heads compute into no head, or into a split or broken head. And the boy might remember this when he gets to the workplace: "The boss is no authority! Why should I respect his orders, produce for him? Why should I produce at all?"

Even though no state institution lies outside ideology, the repetition of sites of authority cannot *not* exhibit the contingency of authority itself. As noted briefly above, if power must be represented, performed, hence repeated—if the priest must in some way reiterate the message of the teacher; and if the ideological state depends on this staging or repetition—it cannot also be essential. The multiplication of sites of power (state, culture, private sector, family, civil society) conceivably splits domination. At times it may weaken rather than strengthen it.

As introduced earlier, Marx suggests that the liberation of the institutions of civil society from government points the way only for *society*'s emancipation, only for *political* freedom. The break, that is, does not lead directly to a more genuine, *universal* liberty but sets up two separate spheres: a free society or bourgeoisie and a confined/abjected proletariat (as well as, of course, the difference between the two). At the same time, in this state form divided between government and the ISAs (government + ISA = state), the bourgeoisie must grant the proletariat access to the institutions of civil society if it desires to maintain its position. Only in this way can society properly "ideologize" the lower class, persuade it to accept the status quo, thus stave off any threats. And herein lies the problem. The ISAs can surely transmit ideological messages that both favor the bourgeoisie and convince the proletariat that social freedom is universal emancipation (that political liberation is human liberation), that the proletariat, too, is free. These messages cannot, however, guarantee that their reception by the proletariat will reproduce the original intent of the ISAs, of the state. They cannot guarantee that the signs will be heard as they are sent—and sent and heard they must be. Indeed, the proletariat cannot always grasp the communication well since it emits from a removed sector, thus serves as a potential sign/image of alienation, a force of oppression, a sense of discomfort, a call to revolt.

In brief, because the field of the ISAs is a relation of ISAs, and because each particular ISA is itself a relation (between its origin and endpoint), separated from itself, the ISAs cannot assure the reproduction of the conditions of production: as the support of the structures of the workplace, they cannot themselves assure that reproduction. Therefore, the reproduction of the ideological state cannot lie in the ISAs as such, in cultural institutions (especially the family, the schools, and the media) as the "reproducer" of labor relations.

But, as Althusser shows, if economic analyses fail to explain the endurance of social injustice and of class difference, an explanation is not to be found in the study of cultural production or cultural influences either, as cultural studies readings of Althusser's essay would argue. "Cultural studies" will not complete the exegesis of the social where "economics-based studies" have failed to do so.

It is interesting to note, in this context, that Althusser does not list the workplace among his ISAs, an omission too noteworthy, too stunning and fundamental for us to attribute it to the "nonexhaustive" nature of his ISA list. Althusser mentions unions in the context of the ISAs, but not the workplace itself. He establishes, for example, that families, schools, and the media "train" the male laborer to be a good, obedient worker. However the workplace, judging from Althusser's analytic, does not train this man to become a certain kind of father, and then to rear a certain kind of son or daughter. If this were the case, the workplace would not lie outside the list of ISAs, but would be an ISA.[6] And this would be true whether a specific workplace pertained to the public or private sector. As to workers, the "S" of the ISA does not refer solely to official state employees. To emphasize a key point concerning ISAs and civil society, for both Althusser and Gramsci: institutions *outside* of government—notably, the media and the workplace—are proper to the state itself, part of the "S."

We certainly understand why Althusser would exclude the workplace from the ISA realm. He clearly desires that cultural analysis, or his reading of civil society, supplement labor analysis; that the ISAs complete a picture that studies based in labor and class can initiate but not complete—the picture not of production but of reproduction. Thus, in the postscript to his essay, Althusser emphasizes repeatedly that class difference, even if just in "the last instance," is the ground of both ideology and the ISAs: "Ideologies are not 'born' in the ISAs but from the social classes at grips in the class struggle. . . . The ruling ideology . . . is indeed 'realized' in those ISAs, but it goes beyond them, for it comes from elsewhere [from class struggle]."[7] Ideology "keeps going" what class difference, working through labor, "starts." The importance of the ISAs thus lies in their role as supplement or support.

In casting the labor process as primary force and the ISAs as supporting force, Althusser's analysis is largely predicated on the possibility of separating out and then reintegrating distinct explanations of the social: the economic, the cultural, and the psychological. Yet if it turns out that labor *is* an ISA, then the ISAs and labor, as two ISAs offering two forms of "education"—education organic to the workplace and formal education—might contradict each other, just as the Church authority might contradict the school authority. The study of cultural/social institutions (the ISAs) cannot resolve the contradictions within labor (labor as site of production), "fill out" labor since, for Althusser, those institutions themselves must exist in a dialectical opposition to labor (labor as competing ISA).

If the ISAs really explained the persistence of the class difference that is, in theory, their origin, Althusser would have had no reason to go on to the third (Lacanian) section of his essay. Whether he "admits" to this or not, his first two explanations of the "reproduction of the relations of production"—the economic and cultural accounts—have clearly fallen prey to their own discord. The one will neither back nor found the other; but neither can the two be separated. Instead, economics and culture cut through each other; seeming complements, the one tears the other down the middle. And herein lies the crux of the matter: How can the relations of production reproduce themselves if the various powers that seem to induce this reproduction are themselves splintered, "full of holes," thus unable to "complete the picture"? How can ideology persist even when the power base is divided from itself? Is this not a self-contradiction? In other words, the Lacanian section of Althusser's essay is not an extension of the Gramscian section, not a deeper meditation on the foundation of the ISAs or cultural forms. It marks the limit of the ISAs' role in ideology formation, the frontier that opens onto a topos that neither the ideological nor the repressive state can account for.

Perhaps Althusser turns to Lacan, in part, because Lacan proceeds from the simple conviction that social or state domination is insidiously persistent: the split master or split subject does not weaken such domination but only strengthens it. If the various powers of the state divide and turn against one another, but the ideological state persists, this may be because the divisions, pluralisms, rivalries, and competitions that ensue are the state's source of strength: the firm root of the ideological or the market state.

What is certain from Althusser's essay is that the state—as the combination of government and the ISAs, material reality and culture, law and education—cannot account for its own "magical reproduction." By engaging Lacan, Althusser recognizes that a full explanation of the state's perseverance lies outside of or exterior to the state's own existence. The ways and means of the state's maintenance can only be grasped, therefore, by going beyond that existence, by penetrating that exteriority.

To put it another way, turning from labor to ideology as the "cause" of capitalism's reproduction, Althusser fails to find the cause of that cause. If ideology working through the ISAs is that cause, what is the cause of ideology? Even a cursory reading of Althusser leads us to the obvious response: the unconscious. Indeed, Althusser, himself, once toyed with the idea of basing his general project on the pronouncement that the "'unconscious works like ideology.'"[8] In the Lacanian unconscious, he finds a theory of state desire, one that his thought—particularly his meditations on the subject as master (and its Hegelian underpinnings)—urgently demands.

Althusser's critique of ideology as false consciousness discloses that ideological "truths" are indeed *desired*. When the representations that shape and distort reality are pealed away, the "truths" they forged are retained by both state and civil society, government and the ISAs because, at bottom, the subjects desire them. It is as if the maintenance of ideologies, however horrible and false they may be, perhaps even because of their spuriousness, is more desirable than their loss, as if one imagines their disappearance as the disappearance of the world itself. Rigorous critiques of ideology thus ask: What historical circumstances led to the creation, not of a false reality, but of reality emerging from and relying on ideology or ideologies? Whence this *desire* for ideology?

Ideology working through the ISAs persuades the subjects of the state to take their proper places in the proper order of capitalism. Society is partially managed and reproduced by this control. This we have seen. But, as we have also seen, because neither ideology nor the ISAs can necessarily reproduce themselves or one another, neither can guarantee society's existence. The latter task is assumed—insofar as it can be assumed at all—by desire, forcing Althusser (and us) to ask: If unconscious desires reproduce capitalism's relations of production, what produces and reproduces the unconscious desires, indeed, the unconscious itself?

"Language" is Althusser's answer; this is the exteriority to which we referred above. To deploy the terms that Althusser would make famous, language "hails" or "interpellates" the subjects into *desiring* a capitalism that they thereby reproduce. Although generally interpreted as specific calls, particular signs or demands with which the subjects identify so as then to accept their proper places within the laws or norms set by capital, in fact, no specific call can interpellate *all*—Althusser *insists* on this totality—subjects equally. Only language, as a piece of and as the excess of every word (*all* of them), the component of each signifier that is no signifier, as the part that is no part, can.

Particular signs, to be sure, interpellate individual or collective subjects, seducing them to take positions; but they do so as tools of the ISAs, as their representatives and representations. If Althusser intended to impart the notion of interpellation as the representative of a given ideological site that summons subjects to occupy that site, he certainly would not have needed either Lacan or psychoanalysis to do so. But because the ISAs, however *well* they function, do not completely work as ideological "reproducers," Althusser's theory of interpellation could explain the persistence of class difference only by breaking with the theory of the ISAs.

Language, in fact, interpellates "prior to" any specific interpellation or sign, and any subsequent position taking. For, if state ideology ultimately emerges from the "obviousness" of the universe, as Althusser resolutely maintains,[9] but the critique of that obviousness or representation does not necessarily "stop" ideology's reproduction, then both the reproduction of and intervention into ideology demand that one attend to some "thing" that is not apparent. And what is not in evidence—but is not absent either—is the relation, difference, "between," bond, or encounter of things, of classes, ISAs, and discourses. In other words, the *existence* of classes, which is obvious, does not engender the key to an understanding of either class *difference*—the relation of classes—or its possible *overcoming*, both of which must be read or theorized, not viewed. The encounter of classes, folded into the reverse side of the "it goes without saying" or of the world's "obviousness," irreducible to the binaries and discourses that back the state—this relation, closed to observation but never amiss, is the *saying* itself, or language. As to precisely how Althusser reads language (as it is cast by Lacan) *into* a theory of capitalist reproduction through his notion of interpellation, readers will have to wait until the conclusion of this study. There is still much ground to be laid.

7.

Laclau and Mouffe

The Closure of an Open Politics, or, Undecidability on the Left

In his well-known meditation "Postmodernism and the Market," Fredric Jameson works to demonstrate the nonnecessity or nonabsoluteness of the market.[1] Although Jameson argues that the free market is not the perfection of Western history, as others have famously claimed, he does not try to locate an external political structure or economic model, an "outside the market" that would "prove" his point by attesting to the market's nontotality. Rather, he discloses the contradictions or antinomies (his preferred term) within capital that index its gaps, cracks, and limits. It is the finitude of late capitalism's market, and not its exterior, that Jameson works to reveal.

Indeed, for Jameson, such a limit is the condition of possibility for political intervention: if subjects are convinced—if it goes without saying, if it is a matter of common sense—that the open market is inevitable (to say nothing of right and ethical), then any desire to struggle against this market is destroyed in advance. One can hardly expect individuals or collectives to fight if they *know*—this is where knowledge analysis and market analysis intersect—the outcome of the contest: if subjects are certain that the market, as an immutable ground, cannot *not* survive every threat, cannot *not* dictate the success and failure of every decision (every relation, every career, every act, every creation). At such a point, one can only say: "If you can't beat 'em, you might as well join 'em."

Having exposed the market's finitude or nontotality, on the other hand, a subject can at least yearn for intercessions, shifts, breakdowns. If the market is not essential, then potentially, at any moment, in any place, it could fall away—or, more crucially, political action could push it away. Thus, although Jameson sometimes expresses hope for a future socialism (or, nostalgically, recalls a past one), his fundamental task is to unveil the market's incompleteness and contingency, in the here and now, so as to keep extant the condition of any anticapitalist intervention, that condition being the just-mentioned contingency.

To investigate the ramifications of Jameson's thoughts, let us turn or return to a work that was of great influence in the 1980s and 1990s: Ernesto Laclau and Chantal Mouffe's *Hegemony and Socialist Strategy*.[2] The text outlines the possibilities for new political movements, yet from within a state context. I want to reveal how the Laclau-Mouffe model, predicated on the theoretical notion that radical politics today turns on a given project's exposure to a "constitutive outside"—to an exteriority that is foundational to the interior of the endeavor—permits us to rethink the global.

Social interventions, Laclau and Mouffe hold, necessarily take place in and under a specific name. One does not add this name to the political operation. Naming or "articulations," for reasons I will outline, are themselves foundational and material components of any action.

Such naming is not a simple matter. No individual or collective can be captured or defined by a single appellation. The worker is a white, Black, Hispanic, or immigrant worker; the immigrant worker is a man or woman; the immigrant woman is wealthy or poor; the poor person was previously employed or unemployed; the unemployed subject is gay or straight; the gay person is HIV positive or not; the HIV-positive individual suffers or does not suffer from AIDS, and so on. Laclau and Mouffe do not oppose, as they are often accused of doing, discourses based on class, the "classical Marxist" stronghold. They merely argue that a class is never just a class, a worker never just a worker. Class is class plus, just as labor is labor plus. To posit class consciousness as the foundation of a political analysis is to fall short of class since class is always greater than itself. Or to put this in more Laclau-Mouffe terms: class, like any category, is determined by its relation to other classifications. Any determination is overdetermined: determined by more than itself.

Imagine the following scenario. On a small, conservative mid-American campus, a group called the "African-American Organization" (AAO) forms. In one of its first projects, the group protests the underrepresentation of African-American texts in humanities courses, pointing out scandalous omissions. Important figures such as Douglass, Wright, Ellison, Malcolm X, and Toni Morrison have not been taught in any class for six years. Certain women within the AAO, originally enthusiastic about its activities, grow suspicious when they see the platform. What about Alice Walker and Maya Angelou? Receiving, in this particular example, suspect responses—"We can make a pitch for those texts later"—these women form a new group called the "Minority Women's Collective" (MWC), which denounces the absence in the curriculum of "minority women's works." An internal squabble ensues. A number of women choose to stay with the first group, AAO, prioritizing race over gender. Others join the new group, MWC, prioritizing gender over race. The AAO thus finds itself forced to "publicly" address gender issues. Leaders determine that if divisions within the African-American community continue to occur, then the demands made by the numerous splinter groups will cancel each other out. The greater the number of groups protesting, the less the force of each protest, and of all protests added together.

Although every political organization possesses a name—a "name of" that is already an "in the name of" or cause—all such names will capture only certain components of the group that forms under the designation. Inclusion, because it must be named, "includes" *exclusion* as one of its conditions. In the example just presented, the "excluded" gender issue, when brought to the fore, is not an outside component that is then added to the original African-American concerns. Every African-American is already male, female, or some combination. The "African-American Organization" that branches out into a "Minority Women's Collective" simply adjoins to itself an "internal plus" that was already present: gender. Nothing "actually" changes except the name. And yet the name alters a great deal: the organization, the cause, the demands, the texts, the people involved. The new articulation does not necessarily produce a distinct entity (minority women). It exposes the same entity (African-American people) differently.

For Laclau and Mouffe, political practice involves, on the one hand, the endless opening of a group or self to more of itself, to the more than the self, the antagonism, the overdetermination, or the constitutive outside; and on the other hand, the refusal to open, the struggle to hold one's ground. Politics materializes, not when subjects finds themselves in a collective "we" that they defend, as in identity politics, but when the "we" splits into "us" and "them": when the border that divides the "we" surfaces, and demands either to be crossed or secured.

Neither move—crossing, securing—is more "political" or "democratic" than the other. To hold onto one's name, to retain intact the "we" even when it is split into an "us and them," may in fact be the more responsible tactic in a certain situation. Should "African-American" be rephrased as "people of color" when the link between two (or more) American peoples—say, Blacks and Hispanics—grows increasingly apparent? It depends on the cause, the context, the political issue.

On the other hand, when politics materializes from the merger of groups, from the openness to the internal outsider (gender as the internal outsider of African-American movements, class as the internal outsider of Third World discourses, and so on), a poetics, a creative naming, is the condition of the practice. One project hitches on to the other. But neither discourse can supply the name—or more crucially, the "in the name of"—for that contact, communion, or encounter, which, for Laclau and Mouffe, represents the "antagonism," the excess of all discourses that does not permit the social (the collection of discourses and collectives) ever to reach a totality. There are always more encounters and thus more antagonisms and more calls for invention, poetics, communication. In Laclau and Mouffe's politics, *poiēsis* does not only designate a praxis; it *is* one. An articulation (name, in the name of)—or its refusal—does not depict a happening. It makes happen, for, without that name, nothing changes, there is no political event.

As soon as collective (African-American) confronts the outside (women) as its own "plus," it may have to rephrase its "name" and "in the name of" so as to incorporate that excess, so as to account for *itself*. The phrasing is the coming-to-production and the coming-to-politics of that new group. The advent of such an articulation represents both an appeal (one thinks here of the term "African-American," which represents an appeal to all Americans to cease using the term "Black," or at least to stop and think what "Black" means, and what it means to call someone "Black"), and the condition for further appeals. "African-Americans are today demanding . . . ," for example, can be very different from "Blacks are today demanding . . ."; and the difference can be essential to the appeal itself. For Laclau and Mouffe, an articulation, the emergence of "hinge signifiers" that do not sit well with the common sense or with the aggregate of discourses within a given culture, but which must be made into this common sense through processes of intervention, repetition, standardization, and ritualization—which expose sense as an incessant *making sense* rather than as a given—compel this consensus to halt in its tracks, and to take account of the novel articulations and "articulators."

The Laclau-Mouffe production of hinge signifiers thereby seems to accomplish precisely the task advocated by Jameson. If the ultimate goal of the market is to create the consensus or commonsensical idea that this market is essential ("the only choice"), hence to rid the social of all desire to disturb it—if this is true, then the disruption of such a common sense, and the time it takes to "commonsensualize" any new articulation as antagonism, marks the limit or temporality of the same market. Temporal, thereby temporary, a common sense that needs time to sustain itself has already exposed its own "overturnability" or nonnecessity. Or so it would seem.

Such ideas, in any case, lead us to Laclau and Mouffe's understanding, so fundamental to their project, of hegemony,[3] an understanding that grows from the marriage that Laclau and Mouffe forge between Gramsci and Lacan. Perhaps the key to such a union is the Lacanian *point de capiton*, translated as "nodal point" in Laclau and Mouffe's lexicon,[4] and as "headpoint" in mine. In French, *point de capiton* is a play on words that could mean either "headpoint" or "no headpoint." For Lacan, the "headpoint" is the signifier—the element of the Lacanian symbolic—through which subjects or organizations find their place in the order of the social.

Laclau and Mouffe work through this concept as follows. Any component of sociality emerges as a relation to other components: as relational or as contingent. However, one element of the relation or relations, in a particular situation, must rise above the others so as to serve as the headpoint: as the signifier that positions the entire relation, that "threads" the subjects at hand into society. The nodal point *sutures* the social, that is, the gaps between sectors and signifiers. The lesbian student feminist wealthy mother woman African-American citizen makes a demand, at a particular moment, as an "African-American." "African-American" is the headpoint that brings the entire being of this individual into the symbolic. And yet it does so by marginalizing a potentially infinite number of aspects of this person, ones no less essential to her existence. The decision for "African-American" over "lesbian," then, is never completely grounded. One cannot argue that the woman is "in truth" more African than lesbian; unless "as much" lesbian as African (or any other aspect essential to her being), she is not who she is.

On the other hand, a decision for a headpoint must be made, across this field of possibilities; or else there is no subject, indeed, no field. One's position always involves a choice that is never grounded in a reason. (Identification, like identity, is never rooted in the "accident of one's birth" but in relatively arbitrary decisions, in choice: the hypothetical Third World male intellectual who presents himself as "Other" by the accident of birth may neglect to highlight, *by selection*, his identity as a member of the wealthy or elite class.) At the same time, if one does not posit a given choice as reasonable or "within reason," does not elect a signifier that "makes sense" within the given community or hegemony, the choice is not viable. For the particular subject, it is not an option. In other words, the selection of the headpoint has no ground; yet without a ground no selection, thereby no headpoint, can emerge.

The hegemonic "instant," when one signifier/identity assumes the position of the whole, can be dynamic or static, radical or conservative, left- or right-wing. The headpoint signifier can disrupt and then reorganize the field of relations, as might a term such as "people of color." Or it may further naturalize or ritualize an already existing status quo, as might also be the situation with "people of color." In either case, there is no perfect *point de capiton* precisely because the headpoint is no headpoint. It is one constituent of the chain that "unjustly" takes command.

The *point de capiton* (the headpoint) is the *point de capiton* (no headpoint). As invention, the headpoint exposes the fact that there is no transcendental ground or "metabase" for politics. Yet, as head signifier, the articulation always already sits as this very ground. The suture as ground is no-ground (disclosing politics as an open process) and the no-ground sets a ground (closing off that openness). The limit on play is also the border that opens onto new play; the stoppage of the flux is the demand for more flux; the "arbitrary" closure that precludes a novel politics is the intervention that makes that politics run.

Herein lies a key reason why Laclau and Mouffe's work, though easily mistaken for a "Left-leaning identity politics" rather than a truly post-Marxist venture, ought not be reduced to this first designation. The social suture, as already indicated, is the part that stands for the whole. It is thus a metonym both in the traditional sense (part for the whole) and in the more taxing Lacanian sense: the figurative substitution that is contingent rather than necessary. As trope and marker of language as such, the headpoint is at once the finitude that exposes the whole to an internal outside, to the demand for more substitutions and social reorganizations; and the part that *is* this whole, the "essence" that subsumes and hence *excludes* in advance all exterior parts/signifiers.

This paradoxical relation of part and whole recalls Rancière's analysis of the proletariat. The "proletariat," the class that is no class, is the undifferentiated embodiment of the *in common*—this, again, is why the emancipation of the proletariat is, in theory, the emancipation of all humanity—that, without property, inscribes itself into and shifts a political body. Laclau and Mouffe, in fact, virtually repeat this Marxist postulate. To be sure, they liberally *translate* the "proletariat" into other names, ones bound to issues of sex, race, and gender. But even though, in the Laclau-Mouffe paradigm, sex, race, gender can displace the proletariat as the foundation for political organization, they cannot displace one another without *first* referring to this primary site: to the proletariat that *represents* class without having the property of *a* class. Thus, for Laclau and Mouffe, woman *represents* sex (the sex that is a part of all human beings) without being one (since woman has traditionally been posited as the epiphenomenal image of man: the essence of woman is man, meaning that woman is "this sex which is not one"),[5] just as "people of color" stand for the whole of race without existing as one of the races. True, woman and people of color cannot but make their appearance upon the political scene as identities with proper names and specific qualities. Yet, *as if* figures of the proletariat, they can never *be* exclusively an identity for they never represent themselves. Just as the proletariat stands, not for the proletariat, but for class, woman stands, not for woman, but for sex, people of color stand, not for people of color, but for race, and so on.

The underpinning of Laclau and Mouffe's project, in sum, is indeed the proletariat—but it is the proletariat as *figure*, one that can be substituted for and filled in by other names and groups. Marx's proletariat is not the agent but the *form* of a future politics. The class that is not a class (the sole class that is *just* class), the proletariat serves as the "general structure" that makes possible Laclau and Mouffe's supplementation of class with nonclass articulations (such as those concerning race). Laclau and Mouffe's supposed turn away from class is, in the end, a ceaseless "turning about" of class.

Stated differently, for Laclau and Mouffe, no one term, whether bound to class, gender, sex, race, or something else, interpellates all. Each must appear in a "series of equivalents." Race, for example, is not just race but class race (or even race *against* class: a negation of class), gender race, sexual orientation race, and so on. Lacking definitive qualities of its own, race qualifies as a political articulation only through another term or cause. It takes on real qualities, spurring real politics, is indeed a reality rather than abstraction, only over against and along with other markers.

The fundamental sign within Laclau and Mouffe's project is thus *democracy*. There are, of course, many democracies: ancient Greek democracy, postdictatorship democracy, neoliberal democracy, and so forth. No democracy names democracy itself, democracy as such. "True democracy" must be viewed as the trace of an unnamed politics, one that is missing from the list of possible articulations. This is why, in *Hegemony and Socialist Strategy*, democracy is conceived, not by itself, but through a series of equivalents: ecological democracy, gender democracy, sexual democracy, class democracy, and so on. Just as the proletariat is the class that is no class, democracy is the politics that is no politics. When, however, democracy materializes as the bond between all projects—when class democracy must open itself to sexual democracy in order to appeal to democracy at all—the *name* democracy (which is not democracy itself) opens infinitely to a possibility which may or may not be democratic, may or may not be political, but which democracy as *point de capiton* prompts all the same. Within Laclau and Mouffe's scheme, democracy is not realized; it is radicalized.

For reasons that will become clear, I want now to translate these theses about the signifier, contingency, identity, and democracy from a theory on hegemony, political group formations, and "social movements" to a deeper meditation on the specific determinations and actions that these individuals or collectives must make and take. To see how Laclau, himself, addresses this issue through his approach to the notion of "toleration,"[6] let us turn to the question of pedagogy.

It is true that, to be a tolerant teacher, I must be open to the views of my students. It is also true that, as a teacher whose task is in some way to aid the conveyance of the material to the class as a whole, I must at times cut students off, tell them that they are leading the discussion astray, hence impeding the education of others, the general "good." Exactly where to draw this line between listening and silencing is one of the most difficult, undecidable questions a teacher faces. There is no rule, no manual of instructions, no fixed site to etch the limit. Yet teachers attending to their ethical obligations cannot make the cut "just anywhere"; they must do so on good grounds.

Moreover, as a teacher, I have always already decided which ideas are acceptable, and which are not. I have always already set up the class—however unintentionally—in such a way that some students will feel comfortable speaking, and others will feel "silenced"; and I have done so on hard grounds (my own reasons), even if I am unaware of their existence. Those who claim to work without rules (or without "a theory"), with complete "openness," deny the hard, if never articulated, regulations they have already "built into" their "open way." In essence, they situate those rules outside the purview or discourse of the class, hence as the absolute or nondiscursive foundation of the teaching process. "No rules," most often, means "absolute rule."

My tolerance as a teacher, then, is not a matter of my mind's being open or closed. It is a matter of my taking responsibility for the closure/exposure—for the law, the boundary—I have already instituted: for the institution (in all senses of the word) of the class itself. Should I let the borders expand? Should I bar the gates? Or is the matter undecidable?

Laclau and Mouffe's undecidability, we can now see, is not simply about decision between two choices that cannot be grounded in a reason or a rule, as when a Black woman "decides" to identify with her race more than she does with her gender. It is also about the decision between a resolution that is already in place, and the displacement or redoing of that resolution.

Derrida teaches us that the condition of an authentic decision is its undecidability, the lack of a perfect, pregiven reason for the determination (if such a reason exists, no decision is necessary or even possible, for what is right goes without saying, is a matter of common sense). But he also teaches a lesson that has perhaps not caught on: the *condition* of this undecidability is the prior rule or *decision* that frames and structures the vacillation. The resolve of a woman to stand more as "Black" than as "woman" is indeed rooted in an undecidability. But her *decision* for the particular categories of race and gender already forms the hard, predetermined base of that selection process. Within the Derridean model used by Laclau and Mouffe, grounds or rules are "necessary," not because they preclude decisions from being arbitrary, from falling into a rampant relativism, but because they always already pertain to the infrastructure of the *undecidability* that renders such decisions, *as* decisions, conceivable.

Yes, groundlessness is the condition of decision. Yet grounds, and a response/responsibility to those grounds—truth, if you prefer—are the conditions of that groundlessness.

Should the teacher ask students who talk too much in class to think more carefully before making comments? Even if offered gently, such a request might discourage these students from speaking at all, even when they *do* think. Perhaps the best thing to do, then, is to let them be, to deal with the comments as they come, often wasting valuable class time in doing so. Both options are viable; a perfectly right resolution is not within the range of options. However, as a teacher, I must decide—but not simply for practical, professional, or ethical reasons. In fact, as I ponder the undecidability of the matter, I have already made a decision to permit the students to continue commenting at will—for the time being. The reason I must decide is that, even if I cannot come to a verdict, even if I elect to ask myself or others more questions, to "think about it," I cannot *not* decide. My indecision is a determination to allow the students to comment freely *for now*. The hesitation, the "mulling over the aporia," the self-questioning, the thinking, do not preexist an eventual response but are themselves responses, with as many real, material effects as any "final determination."

The "must" of the "must decide," then, may indeed be moral, political, practical, or intellectual. But it is always logical. Subjects must decide because, as subjects, they *must* do so. To put all of this another way, subjects are, not before, but *in* a decisive situation. I am never a subject per se.

I am a teacher, a brother, a father, a friend, a lover, a man, and so on. In the situation above, my subjectivity and subject position are that of a "teacher." Thus the decision I must make concerning overtalkative students indexes the limit of my "right": I cannot make a perfectly right determination, however "strong" my will, however fair my faculty of judgment, however empowering my status. But it also marks the boundary of my self (the teacher): it unveils the limit of my position, being, tolerance, agency, and power. The undecidability exposes the contingency, not of my decision, but of myself as the decider, whose "rightness" is put into question by the decision I cannot avoid—not if I am to emerge as a subject, not if I am to be a teacher.

In short, the subjects of radical democracy, individual or collective, are not Cartesian subjects, who, before an uncertain world, assure their being through their doubt: if they are doubting, if they perceive the world as undecidable, they must be. They are, rather, subjects folded into the undecidability, into a situation they cannot "get out of," but cannot determine either. Subjects do not come across an undecidable situation. Instead, an undecidable situation cuts across subjects, marks their being, scars their bodies. We are not subjects who address "undecidable political situations," and make "tough and risky" selections to do this or that, or to *be* this or that (name). The thinking is as much an act as the "real" acting is (by "only" thinking, I am making or allowing things to happen). We are ourselves undecidables who, addressed by situations, can only proceed politically by putting our very being, and everything we believe in, in question—even if only, eventually, to maintain our beliefs.

The above "I must decide" or "must choose" is not just any choice, however. It is the last choice, the final sell of the market. We know that the global market functions by constructing product choices and distinctions and the freedom to select among those choices as freedom itself. I choose, therefore I am: free, self-determined. The market appears essential, and the neoliberal consensus the only way, because they construct the individual as that very essence. It is desirable, consequently, not because it seems the only means by which (individual, collective) subjects can attain their liberty. It is so because it proffers subjects a plurality of subject positions, each as transcendental, and gives them the liberty to choose each among all the others, but as free from those others: as *themselves,* they make determinations but cannot be determined.

Obviously, the counter to these particular constructions of market subjects is not to limit choice, not to insist that consumers not buy or "buy in": that they not watch television, go to malls, follow trends, eat out, enjoy their money if they have it, even save money. Today, there is no choice but to buy, to enter the market. Buy or die: that is the choice (but when has it *not* been the choice?).

And this is what undecidability reveals: that choice is no choice but a mandate. One cannot choose not to choose. Choice is not free; it is not freedom but obligation. We are not at liberty to choose; we *must.* Choice is impelled, meaning both that no choice is a choice (it is predictated—by the unconscious, Freud would say) and that choice is no choice.

As our obligation to the market, the "must choose" also stamps the limit of this market, which pushes freedom as choice, and constructs the consensus that it is essential through an invitation to that liberty. If market choice proves not to be a choice, however, then the market (which says, "Choice is freedom") cannot deliver what it promises.

Undecidability thus represents a potential "leftist" or "post-Marxist" intervention into the global market. It does so, not only because it helps deconstruct "normalized," established grounds for truth, but also because anytime the "must choose" of choice is exposed—and undecidability is one vehicle for that exposure—so, too, is the limit, hence the death/nonnecessity of consensual post-democracy and the sheer potential for political alternatives.

It is almost natural to assume that, for Laclau and Mouffe, politics is "radical" when open, when the imposed (through power) ground of the social is deconstructed and the possibilities for political organization are allowed to expand without limit. Conversely, politics is "conservative" when those grounds are installed. To be sure, for Laclau and Mouffe, in relation to the state, politics hinges on an openness to the constitutive outside. Yet in relation to the *market,* politics—at least leftist politics—often hinges on closure and limits: on the "must choose" that delimits the "free" of free choice. Perhaps this is another reason why Laclau and Mouffe's political model (as they themselves insist) is as likely to fall to the Right as to the Left. What is "Left" vis-à-vis the state form risks emerging as "Right" (absolute openness: openness without law or limits) vis-à-vis the market-form-lessness.

Both leftist politics and "toleration," then, are not a question of opening to more, to greater multiplicity, to more choices and displacements, to less fixity. If we need nodal points, it is because the market is already too open. And it would like to be more open, almost absolutely deregulated, perennially displaced, contingent, discardable, and upgradable. The question today is closure (the closure of the West, the closure of metaphysics, the closure of capital), drawing hard lines in the wake of hard rules. Where do I close off the obscenity, the openness of the market? How do I combat one nihilism (lawlessness, pure openness, absolute obscenity) without falling to the other (rigid law, total closure, complete prudishness)? Laclau and Mouffe, in fact, emphasize that "neither absolute fixity nor absolute non-fixity is possible."⁷ Or they may have said: absolute fixity, like absolute nonfixity (pure difference or pure relativeness as much as no difference), is absolutism and totalitarianism themselves, and is therefore logically "impossible" (for there is always an excess to the totality).

Here it is worthwhile to review Simon Chritchley's analysis of the Laclau-Derrida link. Chritchley agrees with Laclau "that the question of the passage from undecidability to the decision is political rather than ethical—every decision is political."⁸ Chritchley posits or accepts a distinction between ethics and politics; this, not coincidentally, is the same line he draws between knowledge and action. Nongrounds and undecidability are the conditions of a "good" decision. Careful and ethical deliberation (knowledge) never counts on an a priori or *proper* ground in making its determinations. Politics, however, must betray these ethical considerations. It acts in ways that may or may not end up "good" since "the instant of political decision is madness,"⁹ without foundation. Genuine political *action* (decision) responds to ethical *thought* (revelation of the undecidable), even if the action turns out bad.

But to reiterate, in the Laclau-Mouffe model, these separations do not hold (even if Laclau and Mouffe themselves may want them to hold). If decisions and actions are political, then ethics—and thought—is always already also political since, as just indicated, a determination is the condition of indeterminacy (and vice versa, of course). Indeterminacy is nothing but the determination to hesitate "for now," an act that benefits or hurts those involved in that "now." There is no "hesitation" (Chritchley: "*Deconstruction is a 'philosophy' of hesitation*")¹⁰ between ethics and political action (insofar as one draws this distinction in the first place), thought and praxis, because the hesitation, indecision, is itself action.

Yet there is one more matter that must be addressed if we are to arrive at a fuller understanding of the Laclau-Mouffe undertaking in the context of the market: the matter of time. Distinguishing *moments* from *elements,* Laclau and Mouffe observe that moments always form parts of an endless totality, whereas elements interrupt this totality, divide it into temporal or contingent units. A practice of articulation, they explain, "involves working on *elements,* while here we would be confronted only with *moments* of a closed and fully constituted totality where every moment is subsumed from the beginning under the principle of repetition. As we shall see, if contingency and articulation are possible, this is because no discursive formation is a sutured totality and the transformation of the elements into moments is never complete."[11]

I have suggested that only an interruption of consensual post-democracy, which forces the market to stop in its tracks and address the disruption, can disclose the "when," hence the temporality and contingency of the market. And only through that disclosure—of the market's finitude, mortality, or nonnecessity—is anything like an intercession (into the market) possible. For Laclau and Mouffe, such interference is the "element" that has not yet become a signified or part of the symbolic order, "subsumed from the beginning under the principle of repetition."

The question is: *When* does this "element" emerge, when does it disrupt? Or is the difference between "moment" and "element" precisely that the "element" is never a "moment," never temporal but ideal? Perhaps it is a force of negativity?

The difficulty of the query, within the Laclau-Mouffe discourse, rests in a debate touched on previously. An "element," "surplus," or "constitutive outside" cannot *not* already be marked by a signifier. "Elements" are themselves, by logic, a result of "the principle of repetition": of convention. All signifiers, "names" and "in the names of," but also every "between names," are therefore already *signifieds* taken from an established system, already part and parcel of the neoliberal consensus or totality. This is true even of neologisms (such as Derrida's *différance*), which reuse, hence repeat (in the case of *différance*, "differ" and "defer" are repeated), ritualize, and conventionalize the signs, the common sense into which they intrude, and to which they cannot *not* belong. There is never an instant when the signifier is without meaning or a signified, hence utterly wild, never an instant of total disturbance to the consensus. There is no duration when the signifier is a "coming-to-be" rather than a being, a "making-sense" rather than a sense, a *poiēsis* rather than an established concept. During no interim does a political operation displace without also conventionalizing and standardizing the status quo. The "moment" that subsumes finitude into a universal without ends or extras is the same "element" that inscribes this finitude, as the marker of the changeability and "correctability" of the political body, within the universal as a proper part.

Nonconventional intervention coincides with ritualization and normalization. We are now accustomed to the idea that "originality" is a repetition of other moments/beings, a "mere" copy (which we have forgotten is a copy), a contingency rather than the ground or necessity it frequently claims. Ironically, however, those same repetitions or "cultural performances" are what turned (and continue to turn) the contingencies into necessities, constructions into essences in the first place. As *performance*, iteration dislodges at the origin the hegemony it helps cement; but as *ritual* this same iteration naturalizes what it dislodges—also at the origin. The one act (performance) cannot exist without the other (ritual), meaning that there is no time when there is *just* displacement. Hegemony blocks political gestures at the instant of their emergence; and political gestures dislocate hegemony, take their place in and through the very hegemonic block that pushes them aside.

The termination of one institution and the opening to the other is so difficult to effect because, as Alberto Moreiras has pointed out, the death of one world and the birth of another require another step, namely, mourning. And as Laclau and Mouffe intimate, the signs or marks that would perform that closure, the *point de capiton*, cannot help but revive and stabilize the very "thing" they are trying to bury.[12] Closure hinges on bereavement. Yet one cannot mourn without repeating, thus endlessly restituting the body (of the state) to be entombed.

Laclau and Mouffe, one might then say, establish that the hegemonic state, which strives to fix social flows and control political intervention, always leaves a constitutive outside: the marker of its contingency and death and the site of potential for radical democracy. Yet Laclau and Mouffe's text also represents an important meditation on the global. Indeed, it presents the thesis that no constitutive outside of the state form—because every such "outside" counts, by logical necessity, on an articulation—does not emerge *also* as an alternative signifier, an alternative choice, hence as a potential reproducer of the neoliberal consensus (the market) that sustains itself by constructing series and selections within series (one such series being the state and the market). And the *option* between this duopoly, between these two, because it is the vehicle of the subject, sustains both: state and market. The market mourns the end of the state that it simultaneously resurrects. The leftist activism that shifts the arrangement of the state (one set, one count) cannot avoid sustaining the arrangement of the market (another set, another count). This is why Left and Right, revolt and conservation, displacement and stabilization, are today inextricable.

I have emphasized in this chapter that undecidability between political action of the Left and of the Right indexes the possible limit on choice itself, thereby the contingency not of the state but of the market. The "leftism" of Laclau and Mouffe, insofar as their work represents a meditation on the global, lies here. Yet because this limit is always already indexed by a signifier, *is* a signifier, it adds to the field of choices, continues the very market development that it interrupts. How do we know that the limit of consumption and choice—death itself or finitude as such—is not another product to consume, another choice to select?

There is no completion of the state/market without the signifier, the closure, that exposes this system as open to an infinite "otherwise" (one "headed" by democracy). Yet that very signifier, as another choice, may itself represent this same "completion" as participant in a "bad infinity." Openness to the other is the mark of a liberated and liberating institution—unless that institution's name is "the open market."

8.

Negri and Marx on Language and Activism
Has Deconstruction Anything to Say Now to Marxism?

My purpose in this chapter, mainly through a reading of Antonio Negri's *Marx beyond Marx* and Marx's *Grundrisse*, is to respond to a question that, although similar to the one to which I have been replying throughout this study, has not yet been explicitly posed: Why should language as cast by the Heideggerian and deconstuctionist tradition—language as irreducible to communication and representation, hence subjectivity, utility, and all "cultural constructionisms"—matter to Marxism?

Let us begin with a statement put forth in 1997 in a local newspaper by one Frank Pennella, a spokesperson for Telespectrum, a marketing firm located near the State University of New York in Binghamton. Telespectrum announced that it would open 550 jobs. In the depressed area of Binghamton, this was good news for many. Pennella described Telespectrum's ideal worker: "We are looking for people who are articulate—who are assertive to a point, but not pushy. And work ethic is very important. We also like people who have a professional bearing, and—this may sound silly—a neutral accent."[1]

Speaking well, one might assume from this citation, is part of the foundation of the ideal Telespectrum worker. This is not unreasonable; good marketing skills demand a certain articulateness. But, on closer examination, we see that the issue at hand for Pennella is not actually this "speaking well." In fact, many effective speakers—including the current conservative President George W. Bush, the middle-ground former President Clinton, and the liberal/radical Reverend Jesse Jackson—possess rather nonneutral accents. Indeed, in the strict sense, nobody speaks with a "neutral accent"; an accent is by definition not neutral. A particular inflection may be characterized as ideal, mainstream, or perfect (we may even hold that someone possesses "no accent"). But these are hardly the same as "neutral."

The undesirable accent, it is important to emphasize, is not an allusion either to a "foreign" language/individual or an immigrant. Nor can one say that the demand for a "neutral accent" necessarily points up Telespectrum's covert effort to exclude certain minority groups. Someone from southern Texas or northern Minnesota, someone straight from the country—any of these could have as "nonneutral" an accent as an immigrant or minority person. In fact, anybody could: "neutral accent," if we recall Pennella's statement, is related not only to a way of pronouncing words but also to too much and too little assertiveness. Directly opposed to both pushiness and nonaggressivity—these are deemed as undesirable qualities, whereas "neutral accent" is presented as a desirable one—Pennella's "neutral accent" is also about neutrality as such. For Pennella, anyone who speaks too loud or soft, pushes too hard or too easy, asserts him- or herself beyond a certain point or not enough—such a person is nonneutral, and would therefore not properly "fit into" the Telespectrum mix.

The nonneutral accent, in fact, is nothing less than the sign of language itself: the linguisticality of language. The accent is language displaying itself as language. This, indeed, is what a nonneutral accent does. Like a trope or "literariness," it exposes the "nonnaturalness" of language. It reveals that a person is speaking and not simply using language easily, naturally, mindlessly, articulately. When one encounters or uses a "nonneutral accent," language is not functioning as an epiphenomenal vehicle that immediately accomplishes acts, obtains and refuses goods, spreads information, communicates messages, and dissipates into the "things that matter." Language itself surfaces as matter and as *the* matter. No longer merely an articulation within a given habitus or field of representation, the nonneutral accent is language emerging as itself, as language.

Of course, "neutral accent" seems to be only a metaphor. Literally, Telespectrum desires workers who speak transparently. The ideal language is one that "displays" or represents objects (products) without itself appearing. The marketer who sells without too much accent, force, rhetoric, or persuasion, without allowing language to interfere, but through the product itself, is the most productive. Thus the proper language for the late capitalist market is one that vanishes into the commodity, thus making it seem as if the goods were speaking for themselves, as if their value were intrinsic and natural, not fabricated or imposed. A nonneutral accent, on the contrary, adds an unwanted, unprofitable, and nonexchangeable extra to the Telespectrum sales pitch and goods—language itself— and is therefore intrusive, inarticulate, improper.

Indeed, every Telespectrum moment spent trying to translate the nonneutral accent of new employees into direct communication is time and money squandered. Take a new female salesperson. Let us say, on a given day, she needs some advice or instruction from her supervisor in order to continue producing. The interim between this salesperson's speech, the superior's understanding, and the return instruction/advice is potentially unproductive time. If she has an accent, or if her language skills are such that she needs time in order to process the boss's return address; or if, during a potential sale, the consumer does not grasp perfectly and immediately her words due to her accent—in such cases, production and the rate of profit are slowed in direct proportion to the time it takes to make the various translations. The market wants command and obedience, and therefore labor, to go without saying, so that one need not waste production time—through misstating and miscomprehending—on the giving and receiving of orders.

According to Pennella, then, it is not enough that there be a common speech and common understanding patterns among Telespectrum employees, that they comprehend and use the same signifiers and signifieds. Communication, hence the line of production, can be disturbed if there is not also a common *accent*. Authority, consensus, and capital hinge on the reduction of language, not to obvious signifiers with obvious signifieds or "easy meaning," but to signifiers and signifieds, alone, so that those components of language (nonneutral accents or tropes) which expose "language as such" disappear into the binary between these two.

The threat to pure productivity is thus rooted—according to spokesperson Pennella—not in racism, classism, sexism, "laborism," or any other sort of bias but in language as such, which must therefore be eradicated. To be sure, this loathing of language lends itself, for reasons I will clarify below, to ethnic bias; but ethnic bias itself does not ground the loathing. Language does. The company lets language into the workplace; but only in order not to hear or see it.

Telespectrum's hiring policies may potentially violate everyone. But they are not necessarily discriminatory. Hate of language is not hate language. People who speak with an accent, a tone, who speak up or down—the law, including the law of free speech, does not protect them. Anybody who is excluded from Telespectrum before even applying—which, technically, could be anyone—is a victim of unfortunate circumstances, of the free market, but not necessarily of illegal or even unfair activity.

Pennella's claims, in fact, permit us to comment on our two nihilisms, first presented in the introduction and touched on in chapter 7: the nihilism of absolutism, of hard grounds, of the state form; and the nihilism of no grounds, of groundlessness, of the market form. Discrimination falls to the first side, the nihilism of the state, where harsh but arbitrary divisions are established. The decision as to who does or does not fit into the categories (who is or is not a "minority") is equally strong, equally arbitrary. And yet this arbitrariness, through repetition, is ritualized into naturalized, legalized, and normalized foundations that justify the nonetheless arbitrary determinations of whom to include and whom to exclude.

In the second nihilism, that of the market form, there are no bases for exclusion, no hard laws. To bar on grounds such as race or sex is not simply illegal. For firms such as Telespectrum, it is bad for business, stocks, and profits: bad publicity and bad public relations. Thus the market sets up "soft," porous (a "net" not a "wall"), or even absurd grounds for inclusion and exclusion, such as "neutral accent." On such grounds, nobody is quite qualified for employment or acceptance (nobody's accent is neutral), and therefore anybody could be. There is no law. Entry is free and open: as open as the market. Anybody with the right stance, the right tone, the right look, the right push, the right contacts, the right clothes, the right signifiers, the right (ethnic, economic) background, the right discourse on the right day, in the right place, at the right time—regardless of race, religion, sexual orientation, disability, age, or gender—is in. It is a question of the "just right" power. Anybody with the wrong look, the wrong words, the wrong speech pattern, who is too pushy or not pushy enough, may be out.

Today, we see once more, exclusion is still happening as terribly as ever. The excluded, however, are not only those of a certain race, gender, class, sexual orientation (and so on). Excluded as well are people who *embody language*, regardless of race, gender, class.

Now, it is worth repeating that, if the embodiment of language is indeed the abject, no group, identity, or collective subject stands for the "thing" being excluded. Given that everybody speaks, nobody specifically exemplifies language. When language is banished, nobody is the offended part or party. And this fact, for a neoliberal consensus, is useful: if few can be rightfully excluded from the "free market," but if the market must (by logic) exclude, then the expulsion of a "Common" whose disappearance offends no one in particular—of language, or of the embodiments of the "nonneutral accents" that index language—is most expedient.

To explore the above matters further, let us turn to Negri's refutation of two "classical" readings of Marx, put forth in *Marx beyond Marx*.[2] Through his exegesis of the *Grundrisse*, Negri first rebuts the deterministic approach to Marxism: the idea that capitalism will tumble down on its own accord, due to its structural, logical, and ontological faults or contradictions. Although, for Negri, those contradictions do indeed exist, in themselves, they will not compel capital to transform itself and ultimately to fall. Only the force of organization can expose the contradictions, convert them into sites of or for political intrusions and renovations.

In this regard, Negri's most important topos is living or necessary labor. Such labor, for Negri, is not the portion of toil that comes back to workers in the form of the objects that meet their physical needs, satisfy their desires, or give them pleasure. It is not then an economic matter, bound essentially to the components of labor that workers receive as returns, such as salary, working conditions, living circumstances, free time, and so on. Instead, living labor names the labor organization and activism that, from the standpoint of commodification, are "unproductive": the unworking of work, an interruption that is "useless" for the capitalist but "useful" for labor politics. And since, for Negri, the logical condition of a workplace and of work—production, exploitation, commodification—is organization (or at least organizational potential), the prospect of living labor's insurgence, or capital's disruption, is proper to capital itself. Stated in other terms, living labor or labor organization *performs* the internal limit of capital, its contradictions and mortality/transience, and thus (all limits, borders, and frontiers being in fact openings) opens onto a politics that, irreducible to that of the free market, can prove most of use, of *use value* for the workers.

However, this does not mean that, for Negri, capitalism's ruin results from the agency or subjectivity of the worker. Communal or individual subjectivity is in fact a product of capital (in the conclusion to this study, we will see how Althusser develops this point), hence cannot serve as the source that either disrupts or produces it. If capital is not destined to crumble, neither will it disintegrate through the agency of the workers as subjects rising up against its oppression. For Negri, only a very distinct, desubjectivized brand of organizational acts or "living labor" will bring about capital's undoing.

Of course, without communication, there is no such organization, no community. Therefore, Negri's theory of leftist activism, which he grounds on the dialectic between living and surplus labor, use value and exchange value, cannot be completed unless he also scrutinizes the relation of two *exchanges*, which I will call "exchange value" and "language exchange."

Without that investigation, Negri's work would miss key aspects of both the *Grundrisse* and Marx as a whole. Marx, in fact, suggests that language and linguistic exchange—what he calls "material intercourse" and "the language of real life"—are as primary to social experience, actual existence, as class difference itself: "The production of ideas, of conceptions, of consciousness, is *at first* directly interwoven with the material activity and the *material intercourse* of men, *the language of real life*. . . . Men are the producers of their conceptions, ideas, etc.—real, active men, as they are conditioned by a definite development of their productive forces and of the intercourse corresponding to these. . . ."[3]

To be sure, Negri on occasion seems to deny this point, casting language as a kind of antimaterialist "abstraction" or "transcendental domain," a point that lies at the root of his critique of Derrida's *Specters of Marx* (a text Negri, to an extent, admires).[4] Yet it is equally certain that Negri's ideas on activism raise the very question of language they seem—or may even want—to overlook, the question toward which Marx's just-cited comments gesture: If language pertains to material existence ("material intercourse"), what is its exact role in the labor and social organization that Negri advocates?

Like Marx, Negri views labor as the base of all modern political and social constructions. Labor is the materiality that either interrupts or is kept at bay by capitalist social forces, but which is the foundation of capital, and of the social, in either case. Yet, actually, labor cannot ground the social for it cannot ground itself. Indeed, no labor is possible without an exchange of signs between laborers, or between workers and superiors. Either a "boss" or "owner" commands workers or producers (or vice versa); or else workers band together in order to decide what to do, how to do it, who will do what, when, and where. Unless one holds that certain labor or action is instinctive, thus natural to humans (who will just "do it" without any learning, direction, directives, or habitus), no labor prior to the linguistic exchange between laborers, or between capitalist and producers—work before language—is even imaginable (not even in a utopian or precapitalist society).

In *Politics and the Other Scene,* Etienne Balibar discusses Marx's famous statement in *The Eighteenth Brumaire of Louis Bonaparte*: men make their own history, but not under conditions of their own choosing. They do so instead "in conditions always already given and inherited from the past."[5] Balibar indicates that the economic structure, grounded in labor, is one of these conditions: circumstances that determine without predetermining history, determine without predetermining the political. If this is the case, then we must view language also as one of these conditions. "Always already given and inherited from the past," language in fact is a *condition* of the *fundamental condition* (labor and social relations) of "making history" according to Marx.

Marx implicitly raises the point whenever he opposes, as he does in *Capital*, the notion of "simple average labor."[6] The commodity, in fact, insidiously reduces actual labor, which must have itself "attained a certain level of development before it can be expended in this or that form,"[7] to this "simple average labor." Specific toil loses its specificity in the commodity that ultimately represents it. In fact, there is no general "labor" with a uniform value, only concrete efforts: work with a history, tools, forms of training, types of employees, and specific discourses and verbal interaction (by means of which tradition and memory, both key to specific toil and even to invention, are created and maintained). And as such, "real existing labor," actual work, surfaces not "by nature" but through social and historical exchanges, including language.

My intention is not to suggest that language preexists labor (living or dead): that language is the base of work. Nor am I arguing that labor is a "cultural" construction. Rather, I am asserting that the circulation of signs is no more or less essential to work than are tools, food, or the boss-employee relation (class difference). Absent language, no *real* work can occur, and no *real* organization can *organize*.

At this point, it is helpful to address Marx's meditations on circulation and circulation time in the *Grundrisse*. It is certainly true that Marx often discusses circulation only in order to contest the "circulation artists"[8] who argue that value can actually emerge from such circulation. For Marx, circulation, though a factor within capital and production, cannot generate value, which results exclusively from labor and its exploitation; it thus belongs to a "secondary realization process" of capitalism, not to the primary or essential one: "The circulation of capitalism, *realizes value*, while living labor *creates value*."[9]

Yet, if circulation only "realizes value," one of its components, *circulation time*, seems to do the opposite, "unrealize" value. It thus plays a rather subversive role:

> While labor time appears as a value-positing activity, this circulation time of capital appears as the *time of devaluation*. The difference shows itself simply in this: if the totality of labor time commanded by capital is set at its maximum, say infinity, so that necessary labor time forms an infinitely small part and surplus labour an infinitely large part of this infinity, then this would be the maximum realization of capital, and this is the tendency towards which it strives. On the other side, if the *circulation time of capital* were = o, if the various stages of its transformation proceeded as rapidly in reality as in the mind, then that would likewise be the maximum of the factor by which the production process could be repeated, i.e. the number of capital realization processes in a given period of time. The repetition of the production process would be restricted only by the amount of time which it lasts, the amount of time which elapses during the transformation of raw material into product. *Circulation time* is therefore not a value-creating element; if it were = to o, then value-creation would be at its maximum. But if either surplus labour time or necessary labour time = o, i.e. if necessary labour time absorbed all time, or if production could proceed altogether *without* labour, then neither value, nor capital, nor value-creation would exist. *Circulation time* therefore determines value only in so far as a *natural barrier* to the realization of labour time. It is therefore in fact a deduction from *surplus labour time*, i.e. an increase in *necessary labor time*.[10]

Labor creates value; circulation realizes value. Circulation *time*, quite distinctly, curtails value. Marx complements this last point: "Circulation time in itself is a *barrier* to realization (*necessary labour time* is of course also a barrier; but at the same time an element, since value and capital would vanish without it); [it is a] deduction from surplus labour or an increase in necessary labour time in relation to surplus labour time. The circulation of capital realizes value, while living labour creates value. Circulation time is only a barrier to this realization of value, and, to that extent, to value creation. . . ."[11]

We see here that, if labor (whether living or surplus) were eliminated—if the workers were completely replaced by machines, for example—capitalism would cease to exist, for better or worse. The workers and work are *essential* to capital's subsistence. The same cannot be said of circulation. If circulation time, "the amount of time which elapses during the transformation of raw material into product," or the velocity with which "the production process could be repeated, i.e. the number of capital realization processes in a given period of time," were reduced to zero (if "transformation proceeded as rapidly in reality as in the mind"), capitalism would operate at maximum capacity. Capitalism need not retain circulation time to survive or thrive. Unlike labor time, circulation time is a secondary or nonessential topos: it is not necessary.

Now, it may *seem* that capitalism's goal is the complete liquidation of living labor: "If the totality of labour time commanded by capital is set at its maximum, say infinity, so that necessary labor time forms an infinitely small part and surplus labour an infinitely large part of this infinity, then this would be the maximum realization of capital, and this is the tendency towards which it strives." Yet, as Marx goes on to show, this tendency is just that: the *tendency* of capital—not its goal. Capitalism must always maintain *some* necessary labor as a barrier and limit to capital: the limit that allows for capital's perpetual crossing over, its development and expansion, but never for its *absolutely infinite* expansion since, to be traversed, the impediment must always be preserved. Labor (both surplus and necessary) is thus at once the *essence* and the *limit* of capital. It is necessary both for capitalism's perseverance and for its end. Living labor (which Negri alternatively recasts as activism, organization, disruption, or Communism) often functions as one such frontier, exposing capitalism to distinct sociopolitical possibilities.

This, again, is not quite true of circulation time, which stands as a barrier that could be reduced to zero, erased. And this erasure would maximize capital. The best outcome for the capitalist, in short, is the eradication of circulation rather than labor time: of the one blockage or limit that, when eliminated, does not push capitalism to its termination, but spreads it beyond all bounds.

Stated in different terms, necessary or living labor and circulation are significantly different from the standpoint of *value creation*. Yet from the standpoint of Negri's main thesis, to wit, that the increase in living labor—therefore the relative decrease in surplus labor time— *is* the upsurge in political activism and organization; the two topoi play nearly the same role. Indeed, Marx himself argues that an increase in circulation time is an increase in *necessary labor:* "Circulation time therefore determines value only in so far as a natural barrier to the realization of labour time. It is therefore in fact a deduction from *surplus labour time*, i.e. an increase in *necessary labor time.*"

To explore more deeply the connection between Negri's living labor and Marx's circulation time, and between circulation time in the *Grundrisse* and the problem of language, let us turn now to the Hegelian master/slave dialectic as presented in the famous "lord/bondsman" section of the *Phenomenology of Spirit*.[12] Then, to bring the deconstruction/Marxism bond back into the picture, we will examine Paul de Man's recasting of this dialectic.

Hegel's sovereign, we know, is master only when recognized as such by the slave, whether through the slave's production, sweat, escape attempt, transgression, cry, scream, laugh, submission, or love. To be master, the master must make the slave do, say, feel, understand, or know something. These acts serve as recognition of the master's law. And yet the recognition, the production, cannot *not* serve as the mark of the slave's force: of the fact that the slave has not yet been completely mastered. If the master or subject is to be the total master or subject, the slave must be a total slave, a completely "forceless" object, absolutely subservient. But if totally subservient (dead, reduced to an object), this slave cannot offer the acknowledgment that represents the performance of this acquiescence, hence is not a slave at all.

Because the power of the master hinges on the other's capacity for recognition, the master's power is actually a relation of forces. Relative not absolute, bounded not infinite, Power's condition of possibility is the marginal or alternative pulsions it must control but not erase in order to be.

The force of labor, one therefore sees, *always* comes about through a sign. The worker builds "raw material" into a commodity as asked. But this work only emerges as *recognition* of the boss, as *work*, hence as the potential of the worker, if the boss *reads* the process in this manner. A worker *actually* responds to a boss's insistence only if that response—say, production—is *recognized* or *interpreted* as responsive (and, of course, the refusal to respond can be deemed a response). Conversely, the recognition of the worker's production by the boss (through payment of a certain wage, say) must be read as genuine or sufficient recognition by the worker (through acceptance of that wage). Both "master" and "slave" are slaves to reading as the force of the other, which neither subject (neither boss nor worker) can govern: not only to signs and to production *as* a sign, but to the circulation or exchange of signs.

Here we should add that the commonplace assertion that workers are often "treated like animals," as being capable of acting on command but incapable of thought (of reading or exchanging signs), betrays a misunderstanding of the very logic of capitalism. Capital, in fact, demands workers who are able to adapt to new modes of production, on the one hand; and to work without total supervision and command (less wages are thus dedicated to supervision), on the other. For the capitalist, in other words, workers must be *un*like animals. They must not only be able to "take orders." They must also be capable of processing information on "their own," and of reading, adopting, and adapting that information to circumstances ("at the job site") that the boss or supervisor cannot always anticipate.

Which is to say, workers must not only be trainable but *retrainable*: they must possess the potential to modify their "skills," with relative ease, as modes of production change. If workers could not give and respond reasonably and even autonomously to *many* signs, then the rate of profit, and eventually capital itself, would sink. Capitalism requires not animals, but workers with a "certain degree" of self-determination, reason, and linguistic ability. Indeed, let us not forget that, for Marx, the commencement of capitalism, "primitive" or "originary accumulation," is the *freedom* of workers, "liberated" from the land upon which they were forced to toil when serfs. Having been "liberated," these workers are then "free" to sell their own bodies. However devastating this "freedom" may be, it is also why workers always contain within themselves the potential for subversion.

In brief, no matter how events turn out, the slave is never yet a slave/object, and the master never yet a master/subject, since both parties rely on a force/sign of recognition that lies beyond both command and production. This is why Hegel's dialectic is indeed a dialectic, not a mere play of oppositions. If the master could completely objectify the slave (and still remain master), then slavery—including any memory or trace of this phenomenon—would come to an end. But this completion could only take place at the end of history, when Absolute Spirit realizes itself (for better or worse). History, on the other hand, is the battle toward this termination, a fight to the death between two related (thus relative, vulnerable) drives. The command of the master, which tries to induce a sign from the slave while at the same time eliminating the slave's capacity to give signs at all (only such a slave would be an object), is one force. The other force is the slave, who must, at one and the same time, not give a sign to the master (for, in doing so, the slave acknowledges being a slave: the sign is the sign of obedience) and yet also give a sign (that the slave is *not* an object, *not* a slave).

Indeed, even if the master/subject kills the slave, no solution emerges. A corpse acknowledges no master. To be a master through murder, the master would need to force the dead into speech. Such a master would have to be a master of death, able to master the dead body so as to impel it to give signs. And that is what the master cannot do. The slave's death exposes the master to the limit of the master's own mastery, powers, and sovereignty, hence to the master's own death. And such an experience of death, if terrible, does not signify the end of the master but the seeming interminability of the entire master/slave dialectic. Faced with the master's brutality, the slave encounters the menace of death: as the Universal or Absolute Master. To ease the threat, the slave grows servile, works, and produces, all of which appeases as it recognizes the master. Yet the recognition still bears the mark of the universal force, of the death that pushed the slave into servility in the first place. And in beholding this mark of the *true* Absolute in the slave's production, masters experience their own nonabsoluteness or mortality. The dialectic then recommences, albeit in reverse.

Language and the circulation of signs, we can therefore say, are the conditions not only of labor but also of the labor *organizations* for which Negri calls. These hinge on the *force* of the worker, on language as worker pulsion that, as an "add on" (to the capitalist's vigor), exposes precisely the plurality of energies advocated by Negri: "On this level, capitalist relations [i.e., class differences] are reduced to a relation of force . . . above all because the working-side of the relation has subjectified itself and rises up as an antagonistic force."[13]

This antagonistic or extra force, however, is not just "there," suppressed yet a priori, waiting to be tapped. Instead, it hinges on the master's mortality and finitude—if the master were the All of power, there could be no *other* force or labor force—which are, in part, *produced*, as we have just seen, by the communication (of the worker) that the master cannot master. Being mortal, the boss is "surmountable"; being finite, the boss is subject to external forces, such as those of labor. And these conditions—the mortality of the master, the dynamism of labor—are the conditions of rebellion as Negri understands it. Indeed, they are the conditions of revolution, of the workers as a potential source of *terror*. Only if the boss has confronted mortality, limit (language), and thus vulnerability can the menace of revolution/terror dictate the boss's decisions concerning labor. Only then can living labor "push" capital.

At stake in this discussion, I want to stress, is not only the relation of language, labor, and *speech* but also of language, labor, and *reading* (reception). This important point, made before in passing, merits elaboration. If labor is to make a Negri-like intervention through communication, then the most effective intercession will require *reading*. How can I, as one of the representatives of a worker organization, communicate in such a way that I speak to and for the *other* worker's concerns (the other worker who is never just a worker but always also more than the worker, a worker plus: a woman worker, a mother worker, a gay worker, an illegal worker, a Black worker, and so on)? To do so, obviously, I must understand, hence first analyze the desires of these other workers.

Conversely, why should I, as worker, trust the labor or union organizer? I must, to do so, interpret the organizer's words and intentions, as well as the interpretations of other workers.

The notion of "text," seemingly an aesthetic or literary idea more linked, recently, to "literary deconstruction" than any "materialism," now comes into play. We have just seen that the mastery of a subject depends on recognition, or on the force of the other, which blocks this mastery. The same holds for a text, the "other" of the reader. Indeed, in line with the master/slave analytic, a reading subject can master such a text only if the work somehow recognizes this reader. An interpretation is absolutely true if and when it is authorized by the work itself. Otherwise, the reading is either an "uncontrolled" subjective imposition, unauthorized (as when a leader "imposes" meaning and intention, without listening to, the statements of the leader's constituents); or it is an expression of the reader's simple acceptance of previous interpretations, hence not a reading at all (as when this same leader "hears" in the declarations of an authority only the dogma or tradition to which the leader already adheres—"hears" a meaning that emerged prior to the declarations themselves, exterior to the reading process).

And yet this is precisely what a text, as a "withdrawing" of marks or remarks, cannot do: it cannot "give a nod" to the reader. The text is passivity, withdrawal as a force that threatens, by refusing to be "subjectified," the reader's demand and will.[14] Consequently, never gaining the acknowledgment that would prove the rightness, a reading or reader is never "just right."

I draw these last thoughts from de Man, who argues that the interpreter, always involved in a struggle for mastery and truth, is also always confronted with the trope of prosopopeia: the giving of a face, a voice, to the dead.[15] Seeking recognition from an "object" (the text) in the name of a "true reading," the interpreter/reader grants "voice" to this "dead" text which will not respond, displacing or "imaging" onto the still, inhuman work a human voice, which functions as an authority. That voice may be the author, another critic, a school of thought, the teacher, the narrator, a fellow student, the implied reader/author, a political collective, common sense, tradition, or what Lacan calls the "subject-supposed-to-know." All or any of these are "heard" by the reader in the soundless composition; and such a voice serves as recognition of the reader's analysis. Authority emerges because the reader humanizes the text, re-creating the reader's struggle with the work as an inter-subjective one between two subjects that the reader—because the other with whom the reader struggles is only human—can win, and thereby stand as *the* authority.

The dead letter has been brought to life, given voice. Through a fantasy, the limit of human mastery (death) has been "compelled" into emerging as a force of recognition: as another subject. As the work is humanized, the reader emerges via the imaginary as more potent than death, than the Absolute Master, now recast as merely another subject, as a foil, as a slave. As commander of death, the reader now becomes that authority, thereby the beholder of truth.

But, of course, this process only reproduces, for the subject, pre-cisely the limit or the bond-to-the-other that the subject appears to overcome. As "voiced" (even if the voice is imaginary) or as an alternative pulsion, the text reveals to the subject that the subject is not the only force. The reader/subject is instead *like* the other in terms of power: both have "voice," strength. The two fields are *relatively* equal in intensity, meaning that the subject, and the reading that represents him, are relational and vulnerable rather than authorial.

Thus, for de Man, prosopopeia is, on the one hand, the rhetori-cal device by which the reading subjects disavow their limit (dis-avow the Master, death, by giving voice to and controlling the dead letter), thereby affirming themselves as Absolute Subjects. And it is, on the other hand, the figure, the analogon that recalls and desig-nates—as do all tropes—the "like," the relationality and linguisti-cality, the textuality that brought out the mortality or "slavishness" of the Master in the first place: the limit or communication that binds self to other, master to slave.

Within the organizational activities of labor, which Negri addresses, this structure of textuality is in operation at all times. This may not seem to be the case since labor's reading of the "others," of other workers, most often (even if not often enough) counts on the *presence* of those people. Unlike a text, other workers are capable of "voicing" their views, of dialoguing with other subjects so that some kind of intersubjective joint accord can be reached. Yet nothing of the "worker voice" can authorize its interpretation. If those who initiate, announce, write, or lead the actual labor action must first get a "feel" for the collective resolve, no part of this collective's recommendations, however much "back and forth" takes place, will recognize the "rightness" of the way the suggestions are received, deployed, and conveyed. Every such recognition is, in fact, another text that must be analyzed. If labor's relation to itself as a community hinges on communication, thereby circulation—and I see no way it cannot—then it also hinges on textuality as the exposure of the labor community to its limit. The limit concerns the "rightness" of the organizational activity itself, which is never therefore "just right." It is always caught up in a reorganization exigency, in an effort to correct, not only capitalist exploitation, but also itself as exploitative.

Communication is the third party that is the condition of every social relation or political/labor organization for which Negri calls. Yet it does not completely fall—as death does not fall—within the mastery of any human, or of all "humans put together," of any humanism, intersubjectivity, or common sense. According to Marx, language as circulation time is not essential to capitalism. But, according to Negri, it is essential to labor, especially *living labor.*

This extra party de Man calls "the autonomous potential of language."[16] He does not believe that language forms a separate sphere.[17] In fact, the pulsion of the limit cannot even be experienced "by itself," without the cultural representations or human forms that are this pulsion's "carriers." Yet this does not change the fact that communication, as soon it is used, puts language or the limit of mastery in play as a material and social fact, as exposure to the other or "slave" (who, because my existence is relative to the other's force and thus contingent, could take my place). As it does, communication takes on the characteristic of an autonomous force, beyond human agency. The "autonomous potential of language" is this materiality. It is not some literary or abstract reference to "poetic," "complex," or "thick" idioms but language as the physical and real condition of community. And it does not matter whether the community is one of worker and worker or one of worker and boss: in the two cases, the limit and contingency of capitalism are disclosed by language, rendering conceivable both the social bonds and the alternative politics (alternative to the free market) that might arise from these bonds. Certainly, language does not *say* what those alternative ways *are*; it does not represent them. Its "saying" consists only in stating that they are possible.

Such possibility, indeed, is key to Negri's living labor, which is not the fundament of some future, postcapitalist, utopian political program. Rather, it is the incessant organization of labor, here and now, which actually perseveres only if the desire for "other ways" does so as well—a perseverance feasible solely if the finitude of current ways is exposed through social practices. Without living labor and circulation time, which set barriers on capital, capital becomes All. Any possible outside, any *wish* for this outside, surfaces as impossible and unrealistic. The desire for labor organization necessarily desists, as does the activity itself.

Only at this time can we return to the thesis raised earlier: capital's possibly infinite expansion *today*, and the tie of this expansion to the above analyses of Marx. It should now be clear, from our deliberations on circulation time as language, that the capitalist or boss, as one empowered subject, yearns for representations that function without the possibility of difference or deviance as they are transferred to the other, to labor, in the form of an order (so as to situate labor within the "order of things"). These temporal and spatial differences which communication as mediation, as nonimmediate, institutes are, in fact, temporal intervals, which stand as the circulation time within the workplace that represents, in Marx's words, a "deduction from *surplus labour time*." Aspiring for a completed common sense, or for circulation that happens instantaneously, the capitalist actually wants to be rid of this verbiage—of the threat of terror that relations to the worker put in play—and thus rid also of the capitalist's own relationality.

If the boss says, "Lay down a marble floor on Buswell Street by six tonight," and the worker understands immediately and absolutely, acts accordingly (in double time), then the gap, the limit between or of master and slave appears to be eliminated. The command of the master does not separate the speaker and the listener but makes the space between-the-two, and thus the time-it-takes-to-communicate, disappear. This is absolute communication, or communication minus language and difference. It reveals the common site or common sense that the two (worker, boss) absolutely share, as if the two intellects were a single intellect, as if the worker were, in truth, the boss: the transcendental boss without workers, or without "the working-side of the relation [that] has subjectified itself and rises up as an antagonistic force."

I, as master, say, "Lay down"; and the worker hears my words perfectly. I am in control of the other, who now points up my capacity to voyage (by means of my voice) beyond my own space, beyond my temporal and spatial boundaries, my sensual body, and hence, my death. When the master, as represented through the signifiers or commands, travels outside (to the other) and "after" (the time between utterance and reception) the master's physical self without ceasing to be that stable self, without deviation—only then can this master become, in the master's imagination, sovereign.

In other words, communication without the "autonomous potential of language" means the immediate commodification of the inhuman: of death and terror. Commodification subsumes its own limit as communication emerges as a form of immediate circulation, thus as a means for capital's total expansion—but again, only if the barrier that is called "circulation time" is in some way appropriated by circulation itself, by absolute circulation.

On the other hand, when communication between boss and worker takes time, when the connection between the voice of the master and the reception of the worker is not perfect, automatic, or natural, the particularity or finitude, the time and space, the not-Allness, the vulnerability, of the boss—and the terror that menaces the boss—are exposed. And this not-Allness is also the condition of labor organization: "the working side of the relation." Insofar as they emerge as pure representation, as clear and transparent, as part of a common sense whose meaning "goes without saying," signifiers, voice, and commands reveal the master's totality. Insofar as such signs do not communicate fully, insofar as they "get between" existence and subjectivity, they disclose the time and space (the mortality) of this master.

To put these last points another way, the worker cannot stand as the "instinct" or "nature" of the body/mind, physical/transcendent splits (divisions that sustain capital). As far as capital is concerned, the worker must also index the potential for an alternative reason, therefore an alternative political structure.[18] "Language as such," to be sure, is not this other reason, although its loss is the obliteration of that potential, of the very possibility of an alternative reasonable position.

But is circulation without circulation time possible? To my knowledge, this is not a question that Marx addressed. Yet it is a crucial one for us, as technological advances seem to be leading to absolute speed, to "instant messages." What is certain is that there is no workplace element that more impedes the reduction of circulation time to zero than the time it takes to converse.

This is why, at the outset of this chapter, I discussed Telespectum's idea of the perfect employee and, by extension, the ideal of the market itself. As we recall, Telespectrum's desire is for a workplace occupied solely by neutral accents. In such an "ideal" locale, verbal circulation among distinct sectors (worker, bosses, clients, other companies) would take place outside both understanding and misunderstanding, occurring instead automatically, with complete technical efficiency: no time is needed to send or process messages. The language, the "like" or "trope" (the lack of pure clarity, of a "neutral accent") between any two subjects, this "thing" that indexes their commonality *and* separation (two conditions of a social relationship), this "material" that both precludes the Other from disappearing into the One and refuses to allow the One and the Other to exist apart (as separate, therefore noncommunal or apolitical "individuals" or "identities")—these are deleted in favor of a pure homogeneity without language or relations, and theoretically, a capitalism without boundaries.

If capitalism is, indeed, a social as well as an economic relationship, then the creation and preservation of an "asocial" language, the invention of more phrases for the bond between worker and worker and between worker and boss, ought to form part of a leftist politics. At the very least, the "sovereignty of language" should not be the enemy of leftism,[19] as if language were reducible to aestheticism, commodification, and exchange value. Fidelity to Marx after Marxism demands a certain dedication to language. This is not only because the increase in circulation time, the amplification of language, and the subsequent relative decrease in surplus labor are fundamental to labor organization and labor needs. It is also because, without language, no such organization, no community at all, is even possible.

We know that, for Marx, and for Nietzsche after him, the reduction of Being to value is foundational to the nihilism of capitalism. Yet the very fact that the state casts the other as valuable (as a means of production), while indeed founding abuse, is also why this other (other workers) cannot be removed from the capitalist system, and consequently retains might.

Marxism itself counts on this same other: the abjected worker is, at the very least, an "aide memoire" for a reading of the social and historical circumstances from which this worker emerges. Capitalism, for Marx, can therefore never appear as necessary or natural since the violence of its history—historicity and contingency themselves—is written on the backs and products of those it exploits. Inscribed on the "text" of the used (thereby useful) body, history never ceases to remind capitalism of its debt to history, of its culpability before this history, the unjust cause and reason behind its rise.

But in consensual postdemocracy, the other is not necessarily a maltreated being, a human who has been dehumanized, a value that has been devalued. Like "language as such" qua circulation time, the other is without value or utility (similar to a nonneutral accent in the workplace), hence cannot *even* be exploited. The other can therefore be liquidated without being sacrificed; after all, one sacrifices only what is sacred, what contains value. Again, without ritual or guilt, hence without memory, debt, or obligation, the figures that embody "language as such," and thus represent nobody, can be wiped out without a trace.[20]

Contemporary capitalism, while obviously still controlling labor and subduing labor movements, has taken up a supplementary mode of profit building: the abolition not of the living labor but of the circulation time that cannot add (but can subtract from) value. The neoliberalist's interest lies not solely in the abjection of the laborer but also in ridding the world of whoever indexes the market's *valueless* barriers: the people who exemplify not the other but the uselessness of language as such (of nonneutral accents), who incarnate not labor but circulation or communication time.

Earlier in this study, I offered examples of figures likely to stamp the language and death that biopolitics works to eradicate. After William Haver, I dubbed them unmarketable "bodies of this death": the destitute or homeless who possess no property to tender (not even bodies for labor), the AIDS victims, the states in possession of nuclear weapons that refuse to trade them in for proper acknowledgment of the world market through an assurance of deterrence. We can now note that such individuals or groups also incarnate the *time/space of circulation*. The AIDS sufferers who are imagined to circulate among too many sexual partners (and to produce or reproduce nothing), the homeless who seem to be "everywhere all the time," the traffickers of weapons whose nuclear, biological, and chemical agents circulate without barriers or containment, the nationless—these figures of language and death are also, for neoliberalism, the markers of a "circulation" that demands political, social, and economic monitoring: time that is not money.

One desire behind the eradication of "language as such" (non-neutral accents) in favor of a circulation without circulation time, a communication without language, is the creation of an other who can be eradicated without guilt, thereby without recall. Here a Sameness or homogeneity materializes without a past, without cause or reason, not due to historical factors. The market completes itself because it does not result from a historical process but is inherent to existence, like nature or common sense. Without language or accents circulating about, it comes before our commentaries on or evaluations of it, prior to any sign, much less narrative.

Within such a scene, consensus is because it is, not due to temporal factors or actors. And when "is is," circulation requires no time. If everything that "is is," either a pure relativism, in which everything can be exchanged for anything else, in which any message is the right or same message, surfaces. Or else a pure absolutism does, one in which there is no "something else." There is only "is," a possibility that again renders (mis)communication, circulation time, indeed, labor time, inconceivable.

Because the state form (and, by extension, the disciplining of workers into proper subjects of the system) remains a power, leftist activism must continue to attend to labor needs. Yet such activism cannot actually be practiced without care for language as such, so fundamental to labor, yet today so fragile, vulnerable, *almost* dispensable. Indeed, the relation of labor and language is *essential* to Marxism since there is no labor without language, no (use) value without the "valuelessness" that language as circulation time spells.

In sum: no deployment of Marxism can today logically remain faithful to its task (the disruption of capital or, for Negri, the organizational activity that discloses capital as a contradiction-in-itself) *and* refuse to address deconstruction's concern for language. And vice versa.

9.

The Culture Wars, Interdisciplinarity, Globalization
Meditations on Cultural and Postcolonial Studies

In this chapter, I will attempt to analyze the politics of the Academy, in particular the Academy's staging of the "culture wars," in terms of a state/market duopoly. Three introductory comments are necessary, however.

First, one might assume that the politics of the university rests in the struggle between the genuine intellectual pursuits of teachers and students, on the one side, and the crass political interests of bureaucracy—administrators or actual politicians—on the other. Whether informed by neutral, right-wing, or left-wing beliefs, the professor/scholar labors on behalf of knowledge, whereas bureaucracy stymies this labor by operating according to the market: in the name of "the economy," the "cultural logic" of capitalism, or of certain constituencies such as donors, the voting public, and parents. Hence, to understand the standing of the contemporary university, we should examine the way in which economic and governmental concerns shape, and mostly stunt, intellectual quests. Such an analysis, of course, would include a study of the advent of student-consumers: students who attend the university in order to "get their money's worth," that is, to be properly professionalized so that they can succeed in "the real world."

Although these "outside" delimitations placed on the university certainly exist, they are not the cause of academic politics. One cannot grasp such a politics by inquiring into the division between the producers of knowledge (faculty and certain students) and the social conditions in which production and consumption take place. Political and market matters configure the university largely because the fiercest politicians and "vendors" are the intellectuals themselves. Any reading of the academic culture wars must proceed from this fact: the culture of consumption that dictates academic scholarship and pedagogy is, above all, generated by the intellectuals as primary consumers.

Second, the culture wars within the Academy do not involve debates between Right- and Left-leaning academic and social blocs. This postulate is an invention of the culture wars themselves, and serves as their justification. Indeed, these culture wars do not represent typical struggles between conservatives and liberals, traditionalists and radicals, ancients and moderns. The hostilities are far more factionalized and far less delineated. Merely within academic discourses typically situated on the Left, at least ten (actually, many more) fierce engagements take place. Thus Marxism's attacks against Derridean thought (and vice versa) are often as intense as its refutations of free market ideals, if not more so. Moreover, such engagements—between, say, classical Marxism and poststructuralism—tell us more about the particularity of the culture wars than do engagements between conservatives and liberals (which, to be sure, also take place). To tackle the culture wars, one does best to explore controversies, not between friends or enemies, but between nonfriends, such as deconstruction and cultural studies.

And third, few intellectuals, if any, would admit that their projects are grounded in such culture wars: that their endeavors possess little legitimacy outside those battles. Yet no assertion is more proper to the culture wars than the one that avows a position outside these conflicts. Today, "rigorous theorists" who declare that their ventures are rooted in questions that lie outside or above—exterior to—the "trendy" culture wars (or other academic trends) undermine their declarations in advance: such "exteriority" is foundational to the wars themselves.

Having made these comments, let me now name some of the discourses—"armies"—within intellectual skirmishes: feminism, queer theory, deconstruction, psychoanalysis, multiculturalism, post-Marxism, cultural studies, and liberal and conservative humanism (often the discourse that speaks for "the canon"). Each of these discourses, whatever its political leaning, contends that some idea of the global or universal is either injurious to human existence—and must therefore be overcome—or the means or part of the means of that overcoming. In other words, each fights (1) to resist the global in the name of the local; (2) to advance globalization as the overcoming of a restrictive state; or (3) to promote measure, balance, and interplay between the local and the global, the particular and the universal.

Let us assume that a number of these discourses, under the auspices of a "leftist politics," have successfully indexed the limit of a certain articulation of the universal (late capitalism, the West, civilization, Eurocentrism, patriarchy, compulsive heterosexuality). Their claim is that the universal (say, capitalism) is merely a particular that passes for the universal: a single site that controls, hence suppresses, alternatives or differences (say, noncapitalist political structures). The critiques, that is, effectively disclose a site of opposition: the local, the margins, singularity, living labor, queerness, performativity, the feminine, civil society.

Complications arise, however, when we realize that these discourses, though seemingly laboring to perform a similar task—to debunk a universalism that is intolerant of difference—do not complement each other. To dub the universal "Western metaphysics," as do many "deconstructionists," is not equivalent to calling it "the market" or "late capitalism," as do many post-Marxists. Moreover, this "metaphysics" should not be confused with the "dominant forms of representation" of cultural studies, which should not be mistaken for the "compulsive heterosexuality" of queer theory, which should not be misconstrued as the "patriarchy" of feminism, and so on. One might naturally assume that "capitalism," "patriarchy," "dominant discourse," "Eurocentrism," and the like are basically the "same thing." But nothing could be less certain.

Every term for the universal, like every articulation of a locus of resistance, marks the limit of another. The discourse of diaspora studies, which venerates contamination, border crossing, hyphenated identities, multiplicity, and transnationalism as topoi that threaten homogeneity, nationalism, rule of law, and the state, finds its limit in AIDS: nothing is more global, more about contamination, more lawless, more transnational than AIDS. The "positive" aspects of the concept of diaspora encounter an obstacle: not the "restrictive state" but the diaspora itself, now supplemented by the AIDS diaspora. When a thinker such as Haver discusses globalization as the "time of AIDS" (in *The Body of This Death*), he neither offers nor claims to offer a better model of the globe than those provided by diaspora studies.[1] He simply indexes the limit of these models, hence works toward an AIDS discourse, one that maps and addresses the singularity of the globalization or "pandemic" of AIDS.

Globalization is not one process/discourse. Nor is it a collection of processes that add up to the whole. Rather, it is a heterogeneous relation of processes—immigration/emigration, AIDS, Westernization, patriarchy, the market, the New World Order, the United Nations, civilization, heterosexual imperatives, pollution, nuclear proliferation, international terrorism, human rights, humanitarianism, meta-physics—none of which, and no combination of which, can account either for the others or for the All.

This is not a bad situation. Quite to the contrary, if academics interested in combatting totalizing narratives could articulate the relationality of the numerous discourses that undertake this pro-ject, then they might well accomplish their goal. They could demonstrate that no notion of, or name for, the sociopolitical today can in itself account for global developments: for the All. To relate projects is ultimately to demonstrate the relativity—the limit, non-totality, the nonsovereignty, or nonabsoluteness—of every (name for the) universal, the absolute, or the global, hence for the univer-sal itself. And if the market, as one of those names, is revealed, not as the "New World Order" but as relative to other global phe-nomena such as mass immigration, AIDS, or metaphysics—events that the market can affect but cannot completely determine—then the condition (the contingency rather than necessity of the market) of possibility of "the political" as understood by Jameson is exposed.

With these ideas in mind, let us imagine a kind of workplace in the Academy, where the task of the "workers" (the academicians) is to mark the limit of the market. This labor, following the Laclau-Mouffe paradigm, would require that scholars forge the relations of their discourses through "pivot tongues" or "articulations" that, functioning as demands, force each such discourse to assimilate new phrases. Where one discourse or set of signifiers experiences its limit is also the site where that endeavor exposes itself to another. The two projects are then forced to articulate the axis between their foundational notions. In doing so, they potentially fabricate fresh undertakings or radically remodel existing ones grounded on novel foundations: the pivot tongues that emerge through the new relation. This activity, in turn, could well lead to additional campus projects and even additional intellectual institutions (new workshops, programs, departments, faculty), which the reigning homogeneity would have to assimilate or accommodate. The university materializes as an institution where the commonsense signifiers of all the established paradigms, institutions, and discourses endlessly confront and work through their limit, and where new groups—even new friends—constantly form around that work.

The culture wars are precisely the resistance to such a hypothetical undertaking. Rather than relating one discourse to another, these wars set up discourses as competitors—or at least appear to. Each project (say, deconstruction), each component within the projects (say, "philosophical rigor") is given a particular value. Certain paradigms make "politicality" a value. Others posit "close reading" as a value. Still others celebrate—or call into question—"human values." For one endeavor, pluralist or fluctuating identities are held in the highest esteem. For another, the dismantling of all identity, plural or monolithic, occupies this site. Each discourse, concept, signifier, or name has its price. Every paradigm offers a choice with a value; every resistance operates under a label it posits over against the label of another resistance.

Each and every discourse of the culture wars, by itself, may represent a brilliant challenge to the universal or to the market. But none emerges by itself. Every discourse exists, and attains value, by virtue of its relations to others. Thus, by setting themselves up as competing values, these projects perform the very totality that they are trying to resist. By stacking value against value, sign against sign, discourse against discourse, the intellectuals perform the necessity of the very market—the "individual of free choice" that forms the base of the market—and mass consensus they want to displace.

Let me put all of this another way. Just as academic territories seem to be perpetually at war, just as boundaries seem to be ceaselessly breaking down as once-separated academic spaces begin to relate (interdisciplinarity, science across the curriculum, language across the curriculum), so both academic competitions and relations are fast disappearing. In the Academy, no such competitions actually take place since, in competitions (or even in play or in games), one side can lose. And in the culture wars, the "death" (such as the "death of the canon") of a discourse is most often the assurance of its repeated comeback, its eternal life. That is why intellectual debates are no debates.

This last point is key. Because today's academic discourses are endlessly resurrected, the culture wars are just so many *simulations* of war. In saying this, I do not mean to imply that academic conflicts are fake, but rather to assert, as I intimated earlier, that a war or competition—whether a culture war, a market war, an ethnic war, a "burger war," or an international war—ceases to be a real war when the struggles between enemies or opponents erase death, and even the risk of death, from the scene. The culture wars are thus not real wars but the "postwars" of a consensual postdemocracy; they are idealizations and even aestheticized celebrations of war: indeed, by removing death's possibility, they posit conflict as safe, seductive, radical, liberating, *healthy*.

An example: beginning in the 1960s, the literary canon was challenged in American English departments. Despite this challenge, multiculturalists and popular culture enthusiasts of the 1980s and 1990s, seeking to topple the already destabilized canon in the name of "diversity," posited it as "the dominant discourse." Which is to say, multiculturalist popular culture studies raised the banner of the Western canon up to the top of the flagpole so as to haul it back down. These oppositional discourses resteadied their competition so as to then subvert, displace, and replace it.

The conflict has elevated both sides. The humanists who, advocating the canon, were perhaps slipping a bit, now find themselves once again at the center of academic debates, with a "re-firmed" position in the dominant/subversive, traditional/multicultural, canon/anticanon, elite/popular duopolies that ground so many contemporary university discussions. Their opponents, over against this "re-firmed" humanist position, now feel themselves all the more justified in their efforts to subvert it: the "strength" of the "intolerant" humanists supplies them with good grounds. Humanists thus live off their distinction from "deconstructive multicultural radicals"— and vice versa. Without multiculturalism, cultural studies, or popular culture studies, celebrants of the canon or literary studies have no ground; without a strong canon, celebrants of alternatives also have no ground. The various projects are built upon each other. Their banners pulled up and down a phallic flagpole, they are nonetheless grounded—not in the earth, but in these same banners, waving in the air: in the fact that there are at least two signs, never one.

An increase in scholarly conflicts or perspectives thus means a decrease in the desire to open oneself to the Other, to phrase one's relations. If "concept 2" does not threaten "concept 1" but justifies it (as the canon justifies popular culture studies), one cannot expect "concept 1" to address its own bond to this Other. In the culture wars, there exists almost no reason to open to the Other, and no reason to account for one's own position, since the wars between Same and Other vindicate both Same and Other, supplying precisely the reason or ground for a legitimate co-refusal.

Today, the "dominant discourse" is neither "conservative humanism" nor "multiculturalism," center nor margin, canon nor anticanon, essentialism nor decontructionism, patriarchy nor feminism, but rather the debates between humanism and multiculturalism, center and margin, canon and anticanon, essence and construction. "Freedom" and value, that is, lie in neither "tower" but in the production of the distinction/connection between the two. It is obvious that, in the commercial market, "wars" (as in "burger wars") need not yield a winner since they are themselves the foundation of the market's mode of production. The same more or less holds for scholarly conflicts. These need not be resolved since the creation of conflict after conflict is itself the resolution, the means by which intellectuals make a claim on "freedom of thought" and "freedom of expression," indeed, on freedom itself: on their own individual freedom.

Why, then, are academic debates so politically charged? Let us speculate for a moment. Each academic discourse today represents not only a view or ideology, but also an identity, not unlike a "race" (as Foucault uses the term). Ethnic, gender, class, and sexual orientation studies of the 1960s, 1970s, and 1980s revealed that identities are discourses, cultural constructions, and that all such discourses are evaluations, value judgments. Cultural constructions, that is, represent efforts to up- or downgrade the value of the group in question.

Now matters have subtly changed. It is not so much that every identity is a discourse, but that every discourse (with its proper name: deconstruction, cultural studies, Marxism, Deleuze, Lacan) is an identity. Scholars who endorse "deconstruction" have not only embraced a paradigm, a theory, a thinking, a mode, or a method. They have also adopted an "I," and always already stand in a potentially antagonistic relationship to other discourses/identities. The culture wars became "wars" because, in questioning the legitimacy and right of another person's thought, one questions the legitimacy and right of that person's being. Merely to position your thought alongside another's is to pose as a death threat—the death not only of this subject, but of education itself and of a species whose continuance seems to depend on education. The culture wars are, through and through, biopolitical operations.

The idea that academic discourses rarely relate—that debates are dwindling, interdisciplinarity is vanishing—may, I grant, seem ludicrous to academics who believe that they themselves, not to mention everyone around them, are both competing and relating on a daily basis. But the point I am trying to make is easily proven with two analyses of contemporary academic discourses. The first analysis proceeds from the link between two fundamental texts, published in the mid- to late 1970s: Jacques Derrida's *Of Grammatology* and Edward Said's *Orientalism*.[2] Logically speaking, these texts should have generated either a dialogue or a debate between deconstruction and postcolonial studies, the two discourses the works came to found and define in the United States. Indeed, the presence of Gayatri Spivak would seem to have made such a dialogue or debate inevitable. Although not especially involved in postcolonial matters when she translated and wrote the introduction to *Of Grammatology* in 1976, Spivak would later become (willingly or otherwise) one of the leading figures of the postcolonial and the deconstruction projects. Indeed, she represents a tie between the two discourses, one most clearly articulated in her renowned essay "Can the Subaltern Speak?" and pursued in her *Critique of Postcolonial Reason*.[3] One might therefore assume that readers of her work would, at least today, be addressing this link in some way.

But the connection between postcolonial studies and deconstruction remains largely unexamined. To be sure, any number of works conflate deconstruction and postcolonial studies, suggesting that Said and others "deconstruct" the West (or that both discourses pertain to "multiculturalism"). And there have been highly effective applications of deconstruction to colonial matters, such as those of Bhabha and Robert Young, as well as many rejections of deconstruction by postcolonial studies and vice versa. But the nature of the connections and disconnections between the two projects—outside the casting of differences that make no difference—remains largely unstudied, even by those who appear to take up this mission. (And here, loyal deconstructionists and postcolonial studies advocates are equally guilty.)

In fact, *Of Grammatology* and *Orientalism* (and, by extension, deconstruction and postcolonial studies) have a great deal in common—and yet they are also profoundly different. Both are critiques of Eurocentrism. Both address and dismantle a dominant discourse: Western metaphysics for deconstruction, the West itself for postcolonialism. Both view language, and thus reading and writing, not as reflections, but as active creators of reality. Language concerns lives; it is a topos that demands an ethical and political response. Both suggest that dialogue between different peoples, between Same and Other, is crucial, but also risky: the language between Same and Other is not necessarily a common one, and "healthy dialogue" often results in a certain violence.

But there is much more. Difference, for the two discourses, is paramount; so, too, is heterogeneity. Both are concerned with interdisciplinarity. The deconstruction that emerges from *Of Grammatology* tackles this issue by retracing the age-old debate between literature and philosophy, which it may well view as structuring all possible interdisciplinarity. Postcolonial studies (not necessarily Said) undertakes this task, on the one hand, by focusing on the deployment of other disciplines (anthropology, science, law, economics, philosophy) found within the great Third World novels and, on the one hand, by taking note of the fact that "literature" in its traditional sense is not generally produced outside of the metropolis. Therefore, any student truly interested in marginal cultures, or in the margins of civilization, must learn to "read" alternative cultural forms.

Both deconstruction and postcolonial studies have tense relations with psychoanalysis and with Marxism, however much both "use" them. Both have seriously critiqued the Academy, but both have generated huge "markets" and large discipleships within this same Academy.

Of course, these similarities are balanced by crucial differences. Deconstruction investigates language or writing as the finitude of representation, whereas postcolonial studies concerns itself strictly with questions of representation itself. To put this idea in other terms, when the two attack the "dominant discourse," postcolonial studies critiques the representations of Western culture, whereas deconstruction tends to critique representation as such (Western or otherwise)—the reduction of being to appearance—as a key property of that domination.

Or to put it in still other terms: postcolonial studies first demonstrates how the West grounds itself in a series of binaries— idea/experience, human/animal, nature/culture, historical/nonhistorical peoples, controlled/libidinal, clever/instinctive, speech/silence— by means of which the West establishes itself as the whole and the true. It then either undoes those binaries or reveals how the "Other" has subverted them, hence displayed this Other's capacity to resist. Deconstruction, on the other hand, argues that the binaries do not, by themselves, form the foundation of Western intolerance, but are, in fact, a means to displace a third foundational party: the boundary between the opposing terms. Binaries, it concludes, are efforts not to erase or appropriate the Other but to displace the bond to the Other, the subject's frontier, relationality and death, onto the Other.

Postcolonial studies assumes and investigates the Other of the West, whose existence it assumes. Deconstruction exposes the limit of the West: the condition of possibility of an Other, whose actual being, in this view, is not a given. The Other may not *be*.

Furthermore: postcolonial studies is quite concerned with establishing the fact that Third World sites not only possess an imaginary or an art but also a philosophy, a thinking, a reason. The claim is grounded on solid logic: the imaginary and even the arts themselves are too easily subsumed into the idea of "natural talent," thereby into the racist mind/instinct, culture/nature, reason/irrational binaries at the heart of colonialism itself. (Post)colonial artists, like nature, "cannot think," though they possess other gifts.

For deconstruction, however, philosophy is much more the problem than the solution; it too often makes a claim on the totality of thought. Thus deconstruction seems at times to fetishize certain literary works such as those of Mallarmé, Rilke, Holderlin, and Celan as "Other" than metaphysics qua philosophy, as topoi of thought that mark the limit of philosophy's hegemony over thought itself.

Deconstruction and postcolonial studies are further divided by the issue of writing. Derrida's argument that metaphysics and the West are grounded in "phonocentrism," or in the privileging of speech over writing is well known, indeed, too well known. Postcolonial studies has frequently contended the contrary. Third World nations (during the colonial periods) were (and are often still) belittled for supposedly *lacking* a system of writing (which, I should add, they mostly did *not* lack). The point is undeniable: the move away from orality and toward writing has too often been taken as a sign of progress, while "simple" orality has been cast as a mark of underdevelopment and even barbarism.

Derrida's work, however, does not "privilege" writing but addresses (at least in part) a question that, in actuality, has emerged as more central to postcolonial studies than to deconstruction: If, for the Western colonizer, writing is to orality as progress is to underdevelopment, why is this the case? Because, as Anthony Pagden and other scholars of colonialism have shown, writing has been posited in and by the West as the form that preserves oral exchanges, permitting them to be passed down from generation to generation.[4] Each generation receives the learning of the past, conserved in written works. It then compares the more "modern" practices and ideas to the older ones, makes improvements, contributes to progress, and sends the work to its offspring—and the process toward truth and the good continues. Writing, in this paradigm, is the conduit for the speech that antecedes it; it is the faithful reproduction of orality that captures the "present" for future advancement.

And this, for Derrida, is phonocentrism: any thinking that contends that speech is the truth of language, and writing its mere reproduction, a reflection of the spoken word. Derrida's attack of phonocentrism, in other words, is also his attack of "writing as a vehicle of progress," his "deconstruction" of the discourse of developmentalism: of the thesis that writing is passed-down speech that allows peoples to "learn from and correct the past," hence "improve."

When these two pioneering texts, *Of Grammatology* and *Orientalism*, took the U.S. Academy by storm in the late 1970s and throughout the 1980s, almost nobody attempted to articulate these similarities and differences. The unworked link between the two remains a fault between endeavors: deconstruction and postcolonial studies. The thinking of such a relation would have revealed that there are not one but at least two major "critiques" of Eurocentrism. One runs through Heidegger, and considers the limits of the paradigmatic or technological thinking that, Heidegger argued, defines the origin and being of the West. Here—in such Heideggerian and post-Heideggerian endeavors—actual differences between cultures are subsumed into a project that exposes the way in which Being itself is "grounded" on the disavowal of its own difference from itself: the rift at the origin. Cultural difference emerges as an epiphenomenal outcome of the ontological difference: it no doubt bears the trace of the latter difference, but is not foundational.

The other critique of the West runs through the long tradition of colonialism and its resistance that Said so thoroughly gathers, exposes, and analyzes. In this project, the Heideggerian ontological difference is subsumed into a study of the differences between cultures. The distinction between the West and the Other is thereby assumed to account for the distinction between the West and itself. Ontological difference emerges as an epiphenomenal reflection of cultural difference. These two differences form the two sides of a chiasmus or X, but are irreducible to each other. And yet an exploration of the rift/bond between them appears *unthinkable* for both discourses on difference. The difference between differences is what these two academic discourses about difference "as a whole" have not sufficiently addressed.

Touching, exposed, in contact, powerful, right, and legitimate beings-in-common, postcolonial studies and deconstruction coexist through their dis-association or, as neither enemies nor friends, nonfriendship. Grounded on two versions of the West, indeed, on two different grounds for the West, they reveal the more-than-oneness, the relationality, of the West itself. But it is precisely this relation, this dis-association of nonfriends which remains unarticulated some twenty years after the emergence of these projects in the United States.

Instead of trying to state what is meant by "the West" through the fact that neither postcolonial studies nor deconstruction can account for the other, and thus for the West itself, scholars chose to (1) cast Derrida and de Man as embodiments of "Western thought" or "Western ideology," using them as foils for the legitimization of the postcolonial studies examinations of "the Other"; (2) posit postcolonial studies as another identity politics, another example of the spread of Western metaphysics or the transcendental subject, validating deconstructionist critiques that challenge the ontological foundations of the West in the name of difference, politics, and ethics; or (3) advance some sort of balance between the two discourses, a gesture that maintains both discourse in "more or less" strong positions. These unfortunate developments materialized quite openly in the early 1980s, when Derrida and, indirectly through two of his students, Said himself tussled over the issue of apartheid in the prestigious and widely read journal *Critical Inquiry*.[5]

The stakes of the debate for the U.S. public were, in fact, high. Derrida was clearly on trial: Was deconstruction political? Derrida stood by his guns. He contended that even a horrific political situation such as apartheid could never be divorced from the problem of language: not representation, but language. Said's students, on the other hand, held that analyses of apartheid demanded a thinking, not merely of language, but of misrepresentation (racism), self-representation, and historiography. Without entering into the specifics of the debate, I will only note that all players were at liberty to hold their positions, and that all offered legitimate intellectual opinions on apartheid. The problem lay in the *aftermath* of the debate, when scholars did not want, could not, or were not permitted to address what was on the line in this conflict.[6] The ultimately result was a duopoly between postcolonial studies and deconstruction: a debate in which no debate is possible, but in which the taking of sides is.

Let us now examine another, very distinct testimony to the non-war of the culture wars, to the noncompetitiveness of the Academy: the use of deconstruction by Stuart Hall and cultural studies. Hall, on the one hand, holds deconstruction as one of the cornerstones of his work: "Maintaining that [openness] is absolutely essential, at least if [cultural studies] is to remain a critical and deconstructive project. . . . it is always self-reflectively deconstructing itself."[7] Hall's "deconstructive edge," as he puts it, nonetheless is tempered by his strong opposition to the very foundations of deconstruction: "The textual is the moment when culture and the discursive are recovered. . . . Cultural studies is impossible without retaining the moment of the symbolic, with the textual, language, subjectivity and representation forming the key matrix. The moment of the symbolic is critical for me. Nonetheless, I never try to think of it as autonomous. . . . That's where I would draw the line. I think certain literary 'takes' on cultural studies do (in effect) treat the textual moment as autonomous."[8]

Hall thus sees culture as a linguistic construct, never essential or fixed. But language is not itself an autonomous reality. Language is crucial; but one should not mistake it for reality itself. This declaration, whether one accepts it or not, actually contradicts a fundamental conviction of "deconstruction": language does not necessarily reflect or produce practices and the real, but can itself be real. Indeed, Paul de Man, along with Derrida the most famous figure of deconstruction, holds that ideological critique is made possible by precisely "the autonomous potential of language,"[9] by the fact that language can emerge as a separate force. Hall draws a line in the sand at this possibility, crosses off, in the name of a "deconstructive edge," part of deconstruction's very infrastructure. He, in fact, is quite open on the matter: "That's where I would draw the line."

Hall's hard line with deconstruction becomes more manifest in his critique of what he calls Laclau's "deconstructive" politics: Laclau's "last book thinks that the world, social practice, is language, whereas I want to say that the social operates *like* a language."[10] Let us oppose this to another of de Man's postulates: literature "is not a priori certain that language functions according to principles which are those, or which are *like* those, of the phenomenal world. It is therefore not a priori certain that literature is a reliable source of information about anything but its own language."[11] Both Hall and de Man italicize the "like." Yet they do so for diametrically opposed reasons. Hall suggests that language is not itself reality, but is *like* reality, whereas de Man holds that language is not (necessarily) *like* reality, but *is* a reality (the word *cat*, one recalls, is not even *like* the reality it represents).

One could go on to show that, for Stuart Hall, the deconstructionist overemphasis on language leads to, as he calls them, "protoanarchist"[12] discourses—"protoanarchist" because they are not grounded in a reality, but in a "free-floating" textuality. This thesis will in turn lead to Hall's skepticism about Foucault, Derrida, Baudrillard, and Lyotard (the latter two, Halls holds, "have gone right through the sound barrier").[13]

I do not wish to defend deconstruction or groundlessness; if deconstruction were indeed advocating groundlessness, Hall would be right about its "going overboard." Nor do I wish to dismiss cultural studies, whose methods have produced such admirable results. I am only pointing out that, though Hall calls upon deconstruction as a fundamental tool, he elects to draw a line at certain precepts, instead of concentrating precisely on what deconstruction, and thus cultural studies (which includes a "deconstructive edge" as part of its foundation) may or may not be. Lines, to be sure, must be drawn if there is to be thinking. My question is: Why does Hall draw *this* line?

Let us consider Hall's response to the possibility that cultural studies is spreading too far, and thus losing its essential qualities: "I am not interested in Theory, I am interested in going on theorizing. And that also means that cultural studies has to open to external influences, for example, to new social movements, to psychoanalysis, to feminism, to cultural differences . . . cultural studies cannot thrive by isolating itself in academic terms from those external influences."[14]

Because he is "open to external influences," Hall does not want to draw ideological and methodological boundaries around cultural studies. Yet he does "draw a line" at certain influences, as we have just seen. When examined a little more closely, his position turns out to be that displacement as infinite deterritorialization (absolute globalization or "total" deconstruction) is Eurocentric or aestheticist, hence conservative. Yet so too are fixity, empiricism, and essentialist identities. Hall's "line" is etched between these two "unacceptable" positions, as he himself affirms vis-à-vis the names "Lyotard" and "Habermas": "So we are caught between two unacceptable choices: Habermas's defensive position in relation to the old Enlightenment project and Lyotard's Euro-centered celebration of the postmodern collapse."[15]

In this context, it is important to review Derrida's definition of "logocentrism." The "deconstruction" of logocentrism is not the critique of the logos, logic, or reason but, as the word suggests, of the tendency of logos to bring its exteriority or limit back to the center. Derrida usually employs the father (logos) son (logoi) relation to explain this point. To be a true father or logos, a father must produce a true son. If the son stays too close to the father, if he never leaves home, if he remains exactly the same as the father, then he desists as a son, emerging as just a clone of the father: as nothing real. The father (logos), in this case, ceases to be a father: without a father/son difference, there is no father, for there is no other than the father, no son.

Conversely, if the son strays too far, ceases to reflect the father, even poorly, then the father again loses the son, again ceases to be the father. This wanderer is another untrue son, for he does not (re)produce the father. The condition of being a father, therefore, is the father/son *différance* or relation, which the father cannot dictate. He can make the son stay (bad for the family economy since the son does not "make anything" of himself, does not "add" to the family capital), or make the son go away (also bad since this progeny does not bring his "additions" back to the family name); but he cannot make the son go "not too far but far enough." The "not too far but far enough" cannot be defined, hence cannot be dictated by the patriarchal law, or by any other mandate or figure. No signifier for the "just right" command exists. The father (logos) is the commander whose command is limited by his own word or rule since he cannot say, "Go" (far) and "Stay" (close) at the same time.

This paradigm, of course, is at the heart of Derrida's meditations on writing, which, we have already seen, can function as a tool of the Western metaphysical tradition, particularly the discourse of developmentalism. Writing retains and spreads the voice of the father, of authority, to future generations, where its message, as it separates from the oral pronouncement, is adjusted for the times, improved upon in the name of progress. To reiterate: through its *disconnection* with, and its claim to superiority over, orality, writing frequently stands in the West for development: it retains but carries the oral message beyond itself, in the perfect logocentric fashion that Derrida dismantles.

Yet writing can subvert the tradition as well. Since the written word remains in circulation after the death of the father/authority, and can travel outside his domain even when he is alive, it can be reinterpreted, appropriated for purposes and prospects never intentionally advocated by this father but made possible the presence and presentation of his word. A tainted future does not follow but is proper to that presentation; the father is unwillingly responsible. Writing can "go wild," and can do so "in the name of the father."

Writing, then, disturbs logocentrism in two ways. On the one hand, motionlessly "stuck" to the page, writing remains too near and too like the father/origin/oral command. Insufficiently malleable, it does not lend itself to renovation and development: the advancement of the law across generations, the gain in the family's economy. On the other hand, writing, though a "dead ringer" for the voice of the father, can stray as it leaves the paternal hand and is translated. It is excessively flexible. Writing is "bad" because it stretches either too remotely or not at all.

In sum, logocentrism, like the "good father," wants to deploy writing as a means to produce and broaden the scope of its voice/law; and struggles to contain writing so that it (writing) does not extend any missive beyond a "certain" limit. But this very border (between the "go far" but "do not drift too far") is what the father-logos cannot name. It thereby materializes as the limit to the father-logos's own power, to patriarchy.

The boundary on the logos, to sum up, lies within the very structure of the logos. A father is a father only through a "correct son"—a "correctness" the father cannot completely mandate, not even hypothetically or ideally. Translating this father/son metaphor back into terms of logic or reason, we can therefore say: logic/reason needs a certain difference from itself (delusion, fantasy, belief, language, faith, dreams, feeling), one it cannot ordain, in order to be itself. This, for "logocentrism," is the role of literature, religion, philosophy, music, the imagination, the unconscious, art, ideology, government, and, of course, writing: to leave logic behind so as to fulfill or consummate it, to abandon it so as to return to it, and supply it with the necessary returns.

And yet the very discourses that are called upon to complete logic, like any son, only more firmly mark the finitude of the "father-logos." If logic needs its supplement to totalize its thought, this can only be because it is not itself total.

Logocentrism thus strives to bring its supplement back into its own domain: to cast fields both too far outside of it (like sexual desire or passionate poetry) and too close to it (like philosophy) as "logic" that has lost the way. The other of logic is posited as bad logic—either as too different from logic or as not different enough—which needs to be corrected by logic. And this is logo-centrism: not a discourse that rejects or defies logic but any that claims that the truth of domains outside of logic lies in logic itself as the totality of Being.[16]

The importance of such an understanding of logocentrism emerges when we examine Hall's many discussions of the local and the global. For Hall, the "local" that does not open to the "global" is akin to the bad son who never leaves the house. The other untrue son is the global without a local: discourses that focus on global or capitalist thrusts without analyzing their local manifestations. One notes here a parallel with Hall's above observations concerning the relation of textuality and reality. Poststructuralism, when "too tex-tual," is similar to a global (capitalism) without a local. It "breaks the sound barrier" by losing all reference to actual realities and meaning: it goes too far. Essentialism, empiricism, and Marxism, on the other hand, are for Hall too atextual. They are akin to a local without a global, a reality without a textuality, an essentialism without flexibility or flux, and hence are also bad offspring.

Judging from Hall's comments, the critic does best to control both of these "too strong" or dominant tendencies: be just global enough, just textual enough, so as to keep a foothold in "hard theory"; and just local enough, sufficiently grounded, to retain a foundation in reality. Hall's leftism does not lie in the materialism of Marx, the rationality of Habermas, the "irrationality" of post-structuralism, or in the displacements of deconstruction. Radicalism and empowerment instead rest in the possibility of the selection, at any given moment, between all of these: in freedom and nonautocracy as this choice.

Deconstruction, according to Hall, thus fits quite well into the cultural studies discourse. Cultural studies either embraces decon-struction (as a friend) or rejects it (as an enemy, as part of the Eurocentric dominant discourse), in both ways keeping deconstruc-tion within its parameters and control. For as a (too ungrounded) "enemy" or "Eurocentric discourse," deconstruction serves cultural studies as the competition or foil by means of which the project establishes its worth (often presenting itself as "deconstruction with a political edge": as deconstruction with extra value). As "friend," deconstruction is positioned as a sign of "theoretical radicality" within a cultural studies discourse that is now (with deconstruction as an added arm) more able to contest other "dom-inant discourses." Yet, in all cases, the duopoly is held up, for it is through this division that cultural studies speaks not in its own name, as a despotic One, but for the multiplicity, openness, and alternatives it preserves: for liberty in general, and for itself as an agent of that liberty.

Open to all others, cultural studies is nonetheless closed to its own closure (its boundary as the opening-to), to an articulation of the border that enchains it to those others, and without which there is no Other. Thus cultural studies never articulates its relation to decon-struction, for to view itself as that relation, as bound or obliged to a nonfriend is also, for cultural studies, to admit to the limit or death of its own foundations and premises, including and above all the proper name "cultural studies": the label that preserves the endeavor, safeguards its value, and guarantees its progress.

The "dialogue" of cultural studies with deconstruction is therefore not simply one example among others of academic conflict. Deconstruction, as we have seen, works to mark language as such, the "unlike" or boundary between, but not within, fields of representation: the "autonomous potential of language." Indeed, the cultural studies appropriation/expropriation of deconstruction is geared to expunge from the scene, not just another "theory," but the borders that divide up the multiplicity of theories, or the limits of that multiplicity. These frontiers are the "inter" of human discourses (both those grounded in "culture" and those grounded in "nature") for which discourses cannot account. The condition of and a force within the field of choices, discourses, and disciplines that the subject is not at liberty to choose or not choose, the boundary of free choice and thus of the power of the human subject who is "self-determined" insofar as able to construct and make such selections, language is what cultural studies, like the culture wars themselves, must exclude. At language the line is drawn.

What, today, conserves? The answer, I have argued in this chapter, is not "the political Right" but the reproduction of an absolute border between Left and Right. Therefore, today's Left itself includes its own conservatism, a conservatism that lies in all efforts to be, posit, follow, or align itself with a master thinker as master paradigm (linked in some way to Marx or the "true Left" but not simply Marxist) who cannot be disputed except from the *Right*. The border or shared space between Left and Right, which yields contamination between the two, indeed, which demonstrates that no justice without this ill-health is even conceivable, is eliminated by the creation of the master who reconstructs the Left/Right duopoly, and who is master because of this feat. As just indicated, any discussion of the corruption of Left by Right cannot but come from the Right since that is what, in this context, the Right is: the position that challenges the ground of the new Left's authority.[17] Thus, as I hope readers can now see, the culture wars take place to maintain, not the Left or the Right, but the Left/Right division that protects both master- ful positions—safeguarding also their marketability and the mar- ket itself, including, of course, the university as the site for their commerce.

10.

"Empire"

Anti-aestheticism, Leftist Solutions, and the Commodification of the Multitude

Criticism suggesting that deconstruction is "apolitical" is by now commonplace. Such allegations, though emerging from a myriad of perspectives and ideologies, have until recently been humanist, identitarian, or classically Marxist in nature. Materializing today, however, are a series of political-theoretical discourses that, even as they discount most key components of identity politics, humanism, and even classical Marxism—including the key issue: the subject—continue to serve up, directly or obliquely, the idea of deconstruction's "apoliticality." I am thinking of the writings of Giorgio Agamben, Slavoj Zizek, Michael Hardt, and Alain Badiou, among others. In this chapter, through a reading of Hardt and Negri's *Empire*, I will attempt to analyze these projects: not only their claim on the political but also the fact that they make this claim through a dismissal of deconstruction. Is anti-deconstruction central or peripheral to these assertions about the political? And why is the question even relevant?

As suggested previously, *Empire* proceeds from the difference between the state (which includes the international) and "empire" (globalization), disciplinary and control societies.[1] Its authors find in "empire" a topos that, even though despotic, offers new possibilities for political activism.

A main distinction between control and discipline lies in the distribution of power. In a disciplinary society, founded on the state form, power is centralized, whereas, in a control society, it is dispersed. More sites of command exist, but no one site is cardinal. Indeed, according to Hardt and Negri, the proliferation of power in "empire," and thus the limitation on any single site ("limited" relative to the centralized power of the state form), lends itself to even greater proliferation, to the emergence of subversive might, of the new empowerment of certain peoples. By their very structure, control societies provoke the possibility of the upheaval that they quash through management. They work to map, chronicle, and order alterity rather than to eliminate it. The "Other" who eludes the state is manipulated by an "empire" that fears not the emergence of novel, autonomous territories (control society in fact banks on this territorialization of the new) but "deterritorialization" and nomadic "lines of flight." We suggested above that control societies render dissidence conceivable. We now understand that such insubordination, on the map of empire, rests in the Other's refusal to take a place or fixed position. Instead, the Other shifts, reforms, incessantly adopts new poses, organizes fresh collectives, and thus resists administration.

"Deterritorialization" and "nomadic lines of flight," topoi also borrowed from Deleuze (and Guatarri), designate for Hardt and Negri the true leftist tactic in the age of globalization. The goal is no longer to situate oneself over against the state since empire registers all such "situating." We know this, I should add, from empirical experiences in the Third World, where efforts by postdictatorship populations to tear the media away from state control yielded, not "rebellious channels," but the market's management and territorialization of these same media. Indeed, because the market is one of the strongest antistate sites, capable of subsuming all others, the "outside the map" of empire cannot be simply an antistate topos. It is a power that will not lend itself to mapping, which is to say, to the deterritorialization that empire fears.

Hardt and Negri name the agent of the deterritorialization "the multitude," which they define as political force that is "singular" and "incommunicable." Citing the 1994 Zapatista uprising in Chiapas, they argue that leftist political activism no longer issues from a specific leftist program or concept, not even from Marxism. It springs, rather, from singular circumstances—such as the oppression of the indigenous peoples in Chiapas, exacerbated by the initiation of NAFTA—in which the multitude rises up against "empire," with no clear agenda except an absolute "being-against": the concrete situation spurs the insurgent multitude, which "organizes" precisely for that insurgence. Where, before, there was an obvious connection between distinct instances of political unrest such as the events of 1968 in Mexico City and Paris, in the contemporary period, there exists no definitive ideological or situational link between them, between, say, the incidents in Chiapas (1994) and Tiananmen Square (1989).

But Hardt and Negri are not satisfied with this destruction or "being-against," which they associate with contemporary political paradigms they find to be somewhat empty, such as those of deconstruction. They advocate alternative paradigms: forms of production and of living labor grounded on novel deployments of the body, creativity, artifice, and "tools." Without a pregiven agenda, the multitude invents political configurations for the unique circumstances from which it arises.

As outlined by a tradition stretching at least from Nietzsche through Lyotard, production is by a logical necessity the establishment of a subject (individual or collective), hence of a territory. Production, especially that of art and artifice, is the reterritorialization of any deterritorialized movement, and not its invention. If Hardt and Negri are interested in espousing new sorts of creativity and production (their "living labor"), I welcome the contribution. Investigation into a *poiēsis* irreducible to production is, after all, at the center of the philosophical tradition just mentioned; Heidegger's "Letter on Humanism," whose concern is Marx and Marxism, is most likely the most famous document within that tradition. But I find not entirely convincing Hardt and Negri's simple advocacy of alternative production, unaccompanied by a dialogue with that tradition's critique of the metaphysics of production—hence absent any inquiry into whether such an alternative is even possible.

Without delving into the finer points of "incommunicability" or "singularity," I believe the "incommunicability" of incidents such as the Zapatista uprising could be interrogated. The point is not that messages to the West, often conveyed by computers and the Internet, were fundamental devices for the indigenous peoples who rebelled. These helped gain the global support that, however short-lived, sustained and justified the activism. The point, rather, is that this communication appealed to the Westerners' and the Mexicans' identification of the indigenous cause with other or former revolutionary endeavors (including of course those of Emiliano Zapata during the Mexican Revolution). As we have noted, it was this identification—counting on Chiapas's nonsingularity, its forming part of a pattern, a program—which (with international or metropolitan backing) rendered the revolt viable. Every political situation may well "be" unique, singular "in truth," an "event," hence demanding, on some level, an "unprecedented" response. Yet if an event actually emerged without historical model, it could neither generate nor attract a multitude; indeed, it could not logically transpire at all. It could not even be recognized.

The last point is illustrated by the recent history of the signifier "the multitude" itself. For Hardt and Negri, this term indexes a general topos onto which a potentially endless series of political groups might congregate, rally, disperse, and later regather differently. In fact, however, multitude is itself already an identification, model, and signifier, perhaps due to *Empire*'s impressive circulation. Consider, for one of many possible examples, the February 2002 protests against the World Economic Forum (WEF) in New York City. Although a multitude may have demonstrated there, the event itself did not generate it. In the first place, the rally was already a spin-off of other such demonstrations against global economic institutions held in Seattle, Milan, and São Paulo. Before it even materialized, "the multitude" of the 2002 anti-WEF protesters was a well-commodified program. The protests against the WEF in New York actually gathered *under the name "the multitude."* Indeed, the signifier "the multitude" was at the foundation of the political assemblage, not a mere name for it: "As the World Economic Forum meets, outside will be the glimpse of the new movement— global, like the system whose crimes it is protesting—that is the forerunners of things to come. Each protester speaks for a *multitude* around the world who 'stand outcast and starving amidst the wonders we have made,' in the words of the old union song."[2]

In other words, at the WEF, "the multitude" emerged as the performance of its own impossibility: the impossibility of a gathering that is not always already a model, a cause, and an identity, always already calculated, controlled, and a mechanism of control. "The multitude" cannot mark a politics that surfaces from an event outside any program since "the multitude" is itself a program (which is not to suggest that "the multitude" is "apolitical"; it is, or tends toward, precisely a political program).

Even though it was not the source of "the multitude" as used by the anti-WEF protesters, through its global circulation and market success *Empire* is today responsible for all articulations of the term.

More to the point, intellectuals cannot properly be said to think of the market unless they assume responsibility for the commodification of that thinking—indeed, for the fact that the market is the setting and condition of the political influence of *all* thinking. Thus an analysis of global capitalism that does not respond to the publicity and publication of *Empire*'s analysis, and to the subsequent appropriation of the terms of that analysis, may not be a response to global capitalism at all.

Hardt and Negri's notion of an "incommunicable" political situation is also caught up in a different, though related, problem, to which I would now like very much to turn. Let us begin with *Empire*'s reading of Guy Debord's *Society of the Spectacle*. Hardt and Negri indicate that, for Debord, media spectacles and other aestheticisms lead to (1) the individualization, hence depoliticization of the social: people "partake" in social events without relating to others, as occurs when we watch a television program; and, paradoxically, (2) the production of a community, yet one whose "shared space" are the unreal or virtual images, usually distorted, false, and manipulative, which are projected on the "screen" and which both pass for reality and unite participants.[3]

We should note, however, that this "detached aestheticization" or "false representation," which Hardt and Negri oppose in the name of the urgent, bodily recalcitrance of the multitude, is the condition of *any* community or communal activism. No group is one, a "group," by nature. To be so, an organization must imagine itself as integrated. It must conceive, invent, or feel a common ground. The "workers" of a labor movement, as we noted earlier, do not "naturally" form an assemblage. They join together as a political force when they collectively project themselves solely as workers. Here, they sacrifice the complexity of their "true" identities (woman mother poor Hispanic straight worker, for example), "falsely" represent and communicate their being to others (and themselves), in and through a shared image or signifier ("the worker").

According to Hardt and Negri's reading of Debord, media spectacles suppress radical politics. No doubt. Yet aestheticism, as Rancière illustrates in *Disagreement* (see chapter 3), also makes possible the very activism, the very desire and feeling of "the multitude" that it squashes. Thus, just as the "total rejection" of ideology is the profession of the most rigid ideologue—and the erasure of a key condition of politics—so the negation of the aesthetic in the name of the productions of a multitude is potentially the root of a most thorough aestheticism. Indeed, the denial presents as unmediated—"incommunicable"—outside representation and language, practices that are necessarily established, precisely, through spectacle, image, and the signifier, now disavowed and subsumed into the authentic. Aestheticism is, in fact, exactly this: not "too much" artifice but "no artifice," artifice's disavowal. The assumption of a real without artifice is the subsumption of artifice into the real. Thus, for Benjamin, to state matters more directly and harshly, the push for a politics beyond the distortions and "nonreality" of the field of representation—however problematic that field may be—is also the drive of fascism.[4] Representation may be insidious; but its end is equally so.

In brief, one could contest Hardt and Negri's claim about oppositional activities that originate and proceed without recurring to the aesthetic. After all, is not the movement of a "bodily" multitude without a name or "in the name of" the very formula for the most aestheticized political models, above all certain types of populism? I certainly do not want to label Hardt and Negri "right-wing." That would deny the very real leftist promise of *Empire*'s antiempire politics: such a leftism may well be emerging, precisely as Hardt and Negri sketch it. Yet *Empire*'s theoretical model, no doubt unintentionally, outlines the structure of a "new revolutionary Right" as much as it does that of a "new revolutionary Left." And it does so, to repeat, largely due to its treatment of aesthetics.

Not unlike the consensual universe (albeit with different intentions) we have been discussing, *Empire* indeed espouses an "it goes without saying." It seeks to stand, not as another discourse, but as an essay on a new world of action without discourse. The situation is not simply, then, that *Empire*'s call for multitudinous creations that lie outside aesthetics may be indistinguishable from the mob's emotionalism, from the multitude's emergence as the ground for the complete aestheticism of the political. The case is also that *Empire* appears to tender the idea of a pure political creativity, of the *construction* of a political body that emerges from itself, from its own nature.

Hardt and Negri would like to divide the politics of identity from the politics of "the multitude." The latter forms because the participants possess less a common identity than a common concern. Transnational migration, general dispersion, and mechanisms such as the Internet yield groups who do not share a history, land, language, ethnicity, or religion—almost none of the components of the traditional nation or identity—but who cross borders in order to rally politically. Certainly, any actual "multitude" might assume the status of a collective subject, of an identity, after it gathers. But identity is neither the origin nor the cause of the collective. The event is. (In Chiapas, the event was NAFTA, which yielded a rally not only on the part of the Mexican Mayans but of a whole global field).

Yet, as we have just seen indirectly through our discussion of aestheticism, this partition between identity politics and multitude is impossible to draw. Groups cannot, in reality, form around political urgencies rather than pregiven identities. The classification of the "situation" as an "event," as "political," and as "urgent" results from a shared set of values, a certain view of history, an identification with previous groups/gatherings and, in short, a common consciousness (this consciousness, in fact, is the one component of the traditional nation that the multitude must retain).

A transnational rally (in which the demonstrators share no obvious common identity) on the part of a "multitude" against, say, Israeli mistreatment of Palestinians is not grounded in the gravity of that treatment, however severe and horrific it may be. Nor does it emerge from a particular, fierce "event" or episode in the Middle East. In fact, violent conduct by states, "events" of oppression, occur around the globe and almost around the clock; few make the news, much less lead to demonstrations. If people are *particularly* concerned with the plight of stateless Middle Eastern populations who endure enormous suffering due to despotic political apparatuses, then protest on behalf of Palestinians could well be warranted—but no more so than protest on behalf of the Kurds in Turkey. Why the political response to *this* event (Israeli mistreatment of Palestinians) rather than to *that* one (ongoing persecution of Kurds)? In fact, the rally for the Palestinian cause necessarily emerges from certain identifications on the part of the demonstrators, to a mutual consciousness of *something*—not a consciousness that declares that some event merits protest but one that indirectly or directly pronounces the event as an event—a "something" produced by the media, images, aestheticism, and so on. The event is an event, the demonstration happens and works, *because* it is spectacular. These events arise due to the very publication or representation that they—as singular events—may well seem to resist.

To state these ideas in a different way, Hardt and Negri's model takes the topos of Revolution (the big revolution, the Communist or the bourgeois revolution) and remolds it for the idea of microrevolts. (Their "empire," from the standpoint of Rancière's analytic, would include no politics but solely an "order of domination and the disorder of revolt.") They seem to oppose the conviction, shared by thinkers as diverse as Foucault and Baudrillard, that because the revolution of the Left is no longer distinguishable from that of the Right, revolution itself is over: "Thirty years of experiences," Foucault explains, "lead us 'to have trust in no revolution' even if one can 'understand each revolt.' So what effect can such a conclusion have for a people—and a Left—who only loved 'the later and more distant revolution' so much undoubtedly because of a deep, immediate conservatism? For fear of complete paralysis, one must tear oneself away from conservatism as one renounces the empty shell of a universal revolution."[5] Or, as Baudrillard concludes: "But in the end the Revolution signifies only this: that it has already taken place and that it had a meaning just before, one day before, but not anymore now. When it comes, it is to hide the fact that it is no longer meaningful. In fact the revolution has already taken place. Neither the bourgeois revolution nor the communist revolution: just the revolution. This means that the entire cycle is ending, and they have not even noticed it."[6]

Hardt and Negri contend that Revolution (or microrevolution) "happens" rather than surfaces through organization (one can plan for a revolution, but one cannot "make" it happen; the actual breakout of revolt usually results from an event that could not have been predicted). Revolution is thus the disruption that appears *between* two orders: the existing order of identity/territory/politics; and the new order that might follow from the revolt. Revolution itself is without rule because between rules, so it seems.

Although a milestone such as the Iranian Revolution may indeed appear as the suspension between two sets of regulation—as the radical disobedience that exploded between distinct administrations: that of the pro-Western Shah and that of the anti-Western Khomeini—it does so only as a repetition of other revolutions: the French, the British, the Russian, the Cuban, the Haitian. In the absence of the signifier and concept "revolution" (or its Farsi translation), not only could the Iranian Revolution not be understood as revolution; it could not have occurred precisely as it did since the call to the convention of revolution, the deployment of this signifier "revolution," preparation "in the name of revolution," was fundamental to the occurrence. This is especially true for the Iranian students, indeed, for Khomeini himself, who—from large foreign metropoles, such as Paris—spearheaded the happening throughout the 1960s and early 1970s. The signifier "Revolution" was as foundational to the events of 1978 and 1979—the events as such, not knowledge, reading, or understanding of them—as Khomeini's entrance into Tehran, or the Shah's departure.[7]

I do not mean to suggest, with this analysis of the Iranian Revolution, that all revolutions are the same, or that all are "Western." I mean only to indicate that, without standing as a repetition of other like events, a given revolution is implausible. The suspension of convention, the cessation between rules, is itself conventional, already part of a regulation, a habitus, a system of signs, images and, in short, aesthetics. A revolution does not happen, and then yield to the protocols that "force" it to take its place within an intellectual and political order. The order/ritual is already the condition of the disruption. Upheaval can upset an order but not order itself. Now, in the market, "upheaval" is itself an order, a value. Thus what holds for Revolution holds also for Hardt and Negri's modification, the microrevolts of the multitude, which do not arise as disturbances between territories, but as themselves territories.

So that readers might grasp these points more firmly, I want to introduce the notion of *preparation*. After Heidegger, Lacan has perhaps taken this idea as far as anyone. Consider the analytic situation. Nothing that emerges during meetings between therapist and patient is objectively "an event," an interruption in the "comfort zone" of either person, an "encounter with the Real." At a given moment, however, there often *is* an experience: something *is* disclosed. Exposed to the revelation, the subject adjusts his or her very being, takes account for and endures *this*, the materialization of the repressed: not the Real as that which hurts but the Real as encounter.

The precise nature of the Lacanian process will be outlined in the conclusion to this study. What is important to register here is that this Lacanian encounter does not happen "by accident," as I believe it does for, say, Alain Badiou.[8] The repeated and seemingly "pointless" dialogues between analyst and analysand, in which nothing seems to occur, are the preparation that allows the subject to encounter a realization and realize encounter.

One might think here of the scholar's "chance" discovery in the library of "just the right book" while glancing casually through the stacks. The scholar makes this find, even if not consciously looking for such a book, not "by mistake," but only because the scholar is prepared to "see" it (many times before, the person has glanced at the book, but never "seen" it). Preparation renders the event, the "break," conceivable.

True, an encounter such as this cannot be planned. Yet, as discussed in chapter 5, without preparation, and thus without the designs, conventions, and concepts that subsume a priori the happening as happening, no meeting can take place. Yes, yes, the event may have the suddenness of a surprise; yet absent preparation, one misses the surprise, cannot apprehend it. (A "pure event," in fact, can logically emerge solely as a *trauma* that is immediately disavowed in an act of self-preservation, growing traumatic precisely due to this refusal—either as pure event or as simple accident.)

However courageous, Rosa Parks neither "starts" nor "generates" the Civil Rights movement through the *event* for which she is famous. The movement surfaces because people are prepared for it. They react (and Parks herself reacts) to the Rosa Park incident, turning it into an *event*, due to that preparation, due to concepts and identities already in place.

The multitude should perhaps be affirmed in this fashion. The intervention of the multitude does not offer a "counter" to capitalism, an "other politics," another way. The gatherings, however, represent preparation for the event to come, the creation of people and associations who remain open to an "affair" that is not guaranteed to arrive but, insofar as the potential is kept open by the gathering itself, could occur.

But if empire and multitude, preparation and accident, commodification and event, identity and exigency, aesthetics and living labor are bound, if they coincide in time and in space, wherein lies their distinction? Why would one say, about any particular transnational episode, that it indexes multitude and not empire?[9]

Seemingly aware that this question haunts their inquiry, Hardt and Negri insist that the difference between Left and Right, multitude and empire, is not given by empire itself. They emphasize neither the fresh horrors nor the vast possibilities of empire. Instead, they demonstrate how the former (despotic transnational identitarian claims in the name of a nation beyond the state by, say, religious groups such as Christian or Islamic fundamentalists) is not conceivable without the emergence of the latter (a multitude whose origin is the exigency of the situation). Empire, for the authors of *Empire*, is *logically* neither of the Left nor of the Right but could be the site for either. The difference lies in the choice of action on the part of the citizen-consumer-actor. Leftism—the choice for the multitude over identity—is a matter of character, charisma, courage. Empire opens a new transnational Left and a new international Right: the one that materializes in a given situation depends on the valor of the actor-subjects.

I have tried to counter this position by suggesting that, within the market, the neoliberal Right (identity, aesthetics, the subject of free choice, and so on) has already co-opted the Left. This does not mean that there is no such Left; it means that the Left is not a choice. Stated differently, it means that Left *is* Right, multitude *is* empire, market *is* state, control *is* discipline, event *is* the signifier. If you pick the first, you pick the second, for the two are attached. Empire and multitude are not one but are bound by the "is" that simultaneously merges and separates them, renders them the Same and maintains their difference.

The being of our time, in fact, is this "is" that at once reduces the multitude to empire (multitude equals/is empire), makes one of two, homogeneity of multiplicity through the duopoly; and splits them (multitude *is* empire: the "is" keeps multitude from empire, serves as the boundary between the two), makes two of one. "Is" ("multitude is empire") is a part of the whole, one among others; and the "between" (multitude *is* empire), the *inter esse*, that is no part. The being of our epoch must be thought along these lines, as Rancière illustrates: neither as the whole nor the part nor the between but their sum, the equal sign. Being belongs to control society as an addition to that managed site; and is no portion but the uncounted figure which renders each such division conceivable. *Empire*, a text that in addressing the global maintains a certain distance from most ontological questions, opens up the demand for an ontological inquiry, an inquiry into the globe's being, precisely because the foundation of the divisions the book banks on— between empire and multitude, aestheticism and activism, state and global, discipline and control, territorialization and deterritorialization—is the copula, the "and" that is an "is." For if the "and" is not an "is," it is simply the tool of a bad infinity that utilizes "and" and "and" and "and," without thought of "and" as finitude, copula and being. Indeed, the ontological base of the *Empire* model may well be neither control nor discipline, market nor state, but the divide, the *transition* between the two: either the binary that attaches itself to control society or the finitude that exposes that control to its outside.

Certainly, *Empire* does not claim to address complex philosophical matters. Its focus is instead experience and action. It moves away from the mind and toward the body. Yet because the work reveals, despite itself, that the state *is* the global, multitude *is* empire, it ultimately illustrates also that its politics cannot avoid the question of ontology. One cannot choose acting over thinking because the hinge, the "over," the linkage of the two, demands this thought, *is* that call.

It would appear that the authors, having rapidly read the history of Being (*Empire* reflects that reading), including and especially deconstruction as one account of that history, decided that it was an inadequate story. The narrative of Being, for these authors, calls for politics. They are right. Being calls for politics; politics does *not* call for *itself*. Indeed, if politics, ultimately, does not need thought (is this not what the rally of the multitude really is: politics without intellectualism?), then the *reason* for a politics, the demand for politics, cannot *but* be thought.

Either we think through this "is" that binds and bounds multitude to empire; or we ignore the bond, in which case we set up the binaries that sustain choice, support the association of selection, freedom, and subjectivity, and thus help produce and reproduce the notion of the market as liberating, ideal, perfect, and total.

By positioning empire and multitude, identity and deterritorialization, action and intellectualism as two poles of globalization, Hardt and Negri point a way out from neoliberalism. Leftism, for them, remains a choice, a political solution for those with the moral fiber to choose it. And this is what spectacularly excites, rallies: leftism as a selection.

Deconstruction, soberly, can no longer offer this spectacular possibility (is that not what the "death of deconstruction" means: deconstruction has lost its luster, has ceased to be spectacular? And is this luster not what those who speak in deconstruction's name work to restore?), the excitement of a solution, or of politics *as* solution. It can only index the condition of such a leftism: the naming that does not remove leftism itself, but does remove it *from the range of choices*. In other words, deconstruction's "answer" to neoliberalism cannot avoid reconstituting the very structures to which it responds. The difference between Left and Right *is*; but it is not a choice. The "is," indeed, is not simply one of the alternatives; nor is it the alternative of the nonalternative since, as part (that is no part), it cannot *not* be chosen. You cannot opt out of empire through activism, for the choice of "activism" is the choice of choice, hence of the neoliberal consensus.

We might indeed propose that a contemporary Left that chooses deconstruction as an enemy does so because it cannot do otherwise.

The aporia of deconstruction—the copula that, dividing and uniting, makes groups of choices and thus subjects and even deconstruction itself possible—is no longer a choice. It comes into intellectual models of the world, as a part of that world, whether you want it or not.

The "is" binds and frees, manages and de-limits. Yes, it limits, imprisons, by collapsing differences. It posits the world as a totality and history as a completed process, at its end—yet this end, such as the end of the political, the end of history, and the end of the state, emerges as one element within the totality. But the same end or limit, this boundary on possibility, is precisely what prepares for possibility itself: the "is" is also an "and" that opens up. It releases the Same to the Other. At once and distinctly: being as boundary imprisons us within the impossible limit imposed by state and market, and exposes us to the limit that is our possibility. This finitude of state *and* market, this "and" or "language" that comes between the two, is the condition of free choice ("You can have this *and* that: choose!") and one of those choices. It plays to the neoliberalism that subsumes all limits, thereby all exteriors, within the logic of a bad infinity. But the "and" as "is" is also the "more," the promise of an outside that every perimeter, every "is," embodies.

This (im)possibility of being is the heart of deconstruction. It may or may not, in the end, *be* political.

11.

Biopolitics/Foucault II
Statements on the New Media

Like many before him, Foucault draws a strong connection between language and death. Indeed, in his early work, he describes the aversion of discourse in almost the same terms he later uses to posit the biopolitical "ban" on death (see chapter 2): "I am supposing that in every society the production of discourse is at once controlled, selected, organized and redistributed according to a certain number of procedures, *whose role is to avert its powers and its dangers. . . .*"[1]

What I have been calling "language" or "saying"—language that presents a "danger" to consensus—Foucault calls "statement," for him, the smallest unit of analysis, the site for the commencement of an investigation. The statement is neither a sign or group of signs nor the reality to which the signs refer: "the state anterior to discourse."[2] It is neither a word nor a thing. "'Words and

things,'" Foucault says in reference to his book of that name, "is
. . . the ironic title of a work that modifies its own form, displaces its
own data, and reveals, at the end of the day, a *quite different
task*."[3] Moreover, the "statement" is neither visible (empirically
given) nor invisible (the truth beneath the signifier).[4] Instead, statements mark out the connections and relays, the continuity and
discontinuity between signs and among themselves.

Foucault rejects the provinces of words and things, the hidden
and revealed, the signified and signifier as being akin to disciplinary
sites. A chain of signifiers (even *one* signifier) is, in actuality, a
group of institutions (within larger institutions) in which an utterance
must fall if it is to be deemed meaningful, reasonable, truthful, normal. The field of the signifier *controls* statements. It is the domain
of power that subsumes the *relation* of signs, appropriating the
statement as both the "between" and as the "irreducible-to" the
field of every sign.

The statement is, at least potentially, a happening. For example,
within a narrative of world history the storming of the Bastille as
statement shifts accounts of events both that precede and that follow it (such accounts are analyzed from the vantage point of, hence
are altered by, this 1789 episode). Thus the happening is so, not
because of any intrinsic quality—say, the intensity of the event or
the "objective" import of the declaration—but because it surfaces
as a "dispatch point" in a given chronicle, reshaping past and
future (the event does not happen once but continues happening
after—and *before*—that "once"). Yet it also fashions the present.
The statement cannot be "contextualized": it is not a sign we can
understand from the reality around it, for it helps create the "present," the now, in which it falls.

One might think of the series "2, 4, 6, 8, 10." If we continue "2,
4, 6, 8, 10, *12*," the "*12*" does not index a statement, for it does
not alter the order, progression, or logic of the series. Indeed, it is
nothing but the sign of the order's endless reproducibility, and thus

nothing in itself. If, however, we proceed as "2, 4, 6, 8, 10, *11*," the "11" indeed functions as an event. It forces us to recognize that the "past" (before the appearance of the "11") of the sequence or "discourse" was not constructed "by twos" but in some other manner that opens the demand for an investigation (assuming, of course, that this matter is a given subject's concern). This inserted number also transforms the future of the series/discourse, which (apparently) can no longer commence with 12 (as the sequence "2, 4, 6, 8, 10" would command). The "11" as statement thereby produces its "history," its aftermath, and the series itself: it does not slip into a context but builds one. (Conversely, if, in our research, we determine the sequence to have been "2, 4, 6, 8, 10, 11, 12, 14, 16, 18, 19 . . . ," the "11" ceases to stand as a statement; a novel statement must be located for exploration to recommence.)

The statement *happens* because it stretches back and lunges forward, simultaneously sketching out its here and now. It is, in essence, the condition of possibility of its own repeatability across time and space. It thereby exposes, among numerous other matters, a "same" that is different from itself: the alterations of a single utterance or episode, and the impact of those alterations upon other bodies. "History" is an effect of the statement, just as the statement is an effect of history, even though the tracing of these spiraling effects cannot be performed by any historiographical project. It demands what Foucault labels "archaeology."

But why, again, does Foucault suppose that language (statements and discourses) is "controlled, selected, organized and redistributed" by every society or site of power "according to a certain number of procedures, *whose role is to avert its powers and its dangers*"? Why would power concern itself with the "statement" at all? Is the statement delinquent? A "minority"? A biological menace? In fact, the statement is the boundary on the "it the goes without *stating*," on the norms, discourses, and disciplines that expose the life of the subject (subject as species) to the limit where things cross over: to contamination, hence to risk, illness, and death.

The dream of consensual postdemocracy or neoliberal consensus, I have insisted, is to exist as the absolute nature and essence of humanity. The desire of such a consensus is to stand in no need of a statement, no need of putting forth a reason for its right, for its profession on the way of the world. The consensus, like the market, is because it is, exterior to any reason.

But do such theses really explain anything about *today*? To respond, let us weigh three related issues: the news media, ideology, and consciousness raising. In his examination of Debord's *Society of the Spectacle*, Agamben offers a model for analyzing the role of the media in our discussion of biopolitics.[5] We will discuss Agamben's precise treatment of Debord below; for now, I want to highlight the connection that Agamben draws between the loss of language as the loss of what is common to man, on the one hand; and as a manifestation of the society of the spectacle, on the other.

Consider, first, the still prevalent view of ideology: ideology as false consciousness, which counts on the metaphor of roundness. State and globe are posited as spheres (public and private *spheres*), as ideology presupposes an outer layer, represented by signs, images, spectacles, and an inner core, holding truths, secrets, or material reality. In theory, and working through concealment, the exterior portion induces the "population" to accept as necessary and factual a given set of ideas. The populace mistakes the part for the whole, fiction for reality, beliefs for facts, and the culturally constructed for the natural. This enforced view can therefore be easily dismantled, uncovered by methods such as critique, subversive art, labors of negativity, and activism. It can be shown to be a fiction, perspective, act of faith, or construction because that, in fact, *is what it is*. The ideal outcome of such a discovery is the public's—or, if one prefers a more Marxist paradigm, the proletariat's—consciousness raising: its potential politicization.

Consciousness raising avers the *right* to the hidden truths, actualities, facts, and, most important, the subjects that are freed when unburied from beneath the false convictions that domains such as the media generate. It thereby reveals the "true" reason behind the market and its media, the truth of the dominant ideology itself: its desire to maintain current power relations. Indeed, according to the media's presentation, this world could not maintain itself—it would simply fall apart—without these same relations.

The paradox, however, at least for advocates of consciousness raising, is that the market, the media themselves—above all, new outlets such as cable news—make possible this very consciousness raising. Needing to "fill" twenty-four hours, cable news is quite willing to lay bare its own equivocations, depicting, in show after show, the precise nature of its lies and deviations. Thus, far from undoing media exhibitions, the raising of consciousness today emerges as a competing "exhibition," both an alternative media view and an alternative view of the media. Hence it sells: appending life (the oppressed subject, who had existed unseen below ideology's obfuscations, has now been retrieved and *revived*) to life (the subjects in power who produce this consciousness), consciousness raising permits consumers to select between the two, therefore to choose *themselves* as living occupants of and within the species.

In other words, consciousness raising and false consciousness create the duopoly that represents the right of the subject-consumer. The truth that media prevarications stage lies neither in misrepresentation nor in its "de-subjugated" beneath but in a "democratic I" that is simulated by the competition between the "duped" and the "enlightened" (a competition between the two, in which any subject, liberal or conservative, left- or right-wing, might occupy either side).

Facts, in this consciousness-raising scene, may come to light. But they no longer matter. If present before us, they are insignificant since they do not sway public opinion (the media enjoy sway, no question; but not because they impart facts or lies). Why, indeed, should the truth or the facts impact my political decisions/convictions more strongly than do my own personal beliefs? Why should I appeal to dogma over *doxa*? Are not my values and convictions right even if one particular fact—the *media*'s fact—*seems* to undercut them? Do I not *know* what I *believe*?

We noted earlier that, within Foucault's disciplinary society, one need only gain knowledge in a single area to pass as the expert; and that this expert is the one who differentiates the true from the false. Yet everyone can claim expertise in something. Therefore, theoretically, all can express "relatively well," "more or less truly" their views of the whole: all can state the "whole truth." If knowledge is partial, why should my partialities be any less "expert," any less valid "on the whole" than those articulated by people of greater learning or in possession of more "facts"?

Stated differently, the case is not that the facts are now one set of opinions among others, as the relativist might contend. This relativist position, indeed, only reiterates the assumptions behind the narrative of false consciousness: once one can show that the media's truths are actually biased opinions, one has dismantled their power, hence exercised self-determination—and relativists need not offer an alternative, nonrelative truth because they always already have one, to wit: themselves. The case, instead, is that the experts as consumers find their free or true selves, which precede and thus are unaffected by the media's falseness/truth, through one news perspective or another, one medium or another, *or*—and this is the key—through a truth/perspective, fact/conviction binary.

Stated differently, the interplay of false consciousness and consciousness raising yields wars between words and things, words and words, or things and things, but all without death—war materializes as a technique, an instrument of regulation, and a lure— since what these struggles actually produce is the transcendence of the consumer. And herein lies the spectacle's attraction: it relieves the public from the risks—at times, the deadly risks—of any particular decision since decision itself assures every I its spot, the *same* spot. In the battle between deciders (we report, you decide), no party can lose.

The Foucaultian model of archaeology would nonetheless seem to preclude these nonfatal or simulated scuffles. It presents the world as an interaction of surfaces. Across these planes, the statement is the smallest unit. A field or collection of statements yields the next smallest unit: a *discourse*. And the accumulation of discourses makes up the third or largest component: the *archive*. Like a palimpsest, collage, or a folded object (drapes, for example), these planes exist as a volume of surface displays, as a mounting of monitors that, though not flat, contain no underneath. A thick or thin accumulation of surfaces, the Foucaultian archive contains no "lower" secret, reality, truth, subject, voice, void, or absence. The entire field is public; but rather than a public sphere, it is the intersection and accumulation of public screens.

Thus, in the news media (if we grasp them through Foucault's paradigm), not only are multiple truths and competing facts exposed (rather than hidden or viewed) upon these planes and relations of planes. They are so over and over. Like the same news story that one watches time and again, either from this and that perspective or from the same perspective, the surfaces offer no hidden realm to discover—no "news"—but solely the overexposure of the already known. Too full of images, of life, or real life (reality TV), the exhibition is thereby difficult to read or decipher. In essence, the ceaseless disclosure of truth and reality marks the limit of that very disclosure or openness, of that spectacular repetition, through *over*exposure.

This overfull overshow is in fact striking: on CNN, one perceives the spoken story, a caption summarizing the "talking points" of that narrative, the picture, *another* image in the right-hand corner about a *different* issue, some music, a ticker tape describing all the events of the day, the Dow Jones, NASDAQ, Standard and Poor's, and Nikkei averages, and the CNN logo. And these materialize simultaneously, without cessation. They show or hide nothing; but, in their overabundance, overdisplay, and discontinuity, they demand readings. What is the relationship between a bomb falling in Baghdad and the rapid rise of the Dow Jones average? I *see* the connection as I gaze at the screen; it is a direct diagonal line about twelve inches long that extends from the top left (where I note the bomb) to the bottom right (where the Dow numbers appear) of the TV. But the seeing offers me almost no hint as to how to analyze the relation, how to make or derive a statement about it.

For, no matter how emphatic or repetitive, the too much information that supports A *and* B, the too many polls and statistics cannot mandate the reception, the reading, or the effect of that presentation. Yet control of such reception is necessary if the monitor is actually to monitor the population. The screen normalizes and "dulls" only when consumed. But, given the complexity of the signs that crisscross it, the volume of exhibitions cannot guarantee that the signs *will* be consumed: that they will *not*, instead, be *read* or *stated*.

What, specifically, is to be read? One deciphers, obviously, the crossroads that are not themselves either signs or information but overaccumulation (the rising Dow *with* the falling bomb) as irreducible to the sign. One reads *statements* as the hovering between and among meaning.

The media, I should therefore add, do not generate consensus by "forcing" us to forget or look past the atrocious realities, above all, the history behind those realities which they either display or hide. Consensus production and memory loss do not form a unit (as the narrative of false consciousness would have us believe). Neoliberal consensus in fact often obstructs forgetting; it demands a *certain* recall. Indeed, it deploys this nonforgetting as a consensus tool, an instrument ("Do not forget September 11!"

"Do not forget Pinochet—who, do not forget, overthrew Allende *also* on September 11—Saddam, or how America helped the French in World War II!")

In point of fact, the blur generated both by overexposure of the single event and by the speed of movement from one story to the next, across one plane and through the next, leads the viewer not to "forget" historical or actual episodes, but instead to cast the continuity and discontinuity *between* episodes and images off-scene, as obscene. It is the connection/disconnection between images, the edge, border, or finitude of the image, death itself, that the media atrocity pushes aside. What Foucault labels "bourgeois antihistoricism"[6] is not ignorance of the past but the overpresentation and subsequent overlooking of the division between pasts and presents, of the bonds that allow for history's revelation. Overexposure *strips* (as one strips a screw by overtwisting it) the relations between narratives: it strips the statement. Indeed, it *is* that stripping.

The stripping is indeed obscene. Either one reads it, making the news media, because overexposure is their tactic, a privileged site for the translation of the limit of consensus and, therefore, for the preservation or invention of the links that produce history.[7] Or else one is blinded by the disrobing, in which case the obscenity goes unremarked, death unnoticed, and the consensus without saying. Obscenity is the reality that, insisting on being read rather than consumed, resists commodification and precludes the advent of a totally simulated world. But it is also the product by means of which consumers realize themselves, filling out the society of the spectacle.

The very overexposure that *might* operate like a statement, as limit and interruption, might also stultify through repetition the senses, naturalizing the obscenity (hence leaving nothing ob-scene as "exhibition limit" to scrutinize, nothing "to the side," as the obscenity now passes before us as nature). Bare before us in the form of a continuum of spectacles upon a surface, history is thoroughly consumed as an outer layer with a truer beneath: as consensual seduction and as the seduction of consensus. Or to use the language of Zizek: we know very well that there is no secret truth behind cable news. But we watch awaiting the revelation of that secret anyway, for we believe: not in the media, but in our subject position, sustained by the conviction that the TV is hiding something, that the scene before us is untrue and that we, because stronger than any representation, because subjects, are ourselves the missing viewpoint that will locate the concealed information. We are not *before* but *in* the spectacle as the single perspective that, when added to all the others, completes the scene that, we *suppose*, is minus the one truth it nonetheless promises: us.

Biopolitics, spectacle, and language merge one last time. Let us return to Agamben, who, as I suggested before, labels the linguistic and communicative nature of human beings "the Common": "The extreme form of expropriation of the Common is the spectacle, in other words, the politics in which we live. But this also means that what we encounter in the spectacle is our very linguistic nature inverted." And although the "expropriation of the possibility of a common good" is a "violence [that] is so destructive," this "alienation," or the separation of the Common as language from the social, is also a "positive possibility." Such an affirmation can be asserted even though "language no longer reveals anything at all."[8]

First, let me reiterate that Foucault's "statement" is a name for precisely the "language" from which, according to Agamben, the "society of the spectacle" has been alienated. The statement does not reproduce history as it took place. It *reveals* history; it brings into being the links between and among times, altering past and present. Because of the statement, what was never before now is (or was) for the *first* time. And if language as the statement is not reproductive or representative—only representation is representative—but revelatory, as Agamben argues, it is so as the Common, the shared site, the division between any two that is a portion of all, but that is the belonging of no one or no time. When the Common is *stated*, when an *énoncé* takes place, language and thus history occur.

Within cable news media, overexposure of the Same can function as this revelation. The very repetitions that the viewer consumes as differences that yield choices, thus as vehicles of subjectivity, self-determination, and freedom, also—as overexposure—stand as the performances of the finitude of the media's force. If the spectacle is defined as our separation from language/death, the share of us all, it also names the potential encounter with that very separation, with that very commonness or everydayness (for what is more everyday than the spectacle?). Indeed, our severance from language can be the experience of that disconnection: of language as separation (as what is most separate), as finitude and border, and thus as the "common allotment" that opens to the possibility and promise—opens to a politics to come—which the society of the spectacle seems to appropriate in advance. This is why Agamben insists that the "fully realized nihilism"[9] of the spectacle sustains within it a "positive possibility." When language breaks off and begins to form its own proper or "real" domain, as occurs in the spectacle, we *can* experience—through the overexposure upon which the spectacle counts—precisely this break: division as the Common (communicability as what binds us all, "comes between" us consumers) that is essential to our coming-into-being.

Heidegger illustrated the connection between metaphysics, technology, and information.[10] He viewed the reduction of thought to information gathering—or to the promulgation of data that are already always available (that require, for their processing, not thought but only the tools or technologies that might retrieve them)—as a sign of the slippage of *technē* into technology, of creation and *poiēsis* into enframing, thinking into publicity. Heidegger's assessment of modernity, as much an affirmation as a critique, lies here. Foucault pursues both Heidegger's critique and his affirmation, although rarely in Heidegger's name. Like Heidegger, he resists any facile review of information technology, and of aesthetics in general. For Foucault, the publication and iteration of false representations through the media are not responsible for the West's homogeneity, for our "consensual postdemocracy." Although the broadcasting of spurious images, figures, and statistics certainly functions as an instrument for consensus production, such broadcasts (for reasons discussed above) cannot completely persuade the public, hence cannot be held responsible for the depoliticized accord that ensues. Indeed, the repetition of information, and the subsequent formation of a contingent field of copies, replications, and *over*exposure, unleashes also the finitude, the death drive, that the media can communicate but not control. More specifically, novel information technology cannot help but introduce corrupt data into its representations, data that, like or as a computer virus, menace the well-being of the very consensual postdemocracy that this technology labors both to sell and to support. In short, information technology breeds statements, "pure" or unanalyzed information (such as bad DNA), living facts that resist their proper place in the market, that simultaneously refuse and demand reading, and that—as finitude or frontier—open technology to the possibility that technology itself, the media themselves institute but cannot manage.

For Foucault, information and information technology produce the possibilities of radical statements and radical thought that technology may subsume in advance, but cannot subsume without also leaving behind a trace. True, this vestige—product and vehicle of the death drive—presents or represents a terrible scenario. It tempts and lures us to perform the worst act of biopolitics—the displacement of bare life onto actual peoples, now cast as incarnations of a virulent and disposable humanity. But the "statement" as unread mark, as border of and boundary on technology's force, also exposes modernity to its alternative, or at least holds the place of that alternative. Promising the advent of this alternative, it is promise itself.

The "distancing" of humanity from language (yet language is not at a distance; it is common, everyday, most near, *and* inaccessible), the overexposure of the ex-property that makes community possible, is also humanity's "linguistic nature inverted." As language materializes as its own realm, beyond every human property, it becomes—like any transcendental domain—the ideal with which humanity identifies. The condition of language's emergence as the "secret share" (language's appearance as the cut of man from man) is also the condition of language's disappearance into *marketable* information: of the end of the end and of the Common, the death of the enemy and of the friend, of death in general.

This radical alienation, then, takes place not because we each lose touch with one of our possessions: language. Alienation, as Marx well new, means just the opposite: not expropriation but appropriation, the making proper(ty). The individual appropriates the Common (Marx called it "humanity," Laclau calls it "the people," Heidegger calls it "language"), which belongs to no one, as the individual's ownmost property. The Common reemerges, in the realm of spectacle, as a private domain. Thus the limit, the exposure of the individual to the other as the requisite of both communication and politics, turns into the limitless extension of the subject's territory. The subject (collective or not) cannot be in-common with the other for there is no other with whom to be in common. Subjects are common, communal, with themselves only: themselves as what is privative within the public. There are subjects, yet no others. Individuals are alienated—not, for Marx, from themselves but their humanity.

Thus the "society of the spectacle" not only leads consumers to mistake fiction for reality and pushes them into private or apolitical spaces (such as the television room), where "reality" now resides (in the transcendental individual/collective, entirely set off from the public). It also accomplishes two other tasks. As overexposure (but not in the "old" sense of "showing the camera," behind the scene, hence as a means to the consciousness of the mechanisms of control, but in the sense outlined above), it reveals language or the "bad byte" as the excess of the duopoly between representation and mis-representation, subject A and subject B, and thus as the condition of possibility of a resistance within the market. Yet the spectacle is also the worldwide blunting of the senses and the subsumption of the Common into the common sense. It is the attempted destruction of information (exemplified by a corrupt computer byte) that demands reading, in favor of the (mis)information that represents subjects. A biopolitical performance, the spectacle too easily cures Being of its demise (neoliberalism names the cure), therefore of the forces of this termination: engagement and politics, which are impossible to practice—because there is nothing to do—if language, the stain of death, is not proper to the act.

A final comment: globalization names the appropriation of all time and space by consensual postdemocracy—if that comes. Certainly, then, virtuality designates the next and final field that globalization must assume (since, as I hope to have shown, it has not yet done so). Yet one should not therefore suppose that virtual real-ity is a new or contemporary invention, the product of novel com-munication technology. A real site producing real effects, one that nonetheless refuses—like the virtual—presentation, has always already existed: language. Indeed, the new media and other tech-nology only bring into (mere) appearance language as the virtuality that predates them, and is their condition. Baudrillard's concept of "simulation" is nothing but the elaboration of this fact. To be sure, technology and the virtual—and their cohort, commodification— are language's most potent contemporary carriers, much more so than are art, literature, or theory. They either operate as the frontier of globalization, as its outside or its exposure to an outside; or else they stamp the perfection of the market consensus. These, though, are not choices. We cannot choose technology since it has already been chosen for and by us. The question is whether we can read it, disclose the language that lies and works at its core and fringes—not as last resort but as last resistance.

Conclusion

The Frail Empire and the Commodity's Embrace

Let us begin this conclusion with Althusser's concept of "interpellation" or "hailing," which he in fact adapts from Lacan,[1] and which orients the third section of "Ideology and Ideological State Apparatuses: Notes towards an Investigation." Judith Butler centers her examination of the concept on an analysis of the rather comical "example from life" that Althusser offers: when the policeman calls out in the street, "Hey, you!" nine times out of ten the subject who is hailed turns around (and not only because the subject feels guilty). According to Butler, this means that the law and power, both embodied by the police, hail the subject into existence. And yet, because the injunction must be cited ("Hey, you!"), publicized, exposed, staged, it cannot *not* license, even legalize, its own potential displacement, deviance, or transgression.[2]

Butler's reading of interpellation recurs to a series of familiar Derrideanisms, which I will recite for the sake of clarity. If a mark (in writing) or a sound (in speech) is to form part of a language, it must be iterable. Therefore repetition, citation, and performance do not follow (from) a pregiven sign but are a condition of its possibility: a sign must be citable before it is a sign.

This means that deviance, miscitation, and the possible transformation or loss of meaning—any or all of which could occur in the course of a citation—belong essentially to speech acts and norms. The rituals that yield sense and conventions are the same iterations that undermine them. But this is true not only for speech. It holds as well for the law. The citing, execution, writing, and acknowledgment of the law, thereby the possibility of a given law's shift and even disappearance, pertain to the law's infrastructure. Hence—and this is Butler's point—the policeman's hail, in Althusser's example, cannot *not* produce the possibility of the law's own "legal" demise: an internal transgression that Althusser's theory of ideology, which holds (according to Butler) that the law always "gets you," cannot account for.[3]

The Althusserian policeman's "Hey, you!" is just an example, however. And like all examples, it does not quite coincide with the idea it is geared to illustrate. In fact, Althusser is a good enough Lacanian to know that no command, as such, ever fully hailed a subject into being. Subjectivity does not emerge as a response to ordinances but as the condition of both response and ordinance, namely, language.

To be sure, as already intimated, particular articulations exist. These hail one group rather than another, produce this rather than that identification. But in "Ideology and Ideological State Apparatuses," Althusser addresses, not the way in which individual people, persons, or collectives are interpellated, but the universal manner in which *all* are interpellated.

According to Lacan, the subject (which Althusser posits as the "ideological subject") comes into existence the moment the prelinguistic *infans* (the baby mass that has not yet distinguished itself from the world, is not an individual body or self) makes a demand—with a cry, a breath, a moan, a burp, a smile—on the primary caretaker.[4] The caretaker, by a logical necessity that we will trace, can respond (at best) only by offering an object of need (a hug, a breast, words, a bottle) rather than the desired entity: the caretaker falls short. The subject requires language (demand) to get what the subject wants. But because the meeting of the demand hinges on a reception by the other (who must guess/impose the signified or meaning, the *desire*, behind the cry, breath, moan, burp, smile), which no demand can dictate or regulate, language introduces "his majesty, the baby," to the limit of his powers: to himself as the not-All, as relative to others and, above all, as cut off from *the All* he desires.[5]

Why does this baby *never* receive the object of desire he demands? Because what he desires is to eliminate the separation between himself and the supplier-of-the-All so that he can get whatever he wants: without needing to ask. If the baby is All, if there is no distance between self and supplies, if acquisition does not hinge on the "undictatable" capacity and agency (the understanding) of an other, if the infant need not resort to this "tool" that never seems to get the job done just right (demand, language)—only then is the subject self-sufficient: a master without limits, and without others/ relations who could displace the subject. Thus the paradox: the immobile and "immature" *infans* *must* make demands, communicate to obtain All. But the communication or language *must* fail, *must* mark the limit of the subject since communication itself "produces" the very difference or gap—and the unfulfilled desire to fill it: the illusion of an All in the first place—between the receiver and giver, the closure of which is precisely what the demand *desires*.

It is demand or language, then, that exposes the *infans* to its sociality: to itself as a subject whose power and desire, because relative to other powers and desires (in the form, at the very least, of

the other's force of reception), is finite. And this double disclosure—
of the subject's own contingency/vulnerability *and* of the impact/
force of another—is exposure to castration as death.

The case is not that the demand's incapacity to reach the Other
intact (as the communication of a true desire) results from the
space/time that this message must travel. If this were so, time and
space would be abstractions, given prior to history or to the emergence of the *infans*. In fact, the subject produces time/space, hence
the subject's mortality and finitude rather than transcendence,
when the subject's demand is not met immediately: when it is clear
that sociality takes time, and that it divides the subject (spatially,
temporally) from the subject's self. Communication fails not
because language as materiality must travel through space and
time, frequently "losing" its way. The failure establishes space and
time as real material, as the very "stuff" of subjectivity. (Moreover,
because the subject disavows language as limit in order to take the
subject's place in the world, language is the original *forgotten* that
opens the subject to memory and history. The incessant passing of the
language/limit charges the subject with a disavowed past, but with a
past all the same, as the subject is released to a future time/space.)

Yet the limit does not necessarily represent a prohibition, as Butler
intimates. A border is as much an "opening to" as it is a "closure
from." Language, as Lacan defines it, indeed "impels" the subject
toward the subject's not-Allness. But it does not direct the subject to
"do" or "not do" this or that (we recall "Hey, you!" which is also
not a directive). "By itself," in fact, language offers or decrees no
direction. It only exposes the subject to the fact that there must
be *direction*. You must expose yourself, get out there, face the
Other-who-could-take-your-place, as a condition of growth; or else
you cease to develop, like a defective plant. Either you face death
or you avoid it—in which case you also face death.

Subjects must traverse the threshold, emerge into the social,
engage or refuse relations and their menace, if they are to exist.

Language (like the superego) does not simply say, "Stop!" It says, "Go!" which for Lacan is the root both of the subjects' fears and of their eros: the fact that there is no stop to relations, desire, the exposure-to-the-other. One is not self-determined and free, and then socially responsible. One is free (*if* one is free) through that enchainment or bind to sociality.

On the other hand, wanting more to be a subject than to be free, the subject seeks to transcend this sociality, as well as the linguistic imperative that locks selfhood to an outside force. Indeed, the yearning is played out the moment that the demand is misrecognized as a prohibitive statute rather than as the opening-to or contact-with the other.

This is so because legal injunctions indeed function as Butler indicates: they license their own subversion, although, as we have seen, such injunctions are just one of the many kinds of law, and cannot account for the law as such. By virtue of its own logic and structure, the police law is a "soft" law, open to rewriting, misuse, and (mis)interpretation. By miscasting the limit as this kind of edict, and by unconcealing or taking advantage of its structural weakness in order to displace it, the subject is able to stage the subject's mastery of the "despot," albeit through an imaginary process. The subject casts exposure and death (one limit) as police law (an entirely different, less unyielding sort of limitation). In other words, by enacting language qua exposure to the other as a legal injunction qua "vulnerable overlord," and then by defeating the overlord, the subject achieves absolute transcendence or sovereignty, freedom from exterior forces.

Here it helps to turn to the specificity of the policeman's "Hey, you!" In this example, "Hey!" functions as a nearly meaningless expression (in French, Althusser uses the expression: "Hé, vous là-bas!"). Directed to "you," the "Hey!" itself emits (from the standpoint of the "hailed one") from "out there": from no specific subject or place (after all, at the moment of interpellation

Althusser's subject cannot possibly know for sure whether it is the policeman or someone else who has hailed the subject, but has to *turn around* to meet the call. Yet the "direction" ("Hey!") is not a command for the "you" to do anything specific. It barely possesses any message at all. Indeed, the hailed one who, having heard the hail, turns around to "accept" it, does so by converting the "Hey!" into a meaningful signifier directed from a specific human "you" (another subject with whom the hailed one can dialogue, negotiate), this "you" into a "me," and the "me" into an "I," into the subject itself: "*I* am being called. I *am*!"

The "Hey!" we will soon see, is in Althusser's essay not the incarnation of the legal law, which cajoles the subject to enter the social properly, but of the law of "language as such." It is the limit of the subject that the *infans must* (it is, after all, the law: the law of desire) endure in order to materialize as subject. The I, confronted with this demand, humanizes the "Hey!" by turning it into the epiphenomenal representation of another human subject (for instance, the policeman). Converting language ("Hey!" as language's marker) into representation ("Hey!" as clear mandate), the I is then able to compete on equal ground, through an intersubjective battle (a battle that, because "merely" with another human, is winnable), with the limit of the I, now reposited as the other to be defeated. The *infans* is interpellated as it converts, not simply the "Hey!" or "language as such" into representation or part of an order (the Symbolic Order), but representation into self-representation, into an I.

Althusser's point, however, is that, in outdoing the "master" in this manner, the subject does not subvert ideology but precisely falls into its trap. Indeed, cast as police law qua soft law, "Hey!" is the lure that apprehends the subject for a field that assumes control precisely at that point where the police law surrenders it (where the police officer is outsmarted), namely, ideology itself. One slips from the police only to inscribe oneself freely into the source of the ideological state—not the power of law enforcement, but of the codes or norms (the Symbolic Order) that back the legal system, even and especially in its absence.

Let me get ahead of myself and state Althusser's argument all at once. The subject is interpellated, not by the police law, but by language as *mistaken* for the *representation* of that law. What happens? The first instance of language (the demand: "Hey!"), one "prior" to the self or to the person, hence to self-representation, exposes the subject to existence as a relation to the-Other-who-could-displace-the-subject. Yet the demand appears also as a kind of weak "coverup." As "mere language," or "next to nothing," it seduces the subject into misrecognizing the limit as a despot the subject nonetheless can conquer. Thus the subject stands as an independent individual with no necessary bounds, hence no necessary relations/relationality. In constructing and beating a straw sovereign, the subject emerges as absolute, nonrelational.

And this, according to Althusser, is the *general* way in which the "relations of production," all the structures of capitalism, ultimately reproduce themselves. They do so, not through work or the ideological state apparatuses, but through the ideal of the individual subject because the subject qua private individual emerges in capitalism as the teleology of Being (thus Althusser's essay names the "individual," a word that the author places in quotation marks, as the subject's "lost ideal"). The subject enters into the social order, as individual, by mastering, or by imagining freedom from the subject's enchainment to the other. Public but asocial, the subject is "in the public," but not beholden to any exterior being, hence to any engagement or politics: any that might disrupt ideology. Publicness and sociality split. The public I is the I of publicity, divorced from any *necessary* obligation to society as such.

Stated in different terms, this subject relates to nobody but the subject. To be sure, this "relation" is mediated: by "the boss," the capitalist, the state, or by so-called dominant or normative discourses, which, indeed, often *appear* to the subject as sovereigns. However, precisely because this "boss" surfaces as an appearance, a mirror, a mere representation, the subject can deploy this appearance, mirror, representation as a means to displace that boss. The worker interacts with the boss/police as the "measly" image of sovereignty, thus surmounting this "weak" tyrant so as to assume the place of the master in the master/slave dialectic. And in this manner, the worker maintains rather than disrupts the relations of production, the capitalist/worker (master/slave) division, assuming the realm of the capitalist in the binary.

The subject identifies with, or finds subjectivity in, the Absolute Subject as God—in the subject's own "empowerment," as this self is removed from the social bond, from any political obligation, as well as from history (being transcendental). And this creation of the apolitical, nonrelational, ahistorical individual ("ahistorical" because the individual who enters into ideology does so without grasping the historical forces that yield ideology's generation and constant regeneration) reproduces capital globally, universally, and repeatedly, beyond any specific state or culture. "Which means that all ideology is centered," Althusser explains, "that the Absolute Subject occupies the unique place of the Center, and interpellates around it the infinity of individuals into subjects in a double mirror-connection such that it subjects the subjects to the Subject, while giving in them the Subject in which each subject can contemplate its own image (present and future)."[6]

Faced with the language/limit as a fundamental component of being and as exposure to the other, the subject disavows it: disavows, from inception, being mortal and social. Believing instead to have been only temporarily stripped of immortality and sovereignty, which have been lost or unjustly stolen, the subject is not *not* infinite but currently lacking that absoluteness, that sovereignty whose restitution is promised by the very fact of the "unfair" loss. Just as the ego, for Freud, will often envisage a loved one's death as a *loss* to preserve the possibility of a return, so, for Lacan, the subject will view death as the *lack* of an immortality that—because only misplaced—can be recovered. The lack, in short, *is* the phallus, *itself* the wholeness. (The idea of the hole produces, even *is*, the ideal of the whole.)

Although discussed in earlier chapters, it bears repeating that capitalism always includes within its borders an imaginary, empty territory, a "hole," by means of which it seduces the individual into believing that capital eternally tenders a "secret," not yet filled property: a plot that is just for this individual, one the individual is free to inhabit or appropriate. Capitalism thus guarantees the universal right to private property by proffering to each "individual" nothing: lack. The individual accesses this lack, in turn, not by gaining material ownership but by seizing on a symbolic property, an identity or name tag to fill in the hole. Having been provided the gift of nothing by capitalism, consumers pay off their debts by freely entering into the phallic order that controls them. Distinct and separate subject or power positions, symbolic appropriations of market territory, of *freedom*, therefore proliferate endlessly and sit side by side—but, since each is self-determined, they need not relate. There is no call for anything resembling an intervention or even a (political? ethical? moral?) relation. The *relations* of production reproduce themselves because no demand, desire, or need to replace current relations. The situation "as it is," through misrecognition, appears to grant all to all: a political Subject whole unto itself.

Leftist scholarship, particularly as inspired by Deleuze, often supposes the foundation of psychoanalysis to be lack—with the above-mentioned unfilled property. According to this view, the subject of psychoanalysis loses its complete self at the moment it enters into the social. The subject therefore ceaselessly directs its desire toward the recovery of this missing object in quest of "full" individuality (over sociality, over politics). The desire for the whole I, surfacing from privation, from the loss of a piece of private property (the complete self as that property), is but the wish for the empty ration that capitalism always already extends, as lure, to the subject. Lacking by its nature, the I naturally desires the capitalist structure, which itself thereby emerges as natural. Psychoanalysis performs and explains the human desire to reproduce the relations of capitalist production, or capitalism itself; it is a psychologism of capitalism.

Yet lack does not in fact institute the psychoanalytic subject. It pertains to Freud's secondary processes, some of which are described below. The institution or ground of psychoanalysis is the unconscious, which never negates anything. On the contrary, it hoards all apparent losses, rendering lack—outside of the illusion of lack—quite impossible. To be sure, privation or a vacant lot is for psychoanalysis the *fantasy* by which the desire for individuality that stabilizes capitalism sustains itself. Yet this fantasy is also the means by which the unconscious and its drives (which cannot be negated), thereby psychoanalysis itself, are disavowed. The repudiation of the fundamental concepts of psychoanalysis will thus tend to support, not a leftist critique of capitalism, but capitalism itself.

The caretaker—who assumes the role of mother by virtue of this lack—bears the brunt of the misrecognition. The baby-subject has made its demands known. But the mother has not provided the goods (the objects of desire: All) and is therefore assumed to be lacking them. The provider-mother, the one-with-all, the one-supposed-to-be-all who fails to deliver, is lacking. And if the All is lacking and castrated, then so, too, no doubt, is this I (who is part of the All: one lackey among others).

The mother is not the biological mother who then lacks. She does not become the mother until she is assumed to lack. Every mother—and every woman posited as mother—lacks, disappoints, for if she does not lack she is not a mother. (So, for the misogynists who reduce woman to mother, woman is never a *good* mother, and thus "deserves" whatever disrespect she may receive.)

I want to emphasize that this analysis of the Lacanian phallus is quite basic. I do not pretend to be offering a complete reading of Lacan or of any single "scene" within Lacan. I am highlighting only *some* Lacanian issues that inform *some* Althusserian points put forth in "Ideology and Ideological State Apparatuses."

To that end, let me restate the above arguments in a somewhat different way. The misrecognition of language as signifier, the "Hey!" as a proper name or identity, pertains to the Lacanian notion of the fantasy . This fantasy posits an *Autre*, big (m)Other, or Symbolic Order that is privative: it is missing something. The Empire of the sign, or the Master, is incomplete. What is amiss? The phallic or transcendental signifier, of course: the signifier without a signified.

Such a signifier, Lacan illustrates, does not (in the fantasy) turn on repetition and ritual, which yield meaning. Iteration, as noted, always points up the arbitrary or contingent nature of the sign. It discloses meaning as conventional, not necessary. This meaning therefore could slide as its representative (the signifier) moves from context to context. The signifier *with* a signified cannot be assured to communicate the subject's desired message or message of desire. To the contrary, it represents the limit of the subject's control, initiating time and again the process just outlined: the misrecognition of limit as lack so as to posit finitude as wholeness, subjectivity.

The same cannot be said of the pure or phallic signifier. Possessing an integrity so sturdy as to resist all change, this signifier cannot under any circumstance be misunderstood by another. It is, of course, *logically* inconceivable (but let us not assume that the psyche, or capitalism, is strictly logical). To reiterate, sense *is* the result of convention and reception. Therefore slippage—through circulation—is the condition of possibility of even the most solid and long-standing definitions.

Indeed, the phallic sign is not one with a conclusive, unassailable meaning. It is a marker without any meaning whatsoever, an utterance that Lacan calls the "name of the father." A "meaningless" sign, a name refers only to the subject, to the I, without deviation, for, within the imaginary we are discussing here, a surname such as "Zane" means nothing but Zane; even if, etymologically, one is able to track a signified or tradition behind the name, this signified is for the subject of the fantasy defunct, inoperative. Yet the signifier without a signified—"Hey!"—is not without a referent, for it refers absolutely to the I.

Whenever "I" am called by my name, "*I*" am called, "I" *always* turn around (not nine times out of ten: always). The expression is addressed to me. It means me, even and especially if "Brett Levinson" seems as though it has no meaning, and if there are other "Brett Levinsons" in the area. It jumps over the signified in the signifier/signified/referent structure of the sign and directly to its subject (the referent). Subject and representation categorically coincide. The "outing" or publication of this Subject surfaces as the infinite extension of this self's field, far beyond any "origin." The phallus is the sign of the Master's mastery.

The *nom de père* or "name of the father" is a double entendre, however. *Nom de père* can be heard as either the "name" (*nom*) or "no" (*non*) of the father. The most obvious thesis about the *nom de père* is therefore: the *nom* as *name* is, for the subject, the desired and desirable *ideal*. The *nom* as *non* or "no," conversely, frustrates the realization of this desire.[7] The name of the father as phallus is the object of desire. The subject (1) imagines its existence; (2) attaches it to itself; and (3) completes the self in the process. Yet this designation is denied its place in the Symbolic Order, which says no to the name. The completion of the subject's desire is the repression of that same desire. The subject takes his place by being displaced from that same place.

Now, as I have implied throughout this study, the phallic signifier is actually, for Lacan, *language*. There is no name for language itself, no particular sign (a part) for the Whole of communication, no symbol for Symbolization itself or for the Symbolic Order as such. The subject as Master or transcendental subject is barred from the order of the social at the very moment the subject imagines entering therein. In fact, the language that would permit the subject to overcome exile is not among the available name choices. The subject, certainly, selects a signifier for language, a name. Yet this choice, because no signifier that represents "language only" exists, necessarily *means* something other than language ("language," for instance, refers to a particular language or notion of language, never to language itself).

It is well-enough known that Saussure, in order to illustrate his theory of signification, uses as his example the word *arbre*, written under a "——" (*barre*), over which he places the drawing of a tree. Lacan, in addition to reversing the "over/under" (he situates the signifier "*arbre*" above the line; the picture of the tree falls below), plays on the anagram *arbre/barre* in order to emphasize that the name, the proper noun, by which the subject accesses the Symbolic Order is just an improper noun that *bars* this admission. The I crosses over into the social, certainly—yet not as Subject but as one signifier/signified relative to others. Crossing in, the subject is crossed out, barred.

Only now are we truly prepared to outline the aforementioned Lacanian fantasy, which Butler's above reading of Althusser in fact stages. The Symbolic Order, cast as Law and Master, is *fantasized* not as whole but as unwhole. Hence, the subject fails to locate the Master word, not due to a "personal breakdown" or "weakness" (castration) but to the Symbolic Order itself, the big Other, which lacks this term. It is missing its key name. The Master, because lacking, is no Master. The Law is not an absolute Law. Yet this portion of the dream must be complemented by another: the subject must *fantasize* possessing this *nom de père* as phallus. For through this *nom*, subjects place their being into the empty slot, complete the Master as missing foundation, as the Master sign that the *seeming* Master does not possess.

The fantasy, one result of interpellation, is thereby complete. The I possesses the Master Symbol, the key to the entrance, of which the big Other is deprived. "I" own the private password that grants me a classified/transcendent space in the Symbolic or public Order. "I" buttress the *apparent* Master by completing that Master with the name that the Master lacks but "I" *am*: through the addition of myself. "I" am thereby the true Master, the Key. Indeed, this other seeming Master, without my name or "I," would disintegrate.

Armed with this *nom/non*, "I" pass over or into the Symbolic Order like any other I: through the repression of that I as "I" take my name. But in the fantasy that blinds the I to this repression, "I" do so without risking the loss of the moniker that safeguards my place since my *name* is "I" ("I" am the referent of the sign), and can never be otherwise.

Structurally, "I" surface *as if* one among others within the empire of the sign (which is no empire but a partial and conditional territory). But, in the fantasy, "*I*" am that empire.

Could this fantasy also uphold the market? "I" enter into circulation as a name among other names, so as to compete with and defeat these labels, these products. Such circulation and competition would apparently result in the subject's exposure, risk, loss, death. Within the fantasy, however, "I" am saved from such peril.

On the one hand, as a sign within a collection of signs, "I" increase my worth through competition: through "mergers," "takeovers," and so on. On the other, as a name without a signified, I transcend that competition. "I" am always already Master of All before "I" enter into the struggle—even if the struggle makes me that Master. "I" vie but, unlike other entrants, "I" cannot fail. My place is saved as long as "I" play, win or lose. "I" war with others, although the wars, because "I" cannot die, are simulations. As already argued, competition is not a simulation of war; war is a simulation of competition.

The fantasy of the privative Empire or frail Absolute has supplied me with a private, untouchable "office" in the Order of Publication or Representation. And "I" need not stay in that office, but can circulate so as to gain more and more—gain above all the recognition from the others among whom "I" travel. For "I" require recognition, just as Hegel insisted, to be Master. Yet, in contradistinction to Hegel's thesis, the reason "I" indeed earn that recognition as "I," mingled as one among others, is that "I" am already Master.

Stated differently, my name travels toward the other, where it receives the necessary recognition, without passing through the time and space that might undercut it. This is because, in the fantasy, such a signifier always already coincides with its message: I is I. Circulation without circulation time, it is absolute communication.

This idea is not impossible. It is, to repeat, a fantasy. As currency, "I" float, at liberty to benefit from—and also to fall from—a drifting, unrestricted, lawless site: the market. But because "I" *choose* to float, to select my destiny among the multiplicity of signifiers, "I" transcend every choice. "I" choose, therefore "I" am (self-determined) the subject of that choice, one that all others must choose since "I" am unavoidable: "I" am the law (of a market almost without other laws).

In sum, the I, like the market that this I supports, is most essential when it is most contingent. To see the importance of this point, let us consider commodity fetishism, which we might relabel the "commodity fantasy." A tag such as Prada, it would seem, need not enter the relation of signifiers/products to attain its meaning and value. Prada means "value." Be the name attached to a bag, sunglasses, a shirt, a ring, a cheap or illegal knockoff sold on the street, or almost to nothing at all—a Prada billboard that refers to no commodity but to itself only: Prada—its worth is given. The value of the bag with "Prada" is valued more than the exact bag without this name, regardless of price. Prada does not garner value by virtue of either its substance (labor, material) or its competition with (circulation among) other brand names. The value of itself, Prada is not the signified—as tag, it does not *mean* anything, not even the name of a family—but is itself *subject*. In other words, Prada refers not to a product of this or that value but to value as such.

Prada, to be sure, exists among other names: Dior, Gucci, Calvin Klein, Armani, and so on. These brands also signify "just value." Their worth, like Prada's, does not hinge on a relation. Prada *and* Armani say "value" not because one says *"more* value" than the other. They do so beyond any "more or less." This, indeed, is *why* Prada's and Armani's referent is value. They are "out there," in circulation, in the market. But their assessment does not turn on anything other than themselves as separate labels, separate subjects. They travel over to the consumer, but beyond circulation time, for they correspond to "value" prior to their production, competition, and consumption. A potential relation of subjects turns into a nonrelation of things.

At the time of this writing, Citibank in New York City is altering its posted advertisements (on phone booths, in subways cars, at bus stops). Given the economic downturn, as well as the scandals that have hit banks and investment firms, the new motto of the bank is "Live richly." Above the adage, one reads proclamations such as "There is no fluctuation in the strength of the compliment." In an uncertain stock market, within which many potential or former investors find themselves short of funds, Citibank markets this lack of currency so as to emphasize the spiritual emptiness of monetary worth in the first place—worth that most consumers no longer possess anyway. For, as it turns out, the unfilled "pocket" is not empty. It is a storage place for higher but heretofore concealed values, ones of eternal merit, such as munificence and generosity of the soul (incarnated by the "compliment"). Citibank is anchored in values that never oscillate. The compliment is as good in bad times as in good. Firmly installed on such a base, the institution will therefore be in good position to bring financial prosperity to its clients should the economy turn.

Prada desires to occupy the place of Citibank's "compliment"—and all other like values: freedom, peace, equality, love, care, and so on—within the market. For if Prada's *label* as value does not hinge on the consumer's recall of any specific product, therefore on any specific labor, the sign's lack of meaning is also its nonreference to the history—for meaning is always a product of repetition, history—that led to Prada's rise. The Prada label is valuable, not because it exploited this or that labor force, this or that natural resource, in this or that location, but because Prada is Prada, just as a compliment is a compliment and freedom is freedom. The history of the brand's meaning/value, which might disclose the constructed, nonnecessary, possibly corrupt core of the company, also might lead to its discredit (the problem Nike faced with the revelation of the corporation's use of foreign "slave labor"); it might even yield revolt. However, as just a name, Prada designates a subject without history, one whose status dwells beyond any reason other than it being what it is. Those who possess "a Prada" are not "of value" because they are rich. Their worth does not lie in the crassness of money, which can—according to Citibank, anyway—be forfeited as it circulates. That merit rests in value beyond money, in the void that the economic Empire cannot fill: the Subject as Transcendental Signifier.

With my Prada label, "I" overcome the fashions of the day that dominate the wills of others, who are thereby unfree. Fashion is the frail Absolute, an "Absolute" that "I" fantasize as lacking, and which I master by *being* the proper name whose worth surpasses this "absolute" (exhibiting also the Other's frailty relative to this "I"). "I" am the value missing from the trendy marks. Each and every label comes and goes because fashion, like money, is lacking the foundation that transcends the coming and going. "I" literally support the market by taking my private place above fashions, trends, the market itself, in a realm the market itself does not own, but that I am. Prada is not Prada; Prada is "I."

This commodity fantasy is thus literally obscene. As commodity, the subject exhibits the public's privation: that which is private. The subject's private part is *un*concealed as what ought to have remained *concealed*, as the uncanny obscenity that, because open, is difficult to *take*, to scrutinize (like an unfathomable wound), and thereby goes unread as the undigestible.

The commodity, in essence, is fantasized as a secret password. (But we should note that all secrets must be shareable, else they fail to be secrets.) On the one hand, it is exposed, available for endless viewing, hence seductive and unconcealable. On the other, it is overexposed, stripped, and therefore, as noted in chapter 11, resistant to interpretation: hence its "secret" worth. It displays my value, granting me eternal access to other values, which I can thus appropriate. Yet it withdraws from those other values, those other meanings, and cannot itself be accessed or appropriated—except, at least in the fantasy, by the I. The commodity-subject-fantasy is the password into the market or Symbolic Order, a means to all values, that itself (given its overexposure) is asymbolic, a signifier without a signified but with an absolute or invaluable referent—I—irreducible to "mere other values."

One merely needs to consider this password in terms of ideology to imagine its function in the market. Ideology, as Althusser argues throughout "Ideology and Ideological State Apparatuses," operates by offering a space outside ideology. For example, intellectuals of both the Left and the Right will seek the site, term, or discourse that "escapes" ideology. Yet, since no such ideal discourse or term exists, every intellectual's assertion—the signifiers of that assertion— to "go beyond" ideology only inserts that individual into the scene of ideology as the "missing piece," the I, that sustains it. "Freed" from ideology, intellectuals are able to create or imagine thought outside ideology, a password to the outside. The capacity to do so bears witness to their liberty; yet they only reaffirm the power of ideology through this very claim. In "going beyond," they unwittingly take the empty spaces within the order of things that this order extends to them as a way of preserving itself. Their "theory" is but the fantasy of the pure commodity, the absolute value. Hence, as Althusser insists over and over, no project is more ideological than the one that "breaks" from ideology; and none is more marketable than the one that betters—beats out—the market. The exceptional password *out* turns out to be the "regular" and regulating word *in*.

One does well to analyze this password label by way of a Lacanian rearticulation of the notion of enjoyment: Lacan's writing of *jouissance* as "*jouis-sance.*" In this "*jouis-sance,*" one might see "*jouis*" (enjoy) "*sens*" (sense), the joy in sense, the enjoyment in the excess of sense, enjoyment in nonsense, and so on. The limit of the Symbolic Order (ideology, the Other, authority), now cast as void, is the lack of sense, of representation. By adding "my" name, to ideology's realm, "I" disclose desire to fill up this fault within the field of sense. The reason the subject reproduces ideology, even while trying to dismantle it, is that the subject takes pleasure there. "I" enjoy myself in the making common sense of "nonsense," enjoying (as Freud emphasized) at the same time the repetition and reproduction (of ideology) themselves.

In fact, in the absence of this pleasure or fantasy, I imagine disaster (in which, of course, "I" might also take pleasure). It is "I" who preserve the Symbolic Order, the fragile order of things that would fall to pieces without my intervention. "I" adds itself *plus* sense to a whole whose meaning and reason-for-being are otherwise limited. The case is not only that, without the boundary or void in the Symbolic Order, "I" would not find my public place, but also that, absent myself as supporting "beam," the sense of the world could not be sustained. "My" desire to reproduce the market, common sense, or consensus—by cementing their cracks—defeats my inclinations to overcome it (I may *believe* that the addition of myself is this overcoming; yet my *desire* trumps my convictions).

For the latter would mean the end of All, a disaster or void into which I could well be devoured.

These propositions—in the end, there is no escape from ideology or the market since the desire for this breakout *is* the desire of/for that market—may seem pessimistic. Let us examine Althusser's essay from a different perspective, that of interpellation, to see why, in fact, it represents an affirmation. As argued, no particular sign interpellates, no proper name, such as Prada, seduces the subject. The subject is cajoled by the language that every such sign carries within it (as the limit of its representation or representations). The finitude of the Symbolic Order is the language that each signifier within this Order bears but never names. Language, if proper to the field of *jouis-sance*, is also the Lacanian *plus de sens,* "more than sense" and "no more sense." And it is this extra sense which interpellates. "I" am called not by sense but by the boundary on sense: language, which pushes me up against the other, who lies on the alternative side of the barrier, and who will satisfy my desire (or whose desire "I" will satisfy). The limit or death of the subject, hence of the ideology that the subject supports, language is the condition of any name taking—for the taking of the name is also the taking of a language that is "more in the name than the name itself."

My desire is to name this language that, as frontier, exposes me to the other (who could take my place). Language, "property" of every sign that "I" select as password, cannot itself be selected because it *must* be selected. It is the absolute law that is also the finitude of the I. The law of language and the law of death are separate but indivisible. They also lure. For if I am to be Master, I must Master the Absolute Master: not just death, but the language that drives me to death.

In *reading*, rather than consuming this language which rests within every name, "I" run up against my finitude/border, hence up against the other. I run into minimal life. To be sure, this reading, as well as the disavowal of the limit demands a name: the designation of the *inter esse*, which is now the sharing, the contact between two or more (signs, subjects), which pertains to none. To escape my bond, "I" must label the part that is no part for being the whole (language). It goes without saying that the novel articulation, *in part*, serves the I as the new secret sign by means of which the I saves itself, fills in the big Other, and reproduces ideology. Yet the enunciation also designates the miscount (the part that is not included in the parts) of ideology, the fundamental flaw of consensual postdemocracy, that democracy itself must address.

Ideology and the limit of ideology are indivisible and irreducible the one to the other. Affirmation and hopelessness cross each other in such a way that they cannot be declared distinct, which is why the subject should *also* rejoice in the fantasy of the reproduction of ideology, indeed, in fantasy itself. Only because there is ideology (and fantasy: aesthetics) and the desire to sustain it through the subject's search for the right name, is there a limit to ideology. Ideology, for Althusser, is the condition of politics, just as the absolute law is the condition of police law's undoing. Thus, although it is certainly true that, in consensual postdemocracy, all politics is ideology, it is also true that this is why politics is *not yet over*. The "end of politics" is more ideological than "politics itself," for the end of politics necessarily declares the "end of ideology," an end that is most ideological. The desire to sustain ideology by articulating the *plus de sens* also precludes politics from coming to an end—there is *jouissance* there too, and no intervention of consequence without it.

Hence, the market label such as Prada, like the media's overexposure of truth, should be embraced as much as scorned by political thought: embraced in its very obscenity. We have already noted the negative impact of commodity fetishism on social engagements. But let us not forget that the label is one of the last public displays, one of the final carriers of language—and the most marked index of this point is the sudden explosion of abbreviations for almost everything, contractions whose original signifier, hence original meaning, often get forgotten: Does "GFF" (Gianfranco Ferré) refer to anything material or just to itself as nonsense, language, *plus de sens*? The commodity is one of the final elements of our world that we cannot *not* read. Its obscenity, the off-scene of the obviousness or "goes without saying" of its presentation, cannot be avoided. It demands deciphering.

Yes, yes, the cult of the label nourishes consensus. Yet this same moniker, and the market by which it takes on value, are sites that exact affirmation since the language that they cannot *not* deploy is that very call to the other, to engagement, that no label labels. It interpellates. The demand remains insofar as the commodity remains, as does the commodification of this demand (is it called "deconstruction," "Heidegger," or "psychoanalysis"?). That is the Law. The will to power of today's subjects goes without saying; it is the market's sustenance. And, for too many, the battle for power is politics itself. Politics risks becoming nothing but the competition among ideologies and parties, in which case politics is no politics. As for the will to read politics, or to read the end of politics, that is far more fragile.

Notes

Introduction

1. The expression "sense of the world" is drawn from Jean-Luc Nancy's *The Sense of the World*, trans. Jeffrey S. Librett (Minneapolis: University of Minnesota Press, 1997).

2. Samir Amin, *Spectres of Capitalism: A Critique of Current Intellectual Fashions* (New York: Monthly Review Press, 1998).

3. This is among the main theses of Michael Hardt and Antonio Negri's *Empire* (Cambridge, Mass.: Harvard University Press, 2001).

4. Jacques Rancière, *Disagreement: Politics and Philosophy*, trans. Julie Rose (Chicago: University of Chicago Press, 1999), 121.

5. Ibid., 101–2.

6. Tomás Moulián, *Chile actual: Anatomía de un mito* (Santiago: LOM, 1997); Willy Thayer, *La crisis no moderna de la universidad moderna: Epílogo del conflicto de las facultades* (Santiago: Cuarto Propio, 1996).

7. Jacques Rancière, *The Ignorant Schoolmaster: Five Lessons in Intellectual Emancipation*, trans. Kristin Ross (Stanford, Calif.: Stanford University Press, 1991).

8. Christopher Fynsk, *Language and Relation . . . The Fact That There Is Language* (Stanford, Calif.: Stanford University Press, 1996), 3.

9. Jacques Derrida, *Of Grammatology*, trans. Gayatri Spivak (Baltimore: Johns Hopkins University Press, 1997), 5.

10. The adage "the signifier is the signified" is the foundation of Derrida's critique of Lacan's work. The latter, in Derrida's eyes, makes a claim on a signifier without a signified—the phallus—while alleging also to call into question metaphysics itself.

11. Etienne Balibar, *Politics and the Other Scene*, trans. Christine Jones, James Swenson, and Chris Turner (London: Verso, 2002), 8.

12. Karl Marx, "A Contribution to the Critique of Hegel's *Philosophy of Right*. Introduction," in *Early Writings*, trans. Rodney Livingstone and Gregor Benton (New York: Penguin, 1975), 254. Emphasis original.

13. Ibid., 256. Emphasis original.

14. Rancière, *Disagreement*, 105.

15. Martin Heidegger, *Contributions to Philosophy (from Enowning)*, trans. Parvis Emad and Kenneth Maly (Bloomington: Indiana University Press, 1999), 84–85.

16. In the quotation cited above, Heidegger does not in fact oppose change in the name of the status quo, but asserts, quite to the contrary, that change itself names that status quo, that "constancy."

17. Rancière, *Disagreement*, 112–13.

Chapter 1.

1. Civil society, for Gramsci, is both a cultural and a social topos: the "civil" portion represents civilization or culture; "society" names the social element.

2. Antonio Gramsci, *Selections from the Cultural Writings*, ed. David Forgacs and Geoffrey Nowell-Smith, trans. William Boelhower (Cambridge, Mass.: Harvard University Press, 1985), 177–78, 183–84.

3. Judith Butler, *Bodies That Matter: On the Discursive Limits of "Sex"* (New York: Routledge, 1993).

4. Gramsci, *Selections from the Prison Notebooks*, ed. and trans. Quinton Hoare and Geoffrey Nowell-Smith (New York: International, 1971), 418.

5. Rancière, *Disagreement*, 58.

6. I should add that individuals do not come to an awareness of their dialect through a comparison with another dialect except through the medium of the center norm. In such a case—dialect/dialect contact—a relation to the national-literary, even if indirect, remains the condition of these individuals' understanding of the correctness/incorrectness of their speech.

7. Gramsci, *Cultural Writings*, 183.

8. Ibid., 181.

9. Ibid., 184.

10. For an excellent discussion of this point, see David Lloyd and Paul Thomas, *Culture and the State* (London: Routledge, 1998), 1–30.

11. Gramsci, *Cultural Writings*, 178.

12. For Gramsci, education is the most important institution of civil society: "Every relation of hegemony is necessarily an educational relationship." Antonio Gramsci, *A Gramsci Reader: Selected Writings, 1916–1930*, ed. David Forgacs (London: Lawrence and Wishart, 1988), 339. See also Gramsci, *Cultural Writings*, 185–90.

13. See Alberto Moreiras's *The Exhaustion of Difference: The Politics of Latin American Cultural Studies* (Durham, N.C.: Duke University Press, 2001). Although the subaltern's possibilities as a figure of the political are addressed throughout the book, perhaps the most important discussions of the political are found in chapters 5 and 8.

Chapter 2.

1. Carl Schmitt, *The Concept of the Political*, trans. George Schwab (Chicago: University of Chicago Press, 1996).

2. For one of Schmitt's direct discussions of this matter, see his *The Nomos of the Earth in the International Law of the Jus Publicum Europaeum*, trans. G. L. Ulmen (New York: Telos Press, 2003), 350–55.

3. See George Schwab on the role of multiplicity in Schmitt's view of the political in the introduction to Schmitt, *The Leviathan in the State Theory of Thomas Hobbes: Meaning and Failure of a Political Symbol*, trans. George Schwab and Erna Hilfstein (Westport, Conn.: Greenwood Press, 1996), xi. Although it may appear that Schmitt is more concerned with the multiplicity or pluralism of the state, where state and civil society form completely separate spheres, and where distinct parties determine the nature of the political, than he is with the pluralism of the market, Gopal Balakrishnan, in *The Enemy: An Intellectual Portrait of Carl Schmitt* (London: Verso, 2000), 260–68, demonstrates that these "two" pluralisms are, in fact, quite connected, and that much of Schmitt's legal theory can be grasped as an *avant la lettre* analysis of neoliberalism.

4. Jean Baudrillard, *Symbolic Exchange and Death*, trans. Iain Hamilton Grant (London: Sage, 1993), 68–69.

5. Balakrishnan, *Enemy*, 262.

6. This is the main thesis, for example, of Michael Hardt and Antonio Negri's *Empire* (Cambridge, Mass.: Harvard University Press, 2001).

7. The phrase "bodies of this death" is William Haver's, drawn from his book *The Body of This Death: Historicity and Sociality in the Time of AIDS* (Stanford, Calif.: Stanford University Press, 1996).

8. Michel Foucault, *"Society Must Be Defended": Lectures at the College of France, 1975–76*, trans. David Macey (New York: Picador, 2003). Hereafter cited in text.

9. I should again mention the link Foucault draws between the classical epoch and the epoch of representation. In the "age" of sovereignty, as we have noted, the other's death revealed the soul or immortality of the master. This, above all, was because God was the master's witness—and guarantee. In the time of representation, subjects who gaze at their own "work" as self-reflection might well offer similar assurance—yet the assurance is itself not assured. The guarantee is erased in advance since subjectivity and self-representation turn on a *historical* witness (again, even and especially if "I" am that witness) whose view cannot be certain to coincide with that of the "original" subject. In essence, the reflection of subjects upon their own "killings"—the representation of the event—puts these subjects' power in question precisely by establishing this I as transcendental principle. Hence

Descartes calls on God "in the last instance" as he works to install the I in God's place.

10. These ideas about the species and the population are to be found in Foucault's "Governmentality," in *Power: The Essential Works of Michel Foucault, 1954–1984,* ed. James D. Faubian (New York: New Press, 1997), 201–22.

11. Agamben addresses the matter most powerfully in *Homo Sacer: Sovereign Power and Bare Life,* trans. Daniel Heller-Roazen (Stanford, Calif.: Stanford University Press, 1996).

12. Foucault, *"Society,"* 254.

Chapter 3.

1. Rancière, *Disagreement,* 123.
2. Ibid., 5.
3. A similar examination of "the people," which informs my reading of Rancière, is found in Giorgio Agamben, *Means without End: Notes on Politics,* trans. Vincenzo Binetti and Cesare Casarino (Minneapolis: University of Minnesota Press, 2000), 29–34.
4. Rancière, *Disagreement,* 8.
5. Ernesto Laclau, *Politics and Ideology in Marxist Theory: Capitalism, Fascism, Populism* (London: NLB, 1977), 143–99.
6. Rancière, *Disagreement,* 14. Emphasis added.
7. Ibid., 36. Emphasis added.
8. Ibid., 35, 40.
9. Ibid., 37.
10. Agamben, *Means,* 81.
11. Rancière, *Disagreement,* 37–38.
12. G. W. F. Hegel introduces "bad infinity" in his *The Science of Logic,* trans. A. V. Miller (Atlantic Highlands, N.J.: Humanities Press, 1989), 149.
13. Rancière, *Disagreement,* xi. Hereafter cited in text.
14. See Balibar, *Politics,* 23–30.
15. Rancière, *Disagreement,* 102.
16. Martin Heidegger, "Letter on Humanism" in *Basic Writings,* trans. David Farrell Krell (New York: Harper and Row, 1977), 222.
17. Alan Badiou, *Infinite Thought: Truth and the Return of Philosophy,* trans. Oliver Faltham and Justin Clemens (London: Continuum, 2003), 100. Emphasis added.

Chapter 4.

1. Jacques Derrida, "Geopsychoanalysis . . . and the Rest of the World," *New Formations,* no. 26 (autumn 1995): 142–62.
2. Ibid., 147–48.
3. Jacques Derrida, "Racism's Last Word," in *"Race": Writing and Difference,* ed. Henry Louis Gates Jr., trans. Alan Bass (Chicago: University of Chicago Press, 1986), 329–38.
4. Derrida, "Geopsychoanalysis," 151.

5. Jean-François Lyotard, "The Other's Rights," in Stephen Shute and Susan Hurley, eds., *On Human Rights: The Oxford Amnesty Lectures, 1993* (New York: HarperCollins, 1993), 145–46.

6. Derrida, "Geopsychoanalysis," 141. Hereafter cited in text.

7. Here it is important to highlight Derrida's thinly veiled attack on Lacanianism. Speaking early in the morning at the IPA conference, Derrida casts himself and deconstruction as symptoms—marks of death—of psychoanalysis. Like Argentina, deconstruction is the margin that psychoanalysis has nonetheless invited into the center (Derrida, after all, is the conference's keynote speaker), the foreigner that the domestic territory seems all the same to need. His speech, Derrida suggests half in jest, is slated for the "wee" hours so that his outside intervention, now inside, can be placed "out of the way" as quickly as possible, so that the psychoanalytic institution can be quickly cured of its inside but alien infirmity. Just as the IPA uses Argentina as support and supplement, only to disavow that peripheral nation when it acts "improperly," so also psychoanalysis calls upon deconstruction, yet refuses to accept the essential relation of psychoanalysis to this exterior discourse, and to all exterior discourses.

Chapter 5.

1. Elizabeth Olson, "At Rights Meeting, Anxiety That Terror Fight Is Taking Lead," *New York Times*, March 24, 2002: 23.

2. "The identity is called humanity." Rancière, *Disagreement,* 124.

3. I want to note here that, whatever "inhuman rights" might be, they could never include any discourse on the rights of the unborn. Once labeled "unborn," the fetus is completely humanized.

4. Alain Badiou, *Ethics: An Essay on the Understanding of Evil*, trans. Peter Hallwood (London: Verso, 2001), 22–24.

5. Emmanuel Levinas, "Useless Suffering," trans. Richard Cohen, in Robert Bernasconi and David Wood, eds., *The Provocation of Levinas: Rethinking the Other* (New York: Routledge, 1988), 158.

6. Ibid., 164.

7. Ibid., 163.

8. Emmanuel Levinas, "The Rights of Man and the Rights of the Other," in *Proper Names*, trans. Michael B. Smith (Stanford, Calif.: Stanford University Press, 1999), 118.

9. Levinas, "Suffering," 159.

10. In fact, one could also read Heidegger's addressing being-toward-death as addressing being-toward the Other's death. For a discussion of this possibility, and its full political and ethical ramifications, see Christopher Fynsk, *Heidegger: Thought and Historicity* (Ithaca, N.Y.: Cornell University Press, 1993), 28–53.

11. Emmanuel Levinas, "Substitution," in *The Levinas Reader,* ed. Sean Hand (Oxford: Basil Blackwell, 1989), 115.

Chapter 6.

1. Louis Althusser, "Ideology and Ideological State Apparatuses: Notes towards an Investigation," in Slavoj Zizek, ed., *Mapping Ideology* (New York: Verso, 1994), 100–140.

2. Karl Marx, *Grundrisse: Foundation of the Critique of Political Economy*, trans. Martin Nicolaus (New York: Viking Penguin, 1993), 539.

3. In this context, capital punishment in the United States presents an interesting case: it has frequently been dubbed "a human rights abuse," although the U.S. government has not taken the accusation too seriously. The point I want to emphasize is that efforts to condemn U.S. politics through these abuses only count on the repressive/ideological binary that such a politics banks on. They suggest that the ground of evil is physical violence inflicted by the state, condemning the United States for its practices, which is precisely the argument of the ideological state itself, the very one that justifies the United States.

4. Slavoj Zizek, "The Specter of Ideology," in Zizek, *Ideology*, 8.

5. This "state of nature," unlike Hobbes's, which precedes the modern state or the state of reason, *follows* the modern state, takes place when culture has completely naturalized habitus, convention, when capitalism as the reason of being is absolutely given, natural.

6. One might argue that the workplace is the educational site that, by teaching workers to curb their instincts to consume so as to produce, grounds all other sites, and thus stands beyond the ISAs. But such a thesis, though it may be present in other Marxist thinkers, does not sit well within the writings of Althusser as the theorist of the ISAs.

7. Althusser, "Ideology," 138.

8. Louis Althusser, *The Future Last Forever: A Memoir*, trans. Richard Veasy (New York: New Press, 1995), 364.

9. Althusser, "Ideology," 129.

Chapter 7.

1. Fredric Jameson, *Postmodernism, or, the Cultural Logic of Late Capitalism* (Durham, N.C.: Duke University Press, 1991), 260–78.

2. Ernesto Laclau and Chantal Mouffe, *Hegemony and Socialist Strategy: Towards a Radical Democratic Politics*, trans. Winston Moore and Paul Cammack (London: Verso, 1985). My study concentrates exclusively on chapters 3 and 4.

3. Ibid., 134–45.

4. Ibid., 112.

5. This, of course, is the title of Luce Irigaray's study *This Sex Which Is Not One*, trans. Carolyn Burke and Catherine Porter (Ithaca, N.Y.: Cornell University Press, 1990).

6. Ernesto Laclau, "Deconstruction, Pragmatism, Hegemony," in Chantal Mouffe, ed., *Deconstruction and Pragmatics* (New York: Routledge, 1996), 47–67.

7. Laclau and Mouffe, *Hegemony,* 111.

8. Simon Chritchley, *Ethics, Politics, Subjectivity: Essays on Derrida, Levinas and Contemporary French Thought* (London: Verso, 1999), 111.

9. Ibid., 110.

10. Simon Chritchley, *The Ethics of Deconstruction: Derrida and Levinas* (Edinburgh: Edinburgh University Press, 1999), 42. Emphasis original.

11. Ibid., 106–7.

12. This is the main theme of Moreiras's discussion of Latin America and the end of metaphysics, *Tercer espacio: Literatura y duelo en América Latina* (LOM: Santiago, 1999).

Chapter 8.

1. "Want to Apply? Be Assertive, but Polite," *Binghamton Sun-Times,* April 4, 1997: 1.

2. Antonio Negri, *Marx beyond Marx: Lessons on the Grundrisse*, trans. Harry Cleaver, Michael Ryan, and Maurizio Viano (London: Automedia, 1991).

3. Karl Marx and Friedrich Engels, *Feuerbach: Opposition of the Materialist and Idealist Outlooks* (London: Verso, 1973), 8. Emphasis added.

4. Antonio Negri, "The Specter's Smile," in Michael Sprinker, ed., *Ghostly Demarcations: A Symposium on Jacques Derrida's Specters of Marx* (London: Verso, 1999), 5–16.

5. I am citing the translation of Marx's *Eighteenth Brumaire* found in Balibar's *Politics,* 8, which claims to be closer to the original German than the previous English translation. In any case, it better speaks to the issues I am raising. For the more standard translation, see Karl Marx, *The Eighteenth Brumaire of Louis Bonaparte*, trans. Daniel De Leon (New York: International, 1963), 15.

6. Karl Marx, *Capital: A Critique of Political Economy*, vol. 1, trans. Ben Fowkes (New York: Penguin, 1992), 135.

7. Ibid.

8. Marx, *Grundrisse*, 545.

9. Ibid., 543. Emphasis original.

10. Ibid., 541. Emphasis original.

11. Ibid., 543. Emphasis original.

12. G. W. F. Hegel, *Phenomenology of Spirit*, trans. A. V. Miller (Oxford: Oxford University Press, 1977), 111–19 and 294–364.

13. Negri, *Marx*, 179.

14. I use the word *subjectified* in order to contrast Negri and de Man. For Negri, politics involves the "subjectification" of the worker who is objectified: "because the working side of the relation has subjectified itself and rises up as an antagonistic force." For de Man, subjectification is merely the condition of the other's appropriation; he is interested in the text as the "withdrawal" from representation, which opens self to the other.

15. Paul de Man, "Autobiography as De-facement," in *Rhetoric of Romanticism* (New York: Columbia University Press, 1984), 67–81.

16. Paul de Man, *Resistance to Theory* (Minneapolis: University of Minnesota Press, 1986), 10.

17. See de Man's comments on this matter in ibid., 100–101.

18. This is why, to reiterate a point presented previously, puns are important for deconstruction: a pun is a component of language that can be uttered with the intention of communicating "reasonably" one message—including the message that "here is a pun"—but that can be heard by an alternative listener/force, just as reasonably, as containing a different message. Puns mark reason's

inequality to itself: the conceivability, to again refer to Rancière's paradigm, of *reasonable* disagreement, therefore of politics.

19. See Alain Badiou, *Manifesto for Philosophy*, trans. Morman Madarasz (Albany: State University of New York Press, 1999), 94–95.

20. For further reading on this matter, see Agamben on "camps," *Homo Sacer*, 83–90.

Chapter 9.

1. Haver, *Body*, 1–10.

2. Derrida, *Grammatology*, and Edward Said, *Orientalism* (New York: Vintage, 1978).

3. Gayatri Spivak, "Can the Subaltern Speak?" in Gary Nelson and Lawrence Grossberg, eds., *Marxism and the Interpretation of Culture* (Urbana: University of Illinois Press, 1988), 271–313, and *A Critique of Postcolonial Reason: Toward a History of the Vanishing Present* (Cambridge, Mass.: Harvard University Press, 1999). I would simply want to note that, however valuable one finds these writings, they certainly do not articulate the link between deconstruction and postcolonial studies. Rather, they pit one against the other. Spivak legitimizes deconstruction by undermining aspects of postcolonial studies, which she sees as ignoring deconstruction; and she delegitimizes deconstruction by pointing up its unwillingness to address Third World issues. In other words, Spivak's work is geared to negate current models of thought, not to embrace or phrase their connection.

4. Anthony Pagden, *The Fall of Natural Man: The American Indian and the Origins of Comparative Ethnology* (Cambridge: Cambridge University Press, 1982), 126–32.

5. These writings are now collected in Gates, *"Race"*: Jacques Derrida, "Racism's Last Word," pp. 329–38; Ann McClintock and Rob Nixon, "No Names Apart: The Separation of Word and History in Derrida's 'Le Dernier Mot du Racisme,'" pp. 339–53; Jacques Derrida, "But, beyond . . . (Open Letter to Ann McClintock and Rob Nixon)," pp. 354–69.

6. Indeed, when Fynsk, who had been working (and is still working) on the politics of deconstruction, sent *Critical Inquiry* a brilliant article analyzing the political and ontological stakes of the controversy, it was rejected as being of little interest. He later published his article. See Fynsk, *"Apartheid*, Word and History," *Boundary* 2, vol. 16, nos. 2–3 (winter/spring 1989): 1–12.

7. Stuart Hall, *Critical Dialogues in Cultural Studies*, ed. David Morley and Kuan-Hsing Chen (London: Routledge, 1996), 150.

8. Ibid., 150, 403.

9. de Man, *Resistance*, 10.

10. Hall, *Dialogues*, 146.

11. de Man, *Resistance*, 11.

12. Hall, *Dialogues*, 130.

13. Ibid., 131. For Hall's full critiques of Lyotard, Foucault, and Baudrillard, see pp. 131–35. For his comments on Derrida, see Gareth Griffiths and Helen Griffiths, eds., *The Postcolonial Studies Reader* (London: Routledge, 1994), 197.

14. Hall, *Dialogues,* 150.

15. Ibid., 132.

16. This understanding of logocentrism is presented in its strongest fashion, in my view, in Jacques Derrida, *Dissemination,* trans. Barbara Johnson (Chicago: University of Chicago Press, 1981), 63–171.

17. Here I should add that those Derrideanists who cast contamination itself as the ground of leftist politics, who espouse contamination as the foundation of leftism, do little more than embrace this same leftist mastery through a contamination/purity partition.

Chapter 10.

1. Gilles Deleuze, "Postscript on the Societies of Control," *October* 59 (1992): 3–7.

2. *Workers World,* February 7, 2002: 1. Emphasis added.

3. One is perhaps most overtly subjected to such a "community" at theme restaurants within strip malls, such as Outback Steakhouse: without any social context except the commodity itself (the mall, the steak, the waiter's enthusiasm, the music), consumers of Outback food and drink are supposed to enjoy "collectively" the experience of "Australia."

4. When one reads the "Epilogue" of the "The Work of Art in the Age of Mechanical Reproduction" against the body of the essay, one cannot but come to this conclusion. See Walter Benjamin, *Illuminations,* trans. Harry Zohn (New York: Schocken Books, 1969), 217–51.

5. Michel Foucault, *The Politics of Truth* (New York: Semiotext(e), 1997), 142.

6. Jean Baudrillard, *Forget Foucault* (New York: Semiotext(e), 1987), 50.

7. For a superb examination of these issues within the Iranian Revolution, see Afshin Matin-Asgari, *Iranian Student Opposition to the Shah* (Costa Mesa, Calif.: Mazda, 2002), 96–147.

8. "There must be an encounter, there must be something which cannot be calculated, predicted or managed; there must be a break based solely on chance." Alain Badiou, *Ethics: An Essay on the Understanding of Evil,* trans. Peter Hallward (London: Verso, 2001), 122.

9. This question was first raised by Alberto Moreiras throughout *The Exhaustion of Difference: The Politics of Latin American Cultural Studies* (Durham, N.C.: Duke University Press, 2001), esp. 1–49.

Chapter 11.

1. Michel Foucault, *The Archaeology of Knowledge and the Discourse on Language,* trans. A. M. Sheridan Smith (New York: Pantheon, 1972), 216. Emphasis mine.

2. Ibid., 48–49.

3. Ibid., 49. Emphasis added.

4. Ibid., 110.

5. Giorgio Agamben, *Means without Ends: Notes on Politics,* trans. Vincenzo Binetti and Cesare Casarino (Minneapolis: University of Minnesota Press, 2000), 72–88.

6. Foucault, *"Society,"* 209.

7. The import of this translation is not to "save" history. How can we be sure that, today, history retains a political function? The key is to translate language so as to block the "it goes without saying" of the world.

8. Agamben, *Means*, 81–82.

9. Ibid., 84.

10. See Martin Heidegger, "The Question Concerning Technology," in *The Question Concerning Technology and Other Essays*, trans. William Lovitt (New York: Harper and Row, 1977), 3–35.

Conclusion

1. For Lacan's discussion of interpellation or of "the appeal," see Jacques Lacan, *The Seminar of Jacques Lacan,* book 3: *The Psychoses*, ed. Jacques-Alain Miller, trans. Russell Grigg (New York: Norton, 1993), 247–309.

2. See, for example, Butler, *Bodies*, 121–22.

3. There is no need to address other, equally important interpretations of the idea of interpellation, such as those of Slavoj Zizek; these will not alter my conclusions. See Slavoj Zizek, *The Sublime Object of Ideology* (London: Verso, 1989), 43–47. I want to add that Zizek, in this particular and indeed radiant analysis, treats Althusser as if he were more or less a "bad" reader of Lacan, as if Zizek had to place the real Lacan into Althusser's essay in order to save it from itself. From my viewpoint, Zizek is a bit too close to positing "Ideology and Ideological State Apparatuses: Notes towards an Investigation" as the more or less "stupid" object that Lacanian theory as subject "enlightens."

4. This reading of demand, desire, and need is drawn from Lacan's "Signification of the Phallus," in *Ecrits*, trans. Alan Sheridan (New York: Norton, 1977), 286–87.

5. One could begin an analysis of this process from any number of places: from the demand of the infant to the demand of the mother, from the need that induces desire to the desire that produces the need. Since I cannot commence my reading in all of these sites at once, I choose one: the demand of the *infans*. Another point to emphasize is that this immersion into the social never ceases: the subject, from birth to death, makes demands for objects of desire, receiving only needs in return. One does not become a subject once and for all; one never stops becoming a subject or going through the mirror stage that I am describing.

6. Althusser, "Ideology," 135.

7. The proposition is not invalid. But, in truth, the opposite claim is equally legitimate: the subject desires, not the *nom,* but the *non,* the "no" that delivers desire *from* its aim, *from* the satisfaction that ends and kills desire. The subject does not desire that this desire be realized since, if it is, the subject, ceasing to desire, dies.

Index